D0085145

Creativity in Primary Education

Creativity in Primary Education

Edited by Anthony Wilson

Learning Matters

First published in 2005 by Learning Matters Ltd

All rights reserved. No part of this publication may be reproduced, stored in a retrieval system, or transmitted in any form or by any means, electronic, mechanical, photocopying, recording, or otherwise, without prior permission in writing from Learning Matters.

© 2005 Anthony Wilson, Anna Craft, Avril Loveless, Teresa Grainger, Prue Goodwin, Debra Myhill, Jane Johnston, Mary Briggs, Sue Chedzoy, Paul Key, Sarah Hennessy, Hilary Claire, Dan Davies, Alan Howe and Ted Wragg

British Library Cataloguing in Publication Data
A CIP record for this book is available from the British Library

ISBN 1 84445 013 9

The right of Anthony Wilson, Anna Craft, Avril Loveless, Teresa Grainger, Prue Goodwin, Debra Myhill, Jane Johnston, Mary Briggs, Sue Chedzoy, Paul Key, Sarah Hennessy, Hilary Claire, Dan Davies, Alan Howe and Ted Wragg to be identified as the Authors of this Work has been asserted by them in accordance with the Copyright, Designs and Patents Act 1988.

Cover design by Topics – The Creative Partnerhisp
Project Management by Deer Park Productions, Tavistock, Devon
Typesetting by PDQ Typesetting Ltd, Newcastle-under-Lyme
Printed and bound in Great Britain by Bell & Bain Ltd, Glasgow

Learning Matters Ltd
33 Southernhay East
Exeter EXI INX
Tel: 01392 215560
E-mail: *info@learningmatters.co.uk*
www.learningmatters.co.uk

Creativity in Primary Education

Edited by Anthony Wilson

Learning Matters

First published in 2005 by Learning Matters Ltd

All rights reserved. No part of this publication may be reproduced, stored in a retrieval system, or transmitted in any form or by any means, electronic, mechanical, photocopying, recording, or otherwise, without prior permission in writing from Learning Matters.

© 2005 Anthony Wilson, Anna Craft, Avril Loveless, Teresa Grainger, Prue Goodwin, Debra Myhill, Jane Johnston, Mary Briggs, Sue Chedzoy, Paul Key, Sarah Hennessy, Hilary Claire, Dan Davies, Alan Howe and Ted Wragg

British Library Cataloguing in Publication Data
A CIP record for this book is available from the British Library

ISBN 1 84445 013 9

The right of Anthony Wilson, Anna Craft, Avril Loveless, Teresa Grainger, Prue Goodwin, Debra Myhill, Jane Johnston, Mary Briggs, Sue Chedzoy, Paul Key, Sarah Hennessy, Hilary Claire, Dan Davies, Alan Howe and Ted Wragg to be identified as the Authors of this Work has been asserted by them in accordance with the Copyright, Designs and Patents Act 1988.

Cover design by Topics – The Creative Partnerhisp
Project Management by Deer Park Productions, Tavistock, Devon
Typesetting by PDQ Typesetting Ltd, Newcastle-under-Lyme
Printed and bound in Great Britain by Bell & Bain Ltd, Glasgow

Learning Matters Ltd
33 Southernhay East
Exeter EX1 1NX
Tel: 01392 215560
E-mail: *info@learningmatters.co.uk*
www.learningmatters.co.uk

CONTENTS

This book is dedicated with gratitude to Alan Booth,
Tim Borton and John Vickery, creative teachers all

Every effort has been made to contact copyright holders. In the unlikely event that permission has not been granted and acknowledgement has not been made, the copyright holder should contact Learning Matters. We will then make sure that suitable acknowledgement is made in the next printing of this volume.

The following items have been reproduced, with permission, from:

Figure 5.1 – adapted from Hayes, J. R. and Flower, L. S. (1980) Identifying the organisation of writing processes, in L. W. Gregg and E. R. Steinberg (eds), *Cognitive Processes in Writing*. Hillsdale, NJ: Lawrence Erlbaum Associates.

Figure 7.1 – Johnston, J. (1996) *Early Explorations in Science*. Buckingham: Open University Press, p. 33.

Figure 7.3 – Longbottom, J. (1999) *Science Education for Democracy: Dilemmas, Decisions, Autonomy and Anarchy*. Paper presented to the European Science Education Research Association Second International Conference, Kiel, Germany.

Figure 7.4 – Johnston, J. and Ahtee, M. (2005) What are primary student teachers' attitudes, subject knowledge and pedagogical content knowledge needs in a physics topic? *Teaching and Teacher Education* (forthcoming).

Table 7.1 – Johnston, J. (2003) *Teachers' Philosophies on Science Teaching*. Paper presented to the European Science Educational Research Conference, University of Utrecht, The Netherlands.

Figure 10.5 – Addison, N. and Burgess, L. (2000) Learning in art, in N. Addison and L. Burgess, *Learning to Teach Art and Design in the Secondary School*. London: Routledge Falmer.

Figure 10.6 – images taken as part of InfoPlay: a collaborative art project involving Mason Moor Primary School, Southampton, Winchester School of Art and King Alfred's College, Winchester, funded by the Paul Hamlyn Foundation.

Figure 12.2 – lithograph by Patrick Holo (original in possession of Hilary Claire).

Figure 12.3 – print of 'Il mondo alla rovescia' (original in possession of Hilary Claire).

Figure 12.4 – photograph of Oscar Niemayer's cathedral, Brasilia (taken by Hilary Claire).

Figure 12.5 – photograph of rural hotel, Ethiopia (taken by Hilary Claire).

Figure 13.1 – Howe, A., Davies, D. and Ritchie, C. (2001) *Primary Design and Technology for the Future: Creativity, Culture and Citizenship in the Curriculum.* London: David Fulton.

Mahy, M. *The Great Piratical Rumbustification* (1981). London: Orion Children's Books (a division of the Orion Publishing Group).

Nichols, G. (2004) 'When you look at a painting'. Reproduced with permission of Curtis Brown Ltd, London, on behalf of Grace Nichols.

INTRODUCTION
ANTHONY WILSON

> *Large numbers leave school with the bitter taste of defeat in them, not having mastered even moderately well those basic skills which society demands, much less having become people who rejoice in the exercise of creative intelligence.*
>
> Margaret Donaldson (1978)

'Creativity' is a quality we are often made to feel we should value in our society. At the very least we feel we should be 'for' it, even if we do not know how to quantify or explain it. We may even feel slightly reluctant to define something so appealing and powerful. Like other nouns we sometimes use to signify qualities of positive value, for example 'genius', 'poetry' or 'art', we feel we instinctively know creativity when we see it. This does not prevent us from being hard pushed to say exactly what we mean by it.

For teachers this unease is compounded by the feeling that we should be planning for creativity and bringing to bear all of our energies on teaching towards it, including the implications this might have for planning, assessment and progression. These feelings can be complicated even further when we take into consideration the weight of curriculum orders and recommendations which teachers need to understand, digest, interpret and deliver.

The last word of the previous paragraph carries its own baggage in the current climate of targets and accountability. As Ted Wragg says in an interview at the end of this book, many teachers enter into teaching not because they are passionate about 'delivery', but because they see it as a profession where they can develop their own creativity as well as that of their pupils. It is possible that we sign up to the idea of creativity when we begin teaching because it is emblematic of something, a quality we want to be known for, perhaps. Conversely, when we detect its absence, in curricular documentation, schemes of work or in our own practice, we are quick to label that as very negative. With so much support, in terms of curricular recommendations, now available to teachers, there has, perhaps, never been a better opportunity to address issues of individual and collective creativity within the profession. As Ted Wragg reminds us, our duty as teachers is to remain creative throughout our careers. Anna Craft reminds us that we are most likely to feel creative about our practice when we have ownership of it. The implications of this are not easy, for it involves self-examination, honesty, risk-taking and the possibility that we may encounter failure.

How to use this book

This book is an attempt to illumine and discuss what this view of creativity means for us as primary practitioners, and how it might be put into practice across a range of curricular areas. Far from being an 'instruction manual', however, the aim of the book is to make you reconsider any preconceived notions of what creativity might be, and to ask that you reconceptualise your own responses to different subjects by trying out the suggested activities in each chapter.

From Part 2 onwards you will also encounter 'Pause for thought' sections within each chapter. Please use these to reflect on the challenge to think about concepts within each subject in ways which you might not have considered before. Recording for yourself how your responses change as you read the book might be a good way of developing the four modes of creativity noted by Guy Claxton (1999) referred to in Chapter 2 by Avril Loveless: resilience, reflection, resourcefulness and relationship.

Intended audience

It is hoped that this book will be of direct interest to primary trainee teachers on all courses of initial teacher training and education in England and other parts of the UK. One of the themes running through the book is that creativity is not the preserve of the arts alone. While visual, performing and literary arts are tackled explicitly within it, the book is aimed at generalists as well as specialists on PGCE courses. The book will also be of interest to those studying creativity within educational and/or childhood and youth studies on undergraduate programmes and all primary teachers looking to reconsider the place of creativity in their practice.

Chapter details

The book is divided into four parts. The two chapters in Part I are placed at the front of the collection in order to contextualise the concept of creativity and how it came to be such an important and well-used term in educational discourse. In 'Changes in the landscape for creativity in education', Anna Craft gives us an overview of how creativity came to be represented in educational thinking in the UK in three distinct 'waves'. As well as providing a historical overview, the chapter contains a summary of different models of how creativity develops, and a critique of the tensions inherent in teaching in a fast-changing world.

Avril Loveless's chapter: 'Thinking about creativity: developing ideas, making things happen' is an extremely useful summary of different models of creativity. The chapter locates its discussion of creativity much more explicitly on personal responses to questions such as: what wider role do teachers play in both being creative themselves and encouraging creativity in others? One of the central tenets of the chapter is that creative people do not work in isolation. How schools and teachers take up the challenge to draw upon local and global knowledge is exemplified by a case study showing how trainee teachers came to further their own understanding of creativity through working with children and ICT.

Creativity in the core primary curriculum

Parts 2 and 3 of this book tackle creativity in the core and foundation subjects respectively. Chapters 3, 4, 5 and 6 explore different ways of teaching the verbal arts in primary schools. In 'Oral artistry: storytelling and drama' Teresa Grainger envisages classrooms which are supportive environments where teachers and children can experiment with ideas, take intellectual risks and find new modes of expression. Highly practical, it offers a range of strategies for storytelling and drama activities centred on dramatic 'conventions' as tools for creating meaning. Not least of the challenges of the chapter is that of releasing your own creative potential to enrich children's own use of written language.

In 'Creative young readers' Prue Goodwin centres on Anna Craft's idea (2001, 2002) of 'little c creativity'. She promotes a view of reading which goes beyond literal comprehension and celebrates personal and emotive responses to texts. This means, in the words of Martin (2005), moving away from 'simplistic notions of likes and dislikes'. How this might be achieved is shown to us in an example of recent classroom research with nine-year-olds.

Debra Myhill's chapter 'Writing creatively' synthesises creativity theory with recent writing theory to give an overview of what psychologists call 'cognitive load' during writing tasks. Underpinned by research findings from a range of studies the chapter offers practical insights into how teachers can help their pupils with three areas of writing: generating ideas, organising and crafting, and evaluating writing.

Chapter 6, 'Poetry, children and creativity', challenges us to revise our views of what poetry can be and do, both in the light of what poets have said about it and from observation of children engaging with it in their own writing. Poetry develops creativity by requiring children to see the world 'with fresh eyes' and to record this in new ways. Teachers can aid this process by emphasising that writing poems is a process of discovery.

In Chapter 7 Jane Johnston asks 'What is creativity in science education?' Creative science teaching, she says, involves teachers adapting their pedagogy to suit the learning objectives, children and context they find themselves in. Promoting a view of science teaching which develops curiosity, motivation and self-esteem, the chapter also reminds us that interaction with peers and supportive adults in the undertaking of exploratory and investigatory tasks are key to successful learning.

Mary Briggs's chapter 'Creative mathematics' is critical of recent curricular recommendations and challenges the reader to re-evaluate mathematics as a creative subject. The chapter argues that children need to be given open-ended and problem-solving tasks which cater for a variety of learning styles in order for their interest and development in mathematics to be sustained.

Creativity in the foundation primary curriculum

In 'Children, creativity and physical education' Sue Chedzoy gives a useful overview of how PE teaching has changed in the postwar period. She sees the key to unlocking creative potential in PE lessons as belonging to individual teachers. Being 'expert', she says, is not as important as feeling secure in setting up safe environments for children and having a basic understanding of how children learn and develop through PE.

Paul Key's chapter, 'Creative and imaginative primary art and design', asks us to consider ourselves as artist teachers, and to base this not only on the standards set by others but on what we believe to be right. Described as a 'pathway of possibilities', this way of teaching art to children is one which demands flexibility, ambition and trust in pupils' and individuals' instincts and ideas.

Sarah Hennessy, in 'Creativity in the music curriculum', develops further the idea of the teacher as artist, a role which involves risk-taking, confidence, imagination and the mutual handing over of responsibility between teacher and pupils. Using creativity theory developed by Wallas (1926) she presents practical ideas for music teaching based on four stages of the creative process: preparation, incubation, illumination and verification.

Chapter 12, 'What has creativity got to do with citizenship education?' by Hilary Claire, asks individual teachers to place their own sense of self-esteem, confidence and identity at the core of their citizenship education. Only when we value ourselves, she argues, can we begin to value the 'worth' of others. Using the metaphor of a 'journey' to describe citizenship education she encourages teachers to set small achievable goals on a road towards greater collaboration, responsibility and autonomy in response to global and societal issues.

In 'Creativity in primary design and technology' Dan Davies and Alan Howe challenge us not to set children artificial problems, but to support them in developing strategies that will help them to think through problems in the midst of designing and making. Synthesising the work of Csikszentmihalyi (1997, 2002) with good classroom practice, they advocate a style of teaching design and technology which is centred on building on children's interests, identifying real opportunities and using relevant contexts for learning.

Looking to the future: trainee teachers' potential for creativity

The book closes on an optimistic note in an interview with Ted Wragg. Ranging over many subjects, Ted Wragg puzzles over many of the questions teachers have about staying creative in the day-to-day business of teaching. While he is critical of the current inspection regime and of recent curricular recommendations, he remains hopeful of teachers' ability to continue to develop new ideas and approaches to help children learn. Far from seeing this as an 'extra', he is adamant that for teaching to thrive it is vital that new practitioners enter the profession confident that their ideas will be adopted. He labels this as 'going against the flow'.

Contributors

Mary Briggs is a Senior Lecturer in Education at the Institute of Education, University of Warwick where she teaches across a range of undergraduate and post-graduate programmes. She is currently the Director of the Primary and Early Years PGCE courses. Her research interests are within Early Years mathematics, assessment and leadership. She is author of a number of books for trainee teachers focusing on mathematics, assessment and ICT.

Hilary Claire teaches history and citizenship in ITE at London Metropolitan University. She has published extensively in both primary history education and citizenship education and is the national co-ordinator of the Primary Educators Network for the Advancement of Citizenship (PENAC).

Sue Chedzoy is a Senior Lecturer in Education at the University of Exeter. Her key interests are promoting physical activity from the early years and throughout life. Her publications include: *Fitness Fun* (Southgate Publishers), *Physical Education at Key Stages 1 and 2 for Teachers and Co-ordinators* (David Fulton), *Physical Education – Access for All* (David Fulton) and *Physical Education in the School Grounds* (Southgate/ Learning Through Landscapes).

Anna Craft is Senior Lecturer in Education at the Open University and Visiting Scholar at Harvard University. She co-ordinates the British Educational Research Association Special Interest Group, Creativity in Education. Her research interests include creativity and wisdom, cultural perspectives on creativity, exploration of 'possibility thinking' and characterisation of developmental issues in creative learning. Her books include *Can You Teach Creativity?* (Education Now, 1997), *Creativity Across the Primary Curriculum: Framing and Developing Practice* (RoutledgeFalmer, 1998), *Creativity and Early Years Education: A Lifewide Foundation* (Continuum, 2002) and *Creativity in Schools: Tensions and Dilemmas* (RoutledgeFalmer, 2005). She is co-editor of *Creativity in Education* (Continuum, 2001).

Dan Davies is Professor of Science and Technology Education and PGCE Primary Programme Leader at Bath Spa University. He is co-author with Alan Howe and others of *Primary Design and Technology for the Future – Creativity, Culture and Citizenship* (2001), *Teaching Science and Design and Technology in the Early Years* (2003), and *Science 5–11: A Teacher's Guide* (2005), all published by David Fulton.

Prue Goodwin taught in primary and middle schools for over twenty years and was an advisory teacher for language development before taking up a post as Lecturer in Literacy and Children's Books at the University of Reading. She has edited *The Literate Classroom* (1999), *The Articulate Classroom* (2001) and *Literacy through Creativity* (2004), all published by David Fulton.

Teresa Grainger is a Reader at Canterbury Christ Church University College. Her work involves research, consultancy and running Masters courses. Her most recent book is *Creativity and Writing: Developing Voice and Verve in the Classroom*, with Kathy Goouch and Andrew Lambirth (2005, Routledge). She is currently researching drama and writing, teachers as writers, progression in creative learning and the nature of creative teaching.

Sarah Hennessy is a Lecturer in Music Education at the University of Exeter where she teaches both specialist and generalist primary music courses. She also undertakes research into music teacher education and children's musical creativity. She is author of *Music 7–11: Developing Primary Teaching Skills* (Routledge, 1995) and *Coordinating Music Across the Primary School* (RoutledgeFalmer, 1998). She is editor of *Music*

CREATIVITY IN PRIMARY EDUCATION

Education Research, director of the International Conference for Research in Music Education (RIME) and Chair of the Orff Society.

Alan Howe is Senior Lecturer in Primary Education and Primary Science Team Leader at Bath Spa University. He is co-author with Dan Davies and others of *Primary Design and Technology for the Future – Creativity, Culture and Citizenship* (2001), *Teaching Science and Design and Technology in the Early Years* (2003), and *Science 5–11: A Teacher's Guide* (2005) all published by David Fulton.

Jane Johnston is a Reader in Education at Bishop Grosseteste College, Lincoln where she is involved in initial teacher training and continuing professional development of practitioners. She has a particular interest in Early Years education and the development of scientific attitudes and pedagogical approaches to science. Her publications include *Early Explorations in Science*, *Enriching Early Scientific Learning* and *Teaching the Primary Curriculum*, all published by the Open University Press, and contributions to the Association of Science Education's *Primary Science Handbook*, *Laying the Foundations in the Early Years* and *The Curriculum Partnership: Early Years Handbook*.

Paul Key is a Senior Lecturer at the School of Education, University College Winchester. His research interests are exploring teaching methods which encourage meaningful art activities for primary school children and examining the relationship between art practice, teaching and 'landscapes'.

Avril Loveless is a Reader in ICT in Education at the University of Brighton and is involved in teacher education and research which focuses on the use of ICT to support learning and teaching in a 'Knowledge Society'. Her particular area of interest is creativity and the ways in which teachers might promote opportunities for children to develop creative approaches in their learning. She has written and edited many books and articles in the area, and is the editor of the international journal *Technology, Pedagogy and Education*. She is also a member of the 'Creating Spaces' network, a group of teachers, teacher educators, software developers, journalists and broadcasters interested in supporting creative development.

Debra Myhill is Professor of Education at the University of Exeter and is currently Head of Initial Teacher Training and course leader for Secondary English with Drama. Her research interests focus principally on the aspects of language teaching, including underachievement, children's writing, and talk in the classroom. She is the author of *Better Writers* (2001, Courseware Publications) and of *Talking, Listening, Learning: Effective Talk in the Primary Classroom* (forthcoming in 2006).

Anthony Wilson teaches English on the Primary PGCE programme at the University of Exeter. A published poet, he has worked as a primary school teacher, visiting writer in schools and writing tutor for adults. He researches poetry teaching, poetry writing by children and creative approaches to literacy teaching. He is a co-editor of *The Poetry Book for Primary Schools* (Poetry Society, 1998).

Ted Wragg is Emeritus Professor of Education at the University of Exeter and the author of over 50 books on education.

Part I: Setting the scene

1 CHANGES IN THE LANDSCAPE FOR CREATIVITY IN EDUCATION
ANNA CRAFT

Introduction

In the last part of the twentieth century and the start of the twenty-first, creativity in education has increasingly become a focus in curriculum and pedagogy. It is now embedded in the Foundation Stage Curriculum and the National Curriculum for schools (England). There has been a substantial investment in staff development and the creation of teaching resources for school teachers.

This chapter explores why the landscape has altered so radically from the policy context which immediately preceded it. It also explores current concepts of creativity in use in education, and strategies used to enhance opportunity for pupils to be creative.

Finally it raises some fundamental tensions and dilemmas that face teachers fostering creativity in education.

What has changed?

The last twenty or so years have seen a global revolution so that in many places creativity has moved from the fringes of education and/or from the arts to being seen as a core aspect of educating. No longer seen as an optional extra, nor as primarily to do with self-expression through the arts, early twenty-first century creativity is seen as generative problem-identification and problem-solving, across life (Craft, 2000, 2001, 2002, in press).

This position stands in contrast to a period of time from the late 1980s until the late 1990s, when the National Curriculum was introduced to schools in England and Wales, during which time creativity in a variety of forms was marginalised. This included creativity relevant to and expressed through the arts, but it also included the nurturing of individuality which had formed an important part of the value-set informed by child-centred principles of learning which had dominated educational thinking and practice from the mid-1960s onward.

We can describe the change in creativity policy as occurring in three 'waves'.

Three waves of creativity in education

The 'first wave' of creativity in education was perhaps in the 1960s, codified by Plowden (CACE, 1967), drawing on child-centred philosophy, policy and practice.

The second wave began in the late 1990s, about ten years after the introduction of the National Curriculum.

And the third is getting under way in the early years of the twenty-first century.

The first wave: Plowden and beyond

The recommendations of the Central Advisory Council in Education in 1967 (which became known as the Plowden Report), formed thinking about creativity in education for the generation which followed it (CACE, 1967). Drawing on a large body of so-called liberal thinking on the education of children, it recommended that children learn by discovery, taking an active role in both the definition of their curriculum and the exploration of it. Active and individualised learning was strongly encouraged, as well as learning through first-hand experience of the natural, social and constructed world beyond the classroom. A core role was given to play.

Plowden made a significant contribution to the way in which creativity in education was understood. It influenced the early years of education but had an impact on the later primary years and secondary education, too. It provided an early foundation for the more recent move in creativity research towards emphasising social systems rather than personality, cognition or psychodynamics.

Through Plowden, creativity became associated with a range of other approaches: discovery learning, child-centred pedagogy, an integrated curriculum and self- rather than norm-referencing.

However, within the Plowden 'take' on creativity, there are several problems.

The first, is the role of knowledge. For while we cannot exercise imagination or creativity in any domain without knowledge if we are to go beyond the given or assumed, Plowden nevertheless implies that a child may be let loose to discover and learn without any prior knowledge.

Secondly, there is a lack of context implied in the rationale for 'self-expression'. Plowden appears to conceive of the child's growth and expression in a moral and ethical vacuum. It has been argued more recently that encouraging children and young people to have ideas and express them should be set in a moral and ethical context within the classroom (Craft, 2000, in press; Fischmann et al., 2004; Gardner, 2004).

Thirdly, Plowden suggests that play provides the foundation for a variety of other forms of knowledge and expression and in doing so appears to connect play creativity within the arts only and not with creativity across the whole curriculum.

Related to the third point is a further problem, which is that play and creativity are not the same as one another, for not all play is creative.

Such conceptual and practical problems, it has been argued (NACCCE, 1999), were in part responsible for creativity being pushed to the back of policy-makers' priorities in curriculum development. Until, that is, the late 1990s, which saw a revival of official recognition of creativity in education: the second wave (Craft, 2002, 2003a, 2004).

The second wave of creativity in education

During the late 1990s, there was a resurgence of interest in psychology and education research. This accompanied policy shifts reintroducing creativity into education.

Three major curriculum-based initiatives occurred.

The National Advisory Committee on Creative and Cultural Education Report (NACCCE, 1999)

The report linked the fostering of pupil creativity with the development of culture, in that original ideas and action are developed in a shifting cultural context. It suggested that the fostering of pupil creativity would contribute to the cultural development of society, since creativity rarely occurs without some form of interrogation of what has gone before or is occurring synchronously. The Report proposed the idea of democratic creativity, i.e. 'all people are capable of creative achievement in some area of activity, provided the conditions are right and they have acquired the relevant knowledge and skills' (paragraph 25). This notion has some connection with Plowden, in that children's self-expression is valued and all people are seen as capable of creativity. But it *contrasts* with the Plowden approach too. First, it argues for the acquisition of knowledge and skills as the necessary foundation to creativity – reflecting the wider research context in the 'situating' of knowledge. Secondly, it has a great deal more to say on creativity than Plowden since that was its main focus. Criticisms of the NACCCE Report are very few. Since its publication, it has increasingly informed the way that creativity is being developed in the codified curriculum for Foundation Stage and beyond.

'Creative development' named as an Early Learning Goal in the Foundation Stage Curriculum (DfEE, 2000)

The codifying of this part of the Early Years curriculum for children up to the age of five meshed closely with the existing norms and discourse about early education. 'Creative development' encompasses art, craft and design and various forms of dramatic play and creative expression, all of which have traditionally formed a core part of Early Years provision. It emphasises the role of imagination and the importance of children developing a range of ways of expressing their ideas and communicating their feelings.

Codifying creativity within the early learning curriculum has been a significant landmark. Nevertheless, there are several difficulties. First, it is implied that creativity involves specific parts of the curriculum and certain forms of learning, only. And yet problem-finding and -solving using imagination and posing 'what if?' questions could (and do) occur within a whole range of domains.

Secondly, conceiving of creativity as something which may be 'developed' implies that there is a ceiling, or a static end-state, and that, given the appropriate immediate learning environment, children will 'develop'. Both presuppositions are problematic.

Thirdly, the implication is that play and creativity are the same. As already suggested, they are not. Play may be, but is not necessarily, creative. For example, 'Snakes and Ladders', being dependent upon a mix of chance and a set structure, is not creative, but 'Hide and Seek' may well be. Similarly, imaginative play may be imitative but it may equally be highly creative.

'Creative thinking' named as a key skill in the National Curriculum (DfEE, QCA, 1999b, 1999c)

This contrasts with the Early Years formulation in seeing a *cross-curricular* role for creativity in the aims of the school curriculum, suggesting that creativity is not the preserve of the arts alone but that it arises in all domains of human endeavour.

Criticisms of the National Curriculum focused on the lack of exploration of how this skill was manifest in different curriculum areas.

All kinds of other policy initiatives have flowed from these major developments in the second wave. These include the following:

- *Excellence in Cities*, a scheme to replace Education Action Zones and designed to raise achievement particularly in the inner city, was launched in 1999. Targeted to start with at secondary schools and then introduced to primary schools too, this programme was believed to have led to higher attainment in both GCSEs and vocational equivalents for pupils whose schools were in the scheme. Some schools and action zones focused on creativity (DfES, 2005a; OFSTED, 2004).

- For several years at the end of the 1990s and start of the 2000s, DfES Best Practice Research Scholarships and Professional Bursaries for teachers enabled teachers to research creativity in their classrooms (DfES, 2005b). From 2004 the theme was continued through the Creativity Action Research Awards offered by Creative Partnerships and DfES (Creative Partnerships, 2004).

- OFSTED took a positive and encouraging perspective on creativity through two reports published in August 03: *Improving City Schools: How the Arts Can Help* (OFSTED, 2003b) and Raising Achievement Through the Arts (OFSTED, 2003b).

- DfES published *Excellence and Improvement* in May 2003 (DfES, 2003), exhorting primary schools to take creative and innovative approaches to the curriculum and to place creativity high on their agendas following this in 2004 with materials.

- DfES established the Innovation Unit with the brief to foster and nurture creative and innovative approaches to teaching and learning.

- DfES funded research, development and CPD initiatives including creative citizenship as well as a research programme which explored the application into education of Synectics, a business model for creativity (Synectics Education Initiative, Esmee Fairbairn, DfES and OU, 2004).

- **The Arts Council and DCMS became integrally bound into the delivery of Creative Partnerships and associated activities (Creative Partnerships, 2005).**
- **A creativity strand was established within the DTI from the end of the 1990s (DTI, 2005).**
- **The National College for School Leadership developed the notion of Creative Leadership for fostering creativity in pupils (NCSL, 2005).**
- **DfES introduced 'personalised learning' (DfES, 2004a, 2004b, 2004d).**
- **QCA developed creativity CPD materials for Foundation Stage through to KS2 (QCA, 2005a, 2005b).**

The work of the QCA in this second wave is particularly significant as a landmark. It attempted to both describe and promote creativity in schools, through its creativity curriculum development and research project launched in 2000, *Creativity, Find it! Promote it!* It aimed to exemplify creativity across the curriculum, through a framework providing early years and school settings with both a lens and strategies for finding and promoting creativity. Specifically, the QCA suggest that creativity involves pupils in:

- **questioning and challenging**
- **making connections, seeing relationships**
- **envisaging what might be**
- **exploring ideas, keeping options open**
- **reflecting critically on ideas, actions, outcomes**

(QCA, 2005a, 2005b).

There are many other aspects to the framework, including suggestions for pedagogical strategies and ways in which whole schools might develop their creativity.

The model of learning which underpins the QCA framework, is found commonly in what might be called second- to third-wave work in creativity, including that which focuses on creative partnerships of a variety of kinds. For it assumes, perhaps unsurprisingly, that creativity is situated in a social and cultural context. A *situated* perspective, then, it emphasises the practical, social, intellectual and values-based practices and approaches involved in creative activities. From this perspective, 'creative learning' is seen as an apprenticeship into these, a central role being given to the expert adult, offering induction to the relative novice.

Aspects of apprenticeship include:

- **modelling expertise and approaches**

When the adults taking a lead role in stimulating young people to work creatively are creative practitioners in their own fields, they offer novices ways into their own artistic practices. This model of teaching and learning could be seen as quite different to that of the traditional classroom teacher in a school (Craft *et al.*, 2004).

- **authenticity of task**

It seems that the more closely the activities generated by the adult expert correspond to those that form part of their normal professional life, the greater the likelihood that pupils will be able to effectively integrate propositional and procedural knowledge, and the greater the chances of learners finding personal relevance and meaning in them too (Murphy *et al.*, 2004). This is sometimes referred to as 'cultural authenticity'.

- **locus of control**

It is very important that the locus of control rests with the young person (Jeffrey, 2001a, 2001b, 2003a, 2003b, 2004; Jeffrey and Woods, 2003; Woods 1990, 1993, 1995, 2002). Connected with this, the *quality of interactions* between adults and pupils determines, in large part, the decision-making authority.

- **genuine risk-taking**

If the locus of control resides with the pupils, this can facilitate greater and more authentic risk-taking than might otherwise have been undertaken. It has been suggested that the role and expertise of the catalyst and mentors for these processes are distinct from the roles and processes generally found in schools (Craft *et al.*, 2004). There could be implications here for the ways in which schools can genuinely foster children's creativity.

When creative practitioners lead the apprenticeship, children can see work created as part of the leader's own artistic or commercial practices, and are therefore engaged in coming to understand the artist's own ways of working.

The model of creative learning as apprenticeship implies ownership by children of ideas, processes and directions, together with engagement in and motivation toward, their own creative journey. But an apprenticeship is finite. Ultimately the novice becomes a newly fledged expert, taking off without the scaffolding, travelling alone or with others, making their own map. Griffiths and Woolf (2004) document the ways in which skilful creative practitioners are sensitised to when it is appropriate to encourage young people to move to the edge of, and then beyond, the scaffolding.

There are two other issues touched on but perhaps not yet adequately explored, by the QCA framework in this particular incarnation.

- **What is the relationship between individual and collective work?**

How do the two interact? Although this question has been examined by researchers over some twenty years at least (Amabile, 1983, 1988, 1996, 1997; Craft, 1997; John-Steiner, 2000; Miell and Littleton, 2004; Sonnenburg, 2004; Wegerif, 2004), it is still not well understood.

One aspect of the individual/collective negotiation is negotiating the balance between the creative needs of the individual and the collective creative needs of a group.

Nourishment and support for the individual occurs in a wider social context. Seeing how ideas are responded to is a part of this, and therefore so is evaluative two-way feedback in written, dramatic, symbol-based and other forms. The creator should be able to negotiate meaning and possible implications with evaluators. Questions we might address in learning more about this include: what are the interactions between wider culture, individual and collective creativity (Craft, in press)? And: what sorts of engagement might we document and detect between the wider ecology of existence on earth, the unconscious and the spiritual (Bohm and Peat, 1989)?

• **Models of how creativity 'develops'**

It may not be fruitful to consider creativity as being 'triggered' in any simple or direct way. As with all social science, it is very hard to be sure of cause–effect relationships. But we do have some working hypotheses implied in some key terms: teaching for creativity, creative teaching and creative learning.

Creative teaching is focused on the teacher. Studies suggest that teachers feel creative when they control and take ownership of their practice, are innovative and ensure that learning is relevant to learners, envisaging possibilities and differences, seeing these through into action (Jeffrey and Woods, 2003; Woods and Jeffrey, 1996).

Teaching for creativity by contrast focuses on the child and is often 'learner inclusive' (Jeffrey and Craft, 2004; Jeffrey and Woods, 2003). A learner inclusive pedagogy involves giving the child many choices and a great deal of control over what is explored and how. It is, essentially, learner-centred (Jeffrey and Craft, 2004).

Research suggests that a teacher who is successful in stimulating children's creativity does some or all of the following:

- **encourages development of purposeful outcomes across the curriculum;**
- **develops children's motivation to be creative;**
- **fosters the study of any discipline in depth, developing children's knowledge of it, to enable them to go beyond their own immediate experiences and observations;**
- **offers a clear curriculum and time structure to children but involves them in the creation of new routines when appropriate;**
- **provides an environment where children are rewarded for going beyond what is expected;**
- **uses language to both stimulate and assess imaginativeness;**
- **helps children to find personal relevance in learning activities;**
- **models the existence of alternatives while also helping children to learn about and understand existing conventions;**
- **encourages additional and alternative ways of being and doing, celebrating, where appropriate to do so, their courage to be different;**
- **gives children enough time to incubate their ideas.**

(*Sources*: Balke, 1997; Beetlestone, 1998; Craft, 2000; Edwards and Springate,1995; Fryer, 1996; Halliwell, 1993; Hubbard, 1996; Jeffrey and Woods, 2003; Kessler, 2000; Shallcross, 1981; Torrance, 1984; Woods, 1990, 1993, 1995; Woods and Jeffrey, 1996.)

OFSTED (2003a, 2003b) would add to this the significance of:

- **partnership;**
- **authentic relationships with the social, economic, cultural and physical environment.**

The middle ground between creative teaching and teaching for creativity has been gradually expanded to include a relatively new term in the discourse: 'creative learning'. So what does this term mean? Some European work (Jeffrey, 2003b, 2004) suggests that it involves learners in using their imagination and experience to develop learning, that it involves them strategically collaborating over tasks and contributing to the classroom pedagogy and to the curriculum, and it also involves them critically evaluating their own learning practices and teachers' performance (Jeffrey, 2001b). It offers them, in many ways, a form of apprenticeship. The Creative Action Research Awards (CARA, 2005) are giving, in their first year of operation (2004–5), 120 teacher–artist partnerships the opportunity to undertake action research projects with the support of mentors, exclusively focusing on aspects of creative learning.

Nevertheless, the teaching profession and other collaborative partners still have a long way to go in characterising creative learning.

During the second wave of creativity, then, there have been common themes to many of the policy initiatives, for example:

- **role of the arts;**
- **social inclusion;**
- **raising achievement;**
- **exploration of leadership;**
- **place of partnerships.**

Within the research community both prior to and during the second wave, there has been a matched growth. After a relatively fallow period from the 1970s until the late 1980s, the last part of the twentieth century saw greatly increased activity in creativity research as applied to education.

Research foci included the conceptualising of creativity (Craft, 1997, 2001, 2002; Fryer, 1996), exploring how creativity could be fostered and maintained (Jeffrey, 2001a, 2001b), investigation of creativity in specific domains such as information and communications technology (Leach, 2001), documenting creative teaching (Woods and Jeffrey, 1996) and exploring creative leadership (Imison, 2001; NCSL, 2005).

In common with other educational and social science research a significant direction of research into creativity, both within education and beyond it, has been to situate within it a social psychological framework which recognises the role of social structures and collaborative practices in fostering individual creativity (Jeffrey and Craft, 2001; Miell and Littleton, 2004; Rhyammar and Brolin, 1999).

Since the 1990s, research into creativity has focused more on the creativity of ordinary people within aspects of education, what Boden calls 'p' creativity (Boden, 2001). The methodology for investigating creativity in education has also shifted, from large-scale studies aiming to measure creativity toward ethnographic, qualitative approaches to research focusing on the actual site of operations and practice, again contextualising creativity in the social and cultural values and practices of both the underlying disciplines and the particular setting. There has also been a move toward philosophical discussions around the nature of creativity (Craft, 2002).

This was – and is – quite distinct from the earlier climate, in its changed emphasis on:

- **characterising, rather than measuring;**
- **ordinary creativity rather than genius;**
- **encompassing views of creativity which include products but do not see these as necessary;**
- **emphasis on the social system rather than the individual.**

The first years of the twenty-first century have seen a gradual move from a second to a third wave, which goes beyond seeing creativity as universalised, to characterising it as everyday (Craft, 2001, 2002, in press; Feldman, 1999) – seeing creativity as necessary for all at a critical period for our species and for our planet. For the children in our schools will help to shape the world in which they grow up and in which we grow old. Their ability to find solutions to the problems they inherit from us and to grow beyond the restrictions we have placed upon our own world-view will – more than in any other generation – define the future of our species and our planet.

But why the changing landscape?

The reasons for this resurrection of interest and the shift from a first to a second and then to a third wave of change to the landscape of creativity emerge from a mix of political, economic and social change.

The globalisation of economic activity has brought with it increased competitiveness for markets, driving the need for nation states to raise the levels of educational achievement of their potential labour forces (Jeffrey and Craft, 2001). Changes in our economy mean an increased proportion of small businesses or organisations, employing less than five people and with a turnover of less than £500,000 (Carter *et al.*, 2004). Employment in no organisation is for life. We have shifted our core business from manufacturing to a situation where 'knowledge is the primary source of economic productivity' (Seltzer and Bentley, 1999: 9).

Education has, of course, a dynamic relationship with this shifting world of employment and the wider economy. In response to changes in these domains, what is considered significant in terms of educational achievement is changing.

It is no longer merely sufficient to have excellence in depth and grasp of knowledge. Critical to surviving and thriving is, instead, creativity. For it is creativity which enables a person to identify appropriate problems and to solve them. It is creativity that identifies possibilities and opportunities that may not have been noticed by others. And it is argued that creativity forms the backbone of the economy based on knowledge (Robinson, 2001).

In the wider social environment, certitudes are in many ways on the decrease. Roles and relationships in family and community structures, unchanging for centuries, are shifting fast; a young person growing up in the twenty-first century has a much more active role than perhaps ever before in making sense of their experiences and making choices about their own life (Craft, 2001).

And alongside all this, information and communication technology plays an increasing role, both offering potential for creativity but also demanding it.

All of this change in the economic, political, social and technological context means that our conceptualisations of creativity, how to investigate and foster it, are changing. An aspect of the third wave in creativity is that the notion of creativity as 'universalised' is now commonplace, i.e. the perspective that everybody is capable of being creative given the right environment (Jeffrey and Craft, 2001).

But the third wave also problematises creativity. It has brought with it exploration of the tensions and dilemmas encapsulated in fostering it.

Tensions and dilemmas

There are some fundamental tensions and dilemmas inherent in developing creativity. They are rather more than mere tensions between policy and practice although these too pose serious challenges in perspective, disconnected curricula and curriculum organisation to name a few.

There are at least three much more fundamental challenges, bearing in mind that in this third wave the education of children must nurture the creativity which will determine their ability to survive and flourish in a chaotic world.

Culture and creativity

There is growing evidence (for example, Ng, 2003; Nisbett, 2003) that creativity is manifested and defined in different cultural contexts. To what extent can and should we take account of this in a multicultural learning environment? It has been argued that it is imperative that we do address these possible differences in the ways that we foster creativity in the classroom (Craft, in press). And yet, in these times when teachers and creative partners are still celebrating the relative freedoms afforded by increased policy support for creativity, and therefore not perhaps critically scrutinising their practices in ways that they might later do, there is little sign of this occurring at present.

Creativity and the environment

How does creativity impact on the wider environment? For the creativity we are experiencing is anchored in a global marketplace that has a powerful influence on values. It is heavily marketised, so that wants are substituted for needs, convenience lifestyles and image are increasingly seen as significant and form part of a 'throw-away' culture where make do and mend are oldspeak, and short shelf-life and built-in obsolescence are seen to be positive. In this marketised context, the drive to innovate ever further perhaps becomes an end in itself. And this occurs against a rising global population and an increasing imbalance between nations in the consumption of redu-cing world resources. How appropriate is this? What significance do we accord the evaluation of *the impact* of our ideas on others or on our wider environment? For to do so might mean seeing creativity in perhaps a more spiritual way, in terms of fulfil-ment, individual or collective. And so it could also mean taking a different kind of existential slant on life (Craft, in press).

Ethics

This is of course related to the environmental point. We want to encourage children's choices, but in a wider social and ethical context. What kind of world do we create where the market is seen as God? And how can we see creativity divorced from its ends? For the human imagination is capable of immense destruction as well as infi-nitely constructive possibilities. How do we balance these? An aspect of the teacher's role is to encourage children to examine the possible wider effects of their own ideas and those of others and to determine worth in the light of these. This, of course, means the balancing of conflicting perspectives and values – which may them-selves be irreconcilable, particularly where they stem from fundamentalist beliefs (Craft, in press).

Such fundamental challenges clearly leave us with pedagogical challenges. For example, if creativity is culturally specific how do we foster it in a multicultural classroom? And how do we rise to the direct and indirect challenges posed by creativity linked to the market? How far does creativity in the classroom reflect or challenge the status quo?

We have a challenging agenda ahead of us in education, but an exciting one.

Pause for thought

- *How familiar are the three creativity waves in your own experience of fostering creativity in education?*
- *How can you go about using the QCA framework to help you identify and promote creativity in learning?*
- *To what extent do partnership and apprenticeship form a part of your own pedagogy?*
- *How can you document children's perspectives about creative learning experiences?*
- *Which of the fundamental tensions and dilemmas could you begin to address in your own practice, and how?*

Changes in the landscape for creativity in education:

a summary of key points

— No longer the preserve of the arts or arts education, creativity has moved from the fringes of educational concern to being seen as a core aspect of educating, which pertains to all aspects of human endeavour.

— Creative teaching focuses on the teacher. Studies suggest that teachers feel creative when they are in control and take ownership of their practice. Teaching for creativity focuses on the learner and includes giving the child many choices over what is explored and how.

— 'Creative learning' is a phrase which explores the middle ground between creative teaching and teaching for creativity. This involves learners using their imagination and experience to develop learning while strategically collaborating over tasks, critically evaluating their own teachers' practices. This mode of teaching often involves an 'apprenticeship' approach.

— In a world of rapid economic and social change it is no longer sufficient to have excellence in depth and grasp of knowledge. Creativity is critical for individuals to thrive and survive in the twenty-first century. This is because creativity enables a person to identify appropriate problems, possibilities and opportunities and to solve them in ways which others may not notice.

2 THINKING ABOUT CREATIVITY: DEVELOPING IDEAS, MAKING THINGS HAPPEN

AVRIL LOVELESS

Introduction

How can teachers recognise and promote creativity in their pupils, without a personal understanding of the experience of being creative themselves? This chapter will address some of the conceptual frameworks that we can use to help us recognise and think about creativity, and illustrate some of these theoretical approaches by describing creative practices in a project using ICT as tool to develop ideas and make things happen.

This chapter will also raise some questions and discussions to help you to think about:

- **how we might recognise creativity in ourselves, in other people, in our communities and in our wider societies;**
- **how these ideas about creativity can be expressed and developed through using information and communication technologies (ICT);**
- **how we might approach our own teaching to reflect creativity for our pupils and for ourselves.**

What makes a person creative?

Poets, sculptors, engineers, photographers, software designers, geographers, jazz musicians, film directors, writers, theologians, political activists and teachers are not often presented together in the same list. This list represents some of the people in my immediate group of friends who I would consider to be 'creative' – but this leaves out many others who express their creativity without having a formal occupation or label. My grandmother Alice, for example, was a 'carder'. She worked in a cotton mill, raised her children in the first half of the twentieth century, and was renowned in the family for her imaginative solutions to practical problems – such as a Heath-Robinson contraption for washing those awkward upstairs windows. Why should I be thinking about a jazz musician, a teacher and my grandmother in the first paragraph of a chapter in a book on 'creativity'? What is it that these people have in common, yet enables them to express their individuality and difference? How do we recognise those qualities in their lives? Why do we think that we – as individuals, communities and societies – are richer for knowing such people and for being engaged by their creativity? What wider role do teachers play in both being creative themselves and encouraging creativity in others?

I believe that teaching is a creative activity that requires approaches to imagination, inspiration, preparation, engagement, improvisation and interactive relationship that the more commonly accepted 'creative' professions demand. Teachers in all stages of their professional lives, from initial teacher education to continuing professional development and postgraduate study, need to make time and space to think about creativity in their own lives, as well as in their teaching.

Pause for thought

- *Make a list – or diagram if you don't like lists – of people you know who you would describe as 'creative', and try to identify what it is that you recognise in them.*
- *Make another list – or diagram – of words and phrases that help you to describe the creative 'qualities' that you see and experience in these people.*

Seeing creativity as an interaction

Creativity is possible in all areas of human activity and it draws from all areas of human intelligence. (Robinson, 2001:138)

There are some challenging questions to consider when thinking about creativity in education:

- **Where do we find creativity? Is it 'in' individual people, or groups, or societies?**
- **Are there conditions under which creativity can thrive more easily than others, and how does creativity express itself in, or despite adversity?**
- **How might our education systems, from classrooms to national policy, provide opportunities for creative experiences which engage in the full cycle of creative interactions?**

A useful way of looking at and trying to describe and explain our understandings of creativity is to consider it as an interaction between characteristics of people and communities, creative processes, subject domains and wider social and cultural contexts. In the 1950s to 1970s, psychologists' interest in creativity focused on areas of personality, cognition and the stimulation of creativity in individuals, but awareness of the influence of social contexts and environments on the creativity of individuals and groups and organisations has developed in the last twenty or thirty years (Rhyammar and Brolin, 1999). *All Our Futures*, the report of the National Advisory Committee on Creative and Cultural Education, defined creativity as 'imaginative activity fashioned so as to produce outcomes that are both original and of value' (NACCCE, 1999: 29). This definition is helpful in that it expresses five characteristics of creativity which can be considered for individual people, as well as the local and wider communities and cultures in which they act:

- *using imagination* – **the process of imaging, supposing and generating ideas which are original, providing an alternative to the expected, the conventional, or the routine;**
- *a fashioning process* – **the active and deliberate focus of attention and skills in order to shape, refine and manage an idea;**

- *pursuing purpose* – the application of imagination to produce tangible outcomes from purposeful goals. Motivation and sustained engagement are important to the solving of the problem. A quality of experience in the creative activities of fashioning and pursuing purpose has been described as 'flow', where the person's capacity was being stretched despite elements of challenge, difficulty or risk (Csikszentmihalyi, 1996);

- *being original* – the originality of an outcome which can be at different levels of achievement: individual originality in relation to a person's own previous work; relative originality in relation to a peer group; and historic originality in relation to works which are completely new, such as those produced by Fermat, Hokusai and Thelonius Monk;

- *judging value* – the evaluative mode of thought which is reciprocal to the generative mode of imaginative activity and provides critical, reflective review from individuals and peers.

Creativity and individuals

If we were asked to name our creative heroines and heroes, it is likely that we would include many exceptional, perhaps famous, individuals who have expressed creative ideas, activities and outcomes which have enabled us to experience the world differently in some way. They are recognised as contributing ideas and work that are considered to be original and of value in our society. My personal list might include such people as Norman Foster, an architect; Jane Austen, a writer; Picasso, a painter; Isambard Kingdom Brunel, an engineer; Rosalind Franklin, a scientist; Bill Evans, a jazz musician; Emeric Pressburger, a screen writer; Akira Kurosawa, a film director; Anthony Gormley, a sculptor; Anthony De Mello, a priest; and Helen Levitt, a photographer. (Such a list might say quite a lot about how I see and hear the world, and how such people have influenced me.) Craft describes the creativity that we ascribe to such exceptional people as 'Big C' creativity, yet she also highlights our concern with the creative potential of all individuals: 'little c creativity' and 'possibility thinking' in a creative approach to life for everybody (Craft, 2000: 3).

There are many examples of the attempts of different writers and thinkers to recognise and describe the personal qualities of creative individuals. Shallcross (1981) described them as: openness to experience; independence; self-confidence; willingness to take risk; sense of humour or playfulness; enjoyment of experimentation; sensitivity; lack of a feeling of being threatened; personal courage; unconventionality; flexibility; preference for complexity; goal orientation; internal control; originality; self-reliance; persistence (cited in Craft, 2000: 13). Another perspective on such personal qualities is described in Sternberg and Lubart's 'confluence model', in which six resources converge: intellectual abilities; knowledge; styles of thinking; personality; motivation and environment (Sternberg and Lubart, 1999). Robinson also offers a useful approach to thinking about individuals being actively creative within a medium, in which they have control, and are able to play, take risks and exercise critical judgement (Robinson, 2001).

Csikszentmihalyi identifies a common characteristic of creative people as 'flow' – the automatic, effortless, yet highly focused state of consciousness when engaged in activities, often painful, risky or difficult, which stretch a person's capacity while involving an element of novelty or discovery (Csikszentmihalyi, 1996). He elaborates the description of this characteristic in identifying nine elements which such activity provides:

- **clear goals;**
- **immediate feedback;**
- **balance between challenges and skills;**
- **merging of action and awareness;**
- **elimination of distractions;**
- **lack of fear of failure;**
- **lack of self-consciousness;**
- **distortion of sense of time;**
- **autotelic activity (enjoyment for its own sake).**

Individual states of intuition, rumination, reverie, even boredom, play a role in creativity and problem-solving and some studies indicate how creativity is enhanced in a state of reverie and imagery (Claxton, 2000). Such states are not just 'letting it flow' or 'leaving it to luck', but acknowledging a way of knowing which is not necessarily conscious and draws upon resources of knowledge, skill and experience in order to make new combinations, explorations and transformations (Boden, 1992).

It is interesting that these descriptions of creative characteristics, can also be recognised in discussions of what it takes to be a good learner. Alice, in her adventures in Wonderland, met the Mock Turtle and Gryphon who told her about their lessons in Reeling, Writhing and the different branches of Arithmetic – Ambition, Distraction, Uglification and Derision. Guy Claxton speaks of a different classification of the '3Rs' – indeed, he names four: Resilience, Reflection, Resourcefulness and Relationship (Claxton, 1999). Good learners, and creative people, need to be able to encounter and cope with puzzles, problems, seeming failure and disappointment in order to learn from these experiences and demonstrate perseverance and resilience. They also develop their abilities to think about patterns and connections, and reflect upon how new situations might relate to earlier experiences or need novel solutions. They know how to draw upon a wide range of resources to help them solve problems, from materials and memories to networks of other people. They also know how to be aware of, and engage in, relationships with other people and places.

Pause for thought

- *Who would you describe as your creative 'heroines and heroes' who have enabled you to think differently about aspects of the world?*
- *How have they demonstrated imagination, fashioning, purpose, originality and value in their field?*

- **How have you been able to demonstrate various creative characteristics in your own life?**
- **How have you been able to demonstrate resilience, reflection, resourcefulness and relationship in your own life?**

Creativity and communities

Generative ideas emerge from joint thinking, from significant conversations, and from sustained, shared struggles to achieve new insights by partners in thought.
(John-Steiner, 2000: 3)

The creativity of individuals can flourish or be stifled within the communities in which they act. These communities can be in families, peer groups, schools, workplaces and the wider society and culture, and are also expressed in the physical as well as cultural environments in which we develop. It is therefore important to recognise the potential of interactions between people and their communities, and the opportunities for the design of environments for nurturing creativity within those communities.

Western individualism — and romantic images of poverty stricken artists struggling to create their work in isolated garrets — have contributed to our ideas of creativity being located within individuals. These people, however, rarely work in isolation. Their ideas and outcomes may be highly original and iconoclastic, but they are likely to have been generated through interaction with other people's ideas and reactions. It is no accident that many exceptionally creative people tell tales of their supportive families, or engaging network of friends, or group of like-minded people in studios or laboratories. Vera John-Steiner's work with creative people explores the essential nature of their collaborations with others, in which they can challenge, discuss and try out their ideas (John-Steiner, 2000). She discusses the influences upon creative work of the intimate relationship between partners such as Simone de Beauvoir and Jean-Paul Satre or Pierre and Marie Curie, and highlights the patterns of collaboration between artists such as Picasso and Braque who encouraged and challenged each other, learned from each other and were transformed by working together. As well as these 'Big C' creative collaborations, she notes a large number of groups who work together and acknowledge the shared nature of their thinking and knowing — from writing plays to scientific discoveries.

An interesting focus of her work is on the importance of mentorship and intergenerational creative collaborations, in which senior participants provide continuity, guidance and a 'new embodiment' of complex knowledge by working with younger people with energy and fresh approaches to questions in the field. Our traditions of 'apprenticeship' are rooted in this type of collaboration in which experts think and work with novices to mutual benefit, and provide interesting models for the relationships between teachers and pupils as 'expert' and 'novice' learners.

Of all the communities and places in our society, one would expect that schools would be creative and enriching learning communities. We are, however, sadly familiar with experiences of schools in which approaches to active learning and the development of creativity have been lacking in the general ethos, the physical environment, the organisation of the curriculum and the appropriation of the pressures for improvement measured by attainment in a narrow range.

One example of a school which addresses these issues and expresses its identity as a creative community is Coombes County Infant and Nursery School. Jeffrey and Woods (2003) offer an inspiring account of the Coombes ethos, described through the themes of dynamism, appreciation, captivation and care which permeates the learning and teaching activities. The everyday knowledge of the wider community is drawn upon and celebrated in the activities of the school that are grounded in the cycles of the natural world, and local and global communities. The learning environment encompasses all the space, both inside and outside the school. It draws upon the imaginative development of the school grounds as extensions to the physical space of the classrooms, corridors, resource areas and meeting halls, attaching the curriculum to the cycles and connections of natural life on the doorstep and in the wider world. The spaces in the school are 'Aladdin's caves', representing the range of activity and experience through resources and displays which provoke responses, questions, enquiry, development of ideas and celebration of the pupils' achievements.

> What matters is not just the substantive knowledge, but the maze-like structure of the knowledge and the interdependence of its many different parts and forms.
> (Jeffrey and Woods, 2003: 94)

Pause for thought

- **Think about the different communities in which you have lived, worked and engaged with other people. What were the characteristics of those you felt encouraged your creativity, and what were the characteristics of those you felt inhibited your creativity?**
- **How would you envisage developing the physical spaces in your own classroom and school to promote a creative learning environment?**

Creative processes

Anthony De Mello described an image of God's relationship with creation developed in Hindu India as God 'dancing' creation.

> He is the dancer, creation is his dance. The dance is different from the dancer; yet it has no existence apart from him. You cannot take it home in a box if it pleases you. The moment the dancer stops, the dance ceases to be. (De Mello, 1984: 14)

Creativity can be thought of as the 'dance', which does not exist separately from the people who are performing the dance. Creative processes are an expression of the individuals and groups engaging in them, not activities that are independent of them. They can be modelled, encouraged and nurtured rather than transmitted. Being able to take risks is the next level in which the person engages in the 'creativity cycle' of preparation, letting go, germination, assimilation, completion and preparation. Robinson emphasises the need to recognise that creativity involves *'doing something'* – in different subject areas, with different media and materials: 'Whatever the task, creativity is not just an internal mental process: it involves action. In a sense, it is applied imagination' (Robinson, 2001: 115). These processes express, shape and encourage creativity as an approach to life.

Trying to identify creative processes helps us to think about how we recognise when creativity 'is going on'. We can't lift off the top of people's heads to see if they are thinking more creative thoughts at one time rather than another, but we can see and discuss how they express creativity through their behaviours, activities, experiences and outcomes. The NACCCE definition of creativity encompasses processes of imagining, fashioning, pursuit of purpose and evaluation of originality and value. We can also overlay these processes with behaviours of questioning and challenging, making connections and seeing relationships, envisaging what might be, playing with ideas, representing ideas and evaluating the effects of ideas (QCA, 2003).

Thus people and communities engage in these processes using a wide variety of tools and media to express and fashion their imaginative ideas. A musician, a mathematician or a marine biologist would each approach their endeavours by asking 'what's going on here and would happen if...'; playing with ideas and materials; paying close attention to cause and effects; practising and refining techniques and skills; standing back and evaluating the outcomes; and learning from experiences in order to engage in the processes in new situations. Sculptors might work with stone; engineers with steel; photographers with film; multimedia designers with pixels – each is working and fashioning with chosen media to represent and express their imaginings.

Pause for thought

- *Think of a variety of creative outcomes or artefacts – from a dance to a design for a new toothbrush – and imagine how the 'creators' engaged in a range of creative processes in order to realise their ideas.*
- *List the different media and tools that were used to create these outcomes.*
- *When do you have the opportunities to pose a problem and apply your imagination?*

Creativity in subject domains

Where is the life we have lost in living?
Where is the wisdom we have lost in knowledge?
Where is the knowledge we have lost in information?
T. S. Eliot

Creativity is, of course, not confined to particular subject domains, such as art, drama, music and design and technology, but can be expressed in all areas of our knowledge and 'ways of knowing'. Our understandings of 'learning domains' as 'subjects' are related to our understandings about the nature of knowledge. It is possible to distinguish four perspectives on the nature of knowledge within the UK education system and traditions. A 'rationalist' view, described by writers such as Hirst and Peters, identifies subject areas as distinguishable by different ways of thinking and the kinds of methods and evidence used in enquiry within the subjects. In the National Curriculum the clear identification of subject boundaries is related to this view. An 'empiricist' perspective draws attention to the structuring of knowledge through active engagement in the environment, that is the application of the intellect to experience. Such an approach is grounded in a constructivist, Piagetian view of learning. An 'interactionist' approach to the nature of knowledge focuses on a social-constructivist perspective expressed by theorists such as Vygotsky and Bruner, in which knowledge is constructed through social interaction and agency. An 'elitist' view, described by writers such as Bernstein, would highlight the role of powerful social groups defining the status and appropriateness of certain types of knowledge. Discussions of learning domains will therefore reflect a variety of approaches to knowledge, concepts, skills, philosophies, communities, ways of working, cognitive demands and ways of knowing (see Pollard, 2002).

The structure of the National Curriculum and the training of teachers to offer a 'subject specialism' in their teaching indicates how school curriculum and assessment systems are rooted in a view of 'subject knowledge'. Pupils also learn from people with recognised subject expertise beyond school settings and many schools offer opportunities to engage with 'experts' or 'practitioners'. These 'experts', such as artists, musicians, scientists, engineers, writers, historians, sports men and women, can model their own high levels of practice which draws upon their deep conceptual understanding, knowledge and skills within authentic contexts in the subject area. This approach to learning from the expertise of others is reflected in theories of learning in 'communities of practice' and by apprenticeship in 'legitimate peripheral participation' (Lave and Wenger, 1991).

It is argued that creative individuals within subject domains demonstrate knowledge and understanding of the concepts and traditions within the domain while knowing how to 'break the rules' in order to present original combinations of ideas. This can be illustrated in the ways a jazz musician, for example, can improvise to high levels when grounded in the history, philosophy, technique and practice of jazz (Nachmanovitch, 1990). The conceptual understanding of subject 'experts' enables them to make decisions about the appropriate use of tools and technologies to support and explore creative processes of imagination, fashioning, pursuing purpose, being original and judging value within the field. Looking closely at how 'experts' are creative in their different areas offers vivid illustrations of the relationship between subject knowledge and creative processes. In my own work in teacher education I have had the opportunity and privilege to work with scientists, artists, photographers, sculptors, film-makers and writers who work alongside pupils and teachers in schools. We have often witnessed how these practitioners – who are immersed in, and passionate about, their practice – can represent and draw out a deeper conceptual understanding from the pupils in their creative work (Hawkey, 2001; Loveless, 1999a, 1999b; Loveless and Taylor, 2000).

Pause for thought

- *Who are the creative heroes and heroines in your own favourite subject areas?*
- *What have they contributed to your knowledge and practice in these domains?*

Creativity in social and cultural contexts

Heavier-than-air flying machines are impossible. (Lord Kelvin (1824–1907), ca. 1895, British mathematician and physicist)

The wider contexts in which we promote and reward, or stifle and disregard creative people and practices act as 'gateways' to recognition or marginalisation of creative activities in our societies. Teachers who are interested in developing creativity need to be able to 'read the world' in order to recognise not only the subject and local contexts in which creativity can be expressed and acknowledged, but also the wider cultural, political and economic spheres in which creativity is encouraged.

Recent research in communities of practice also presents a view of learning as social, situated and characterised by interaction and communication between individuals (Wenger, 1998). Leach (2001) cites examples of creative individuals, such as Nobel Prize winners, who benefit from association with other creative people within their communities which supported and celebrated the creative process. Feldman, Csikszentmihalyi and Gardner (1994) propose that creativity arises from the interaction between the 'intelligence' of *individuals*, the *domain* or areas of human endeavour, disciplines, crafts or pursuits, and the *field*, such as people, institutions, award mechanisms and 'knowledgeable others' through which judgements of individual performances in society are made.

Csikszentmihalyi develops his discussion of the *field* as a component of creativity wherein other individuals act as 'gatekeepers' to a domain by recognising, preserving and remembering creative outcomes (Csikszentmihalyi, 1996). He presents a systems model in which creativity is in the interaction between a person's thoughts and actions, their knowledge and skills within a domain and a sociocultural context which can encourage, evaluate and reward. In such a systems model, the recognition and value of creativity is related as much to the wider context of *domains* and *fields* as much as to *individuals*. This has important implications for thinking about creativity and learning, where the context could be a school classroom, education system or a large corporation that can either nurture or dismiss the development of creative individuals, groups and communities. There can be a tension, however, between the current policy of promoting creativity in education that can be linked to political and economic imperatives, and the place of creative people and communities who can be challenging and disruptive to the 'status quo'.

'Creativity' is currently a term used often in policy and the practice of education in the UK. After many years of concern about lack of creativity in the curriculum (Kimbell,

2000; NACCCE, 1999; Robinson, 2001), government agencies engaged in consultation and policy development to include national initiatives to develop materials to promote pupils' creativity (QCA, 2003), and a national Primary Strategy – named 'Excellence and Enjoyment', for teaching to improve standards in pupil attainment, measured in national testing arrangements (DfES, 2003). Creativity is therefore now discussed as 'a good thing', promoting both personal expression and enhancing opportunities to engage in the complexities of problem-solving in the economic and cultural landscape of the twenty-first century.

There are, however, concerns that both the definition of 'creativity' and the practical experience of creative processes become simplistic, unproblematic and unable to reflect the complexities and challenges of developing creativity in the wider spheres of curriculum and pedagogy for the twenty-first century. There are dangers of creativity being used as a complex and slippery concept leading to confusions and contradictions which do not help educators to focus on the purpose and possibilities of creative processes in the curriculum (Prentice, 2000). Hartley (2003) draws attention to the ways in which government and business are attending to creativity and emotional literacy in education, attaching them to 'practice which remains decidedly performance-driven, standardised and monitored' (p. 16), and harnessing them for instrumental purposes in the knowledge and service-based economy. Craft also acknowledges the tensions and dilemmas which creative processes can raise within teachers' professional practice and development, such as the culturally specific nature of creativity; the desirability of perpetual innovation in a consumerist economy; the potential challenges to the status quo; the organisation of the curriculum; the role of the teacher and 'professional artistry' in a centralised pedagogy; and the tensions between teaching for creativity, creative teaching and creative learning (Craft, 2003).

Being creative is not easy or straightforward, indeed not always desirable in every situation. In our work with creative practitioners, teachers, children and policy-makers engaged in a variety of 'creative experiences' in projects, workshops and consultations in recent years, we have been aware of the dangers of creativity being perceived as just the elements of 'having good ideas' or 'making pretty things', rather than the challenging, and often painful or frustrating, experience that characterises the practices of creative people – the 'hard fun' and the 'flow' (Csikszentmihalyi, 1996; Papert, 1993). Teachers who wish to promote creativity in the lives of their pupils need to be able to model and share the range of creative experiences from their own lives – as individuals working in communities which are shaped by engagement in, and resistance to, the wider social, economic, cultural and political arenas in which education takes place.

Pause for thought

- *How does a view of creativity as an interaction between people and communities, creative processes, subject domains and wider social and cultural contexts help you to understand your own creative experiences and possibilities?*
- *How would you like to describe yourself as a creative teacher?*

Creativity in context: student teachers working with children

I feel that I have been able to engage with creative processes in ways that I haven't had the opportunity to do before. I feel that being able to work in small groups during session one and then in pairs during session two, allowed me to be creative with my peers. I have been able to use my imagination to develop my ideas and to be creative with other people's ideas. I feel that I have also seen that creativity is a process rather than simply one activity. I have seen that there is a process from developing an idea to working with that idea and then developing it further with the technology. (Jan: student teacher, 2004)

If it is useful to think about creativity as an interaction between people and communities, processes, subjects and the wider social and cultural contexts, what might that look like in a real case study for teacher education? The following example focuses not on the technologies used but on the underlying creative processes that bring the activities to life. The Creativity and Professional Development Project at the University of Brighton focused on student teachers, and one of the aims of the project was to develop a conceptual framework for looking at creativity in the context of the use of ICT in primary classrooms. The students were given opportunities to experience working to a creative brief at their own level, as well as working with young children in school (Loveless *et al.*, 2006).

The framework for creativity and ICT attempted to describe the interaction between three elements of creative practices with ICT:

- **creative processes – for example, using imagination, fashioning, pursuing purpose and evaluating originality and value;**
- **the features of ICT – for example, provisionality, interactivity, capacity, range, speed, automatic functions, multimodality (see Sharp *et al.*, 2002); and**
- **ICT capability as an expression of elements of higher-order thinking – for example, finding things out, developing ideas and making things happen, exchanging and sharing information, and reviewing, modifying and evaluating work as it progresses, through a breadth of study (see DfEE, 1999).**

The study focused on the experiences of a group of 16 student teachers, all ICT specialists in primary education, working collaboratively in using digital technologies to support creative digital video activities in primary schools. They worked with ten 'digital media labs' of portable ICT resources which included a laptop, digital video camera, digital camera, music keyboards and software for image and sound editing and manipulation. The student teachers were given two days to familiarise themselves with the resources by investigating what the hardware and software could do, working in groups of four. Firstly, they were shown the key features of the DV cameras and editing software, and then given two hours to make a mini-movie to a brief of getting someone through a door in only 10 shots. The following week they were asked to work with digital still cameras and music composition software to create a slideshow that evoked memories of childhood toys.

After another two half days of visiting schools and planning, the groups spent two days working in small groups in two Primary schools – one class of five-year-old children and one class of ten-year-old children. Each group of children worked on making a digital movie from starting points emerging from the children's ideas – from stories shared in class, to music videos and original dramas. Half a day was spent in viewing and evaluating the outcomes from all the groups, and a final half day was used as an exhibition of the groups' work and critical reflections. Group feedback from this exhibition informed the students' individual presentation of their module assignment.

By engaging with the project and analysing their experiences, the student teachers reflected upon their personal understandings of creativity, the contribution of ICT as a tool and their own professional development. Their own definitions of creativity were wide-ranging, from 'creative' qualities in all individuals to a focus on having ideas or the making of tangible products. Many discussed the experience of being engaged in activities that they thought were creative, and emphasised not only the ideas and outcomes, but also the feelings in that engagement. They described enjoyment, enquiry and excitement which led to their greater involvement and desire to follow things through. Many focused on the opportunities, and frustrations, of working in groups to develop creative ideas. They commented on the experience of offering their ideas to the group and learning how to adjust them, rethink and develop new ideas through discussion. One group highlighted the word 'compromise' in describing this experience and acknowledged the difficulty of having to put aside or compromise their personal ideas within the group activity. After the presentation of all the work, the students remarked upon their feelings of pride and achievement in what they had done. They later observed that their own experiences of generating ideas in groups, excitement and frustration in shooting and editing images, and enjoyment and pride in exhibiting the final movies were echoed in the children's experiences. They also recognised that their earlier experiences with playing and exploring with the equipment had enabled them to support the children's ideas in a more flexible manner. All recognised how they personally had engaged with a cycle of creativity activities and processes, from developing initial ideas, through fashioning and reworking, to presentation and evaluation.

In considering how they thought the technologies have helped or hindered them in being creative in these activities, they highlighted the affordances of ICT to try out lots of ideas, revise and make choices. They described how they felt that they had used their imagination and collaborated to produce a mini video story. In order to do this they had to master the use of the technology, collaborate, pool ideas, discard ideas that did not work, edit their work and show it to their colleagues. The provisionality of the technology enabled them to try things, then discard or edit them easily. The immediacy of seeing their work in progress, without the constraints of limited film footage, allowed them to move on quickly to produce an acceptable product. There were, of course, feelings of frustration and impatience in learning to use new techniques with unfamiliar technology, but the groups developed strategies to share their knowledge with each other.

The focus on creativity and ICT afforded the opportunity to practise and advance their ICT capability in a context that was more challenging than many of their previous school placements. As well as learning to work with colleagues, they acknowledged the need for teaching strategies to support creative and collaborative group work for the children. Despite being experienced and successful student teachers nearing the end of their training, they recognised that they learned much by working with small groups of children.

An important aspect of the project was the challenge it raised for the students' working within the wider context of systems of primary schools and teacher education. They recognised the usual constraints of timetable, curriculum and assessment targets – for the children and for themselves. Designing opportunities for student teachers to experience, model and evaluate creativity in their practice is a challenge in the context of a schooling and teacher training system characterised by centralised pedagogy, monitoring and inspection, and aspirations focused on standards of achievement in a limited range of 'measures'. A conceptual framework for creativity and ICT must describe not only the interaction in the activities themselves, but also the interactions between the activities and the wider contexts of policy and practice as they affect people and communities. By engaging in creative practices within the C&PD project, the student teachers experienced tensions and resolutions that helped them to 'read the world' in which they were acting in a more informed and interrogative manner.

Pause for thought

- *Look back at your own experiences of being creative in your life. What have you learned from those experiences? How will you take this into your own teaching?*
- *How would you like to express and develop your own creativity and creative habits of mind? What practical steps can you take to make that happen? How can you build a network of like-minded people to support and encourage each other?*

Thinking about creativity

a summary of key points

- *A useful way of looking at creativity is to consider it as an interaction between characteristics of people and communities, creative processes, subject domains and wider social and cultural contexts.*
- *Creativity can be described as combining the following five characteristics: using the imagination; a fashioning process; pursuing purposes; seeking originality; and judging values.*
- *Good learners, and creative people, need to be able to encounter and cope with puzzles, problems, seeming failure and disappointment, in order to learn from these experiences and demonstrate perseverance and resilience. They also develop their abilities to think about patterns and connections, and reflect on how new situations might relate to earlier experiences or need novel solutions.*

- *Creative people rarely work in isolation. Their ideas and outcomes are likely to have been generated through interaction with other people's ideas and reactions.*
- *A challenge for schools to think creatively in this regard is to draw upon the everyday knowledge of local and global communities; and to promote imaginative use of school environments as extensions to the physical space of classrooms.*
- *Being creative is not easy or straightforward, indeed, not always desirable in every situation. Tensions can arise when pursuing creativity: for example, between individual teachers, who challenge the status quo of pedagogical and curricular recommendations, and their schools.*
- *Teachers who wish to promote creativity in the lives of their pupils need to be able to model and share the range of creative experiences from their own lives.*

3 ORAL ARTISTRY: STORYTELLING AND DRAMA
TERESA GRAINGER

Introduction

This chapter examines the oral artistry of the spoken word, particularly in the context of storytelling and drama. It also focuses on your role as a fellow oral artist in the language classroom. It aims to help you take a fuller part in the creative endeavour of teaching these language art forms with passion, purpose and pleasure and presents some practical strategies to enable you to develop children's confidence and competence as oral language artists. Children deserve to hear, feel and experience the magic of language and its evocative, as well as provocative, potential. Recent government guidance on speaking and listening highlights the significance of both drama and storytelling, and many teachers are working to enrich their practice in these areas (DfES/QCA, 2003). In addition, the HMI Report (2003) *Expecting the unexpected* and the QCA (DfES/QCA, 2003b) resource *Creativity: Find it! Promote it!* indicate that both talk and these oral art forms can play a key role in enriching creative practice right across the curriculum. Initially in this chapter, attention is paid to creative contexts and the importance of dialogue and language play, and then the key areas of storytelling, drama and your artistic involvement as a teacher are explored.

Establishing creative contexts for talk

A creative context implies an environment of possibility which offers choices and encourages teachers and children to experiment with ideas, take intellectual risks and find innovative ways forward. Such an environment needs to be both supportive and challenging in order to foster children's creative endeavours, yet the creation of playful contexts is not without frames of reference. Teachers who wish to foster children's creative oral engagement do not ignore form and function, rules or conventions of language, but seek to help children explore these in meaningful contexts. Open-ended approaches involving all learners in a stimulating process of exploration and experimentation can be planned and developed from set learning objectives and can embed learning about language within them. Language arts activities in particular can enable you and the children to dwell in the realms of possibility, generating alternatives and developing insights as well as sharing these in more performative contexts. Literature discussions, oral storytelling, poetry performances and drama provide powerful contexts for creatively pursuing oral language. It is in such open scenarios, in improvisation, structured simulations and playful encounters that children discover their voice and verve, their fluency and flair, for creativity develops through interaction with others and with ideas.

As an adult you already know intuitively that learning is often a mutual accomplishment and that collaboration is critical. Many educationalists, leaning on the seminal work of Vygotsky (1978), argue for a pedagogy in which talk plays a central role and highlight that we learn through guided participation and benefit from the support of more competent others (e.g. Bruner, 1986; Wood, 1988; Corden, 2000). Recent research into development through dialogue proposes that learning is a product of inter-thinking, and that for a teacher to teach and a learner to learn, they must use talk and joint activity to create a shared communicative space, 'an intermental development zone' (Mercer, 2000). This conception of cognitive development as a dialogic process has consequences for our classrooms. Such an interactive pedagogy is dependent on the children's active involvement and sees learning as a transformation of participation. If children are creatively engaged in their learning, talking their way forwards and making connections, then high levels of involvement, motivation and imagination are likely to result.

But talk, while it is a tool for learning, is also a mode of communication and has a performative aspect and considerable artistic power and potential. Think of the great orators in the days before our politicians depended on sound bites, think of famous bards and poets, or famous actors who memorably bring others' words to life and consider those of your friends and family who have a marked facility with words. Perhaps you too find pleasure in the sound and savour of words, enjoy tasting words on your tongue, sing to yourself sometimes and experiment with language. Research into everyday talk suggests that language play is a creative social practice which pervades many aspects of our lives (Carter, 2004). Through examination of a large spoken word corpus, the CANCODE corpus, Carter shows that creative language use is not a special feature of some people, but a common feature of all people and that such playful use of language is most likely to develop in dialogic and intimate conditions. Spoken creativity, he asserts, is typically co-produced and works as a process with several individuals in dialogue (Carter, 2004: 112). This too has consequences for our classrooms if we want children to develop their creative capacity to play with words and their confidence as language artists, learners and performers. Meek suggests that as children learn to handle the language of the taken-for-granted in their culture, they 'experiment with parody and impropriety, guile and authority baiting' and become wordsmiths, whose voices creatively undermine or challenge existing forms and functions (1985: 47). Through telling stories and through taking part in both improvisational and performance-oriented drama, children can taste the magic of language, experience the potential of the spoken word and enrich their oral artistry.

Activity

Reflect on the language you use with your close friends. Is there a playful dimension to this at times? Can you think of examples? You might want to share these with others in your group and consider the purpose of such playful language use.

Storytelling

Children all have stories to tell: anecdotes, hopes, warnings, explanations, jokes, family stories, reminiscences, tele-visual tales and tales read, heard and created. They make full use of narrative as a way of making sense of the complexity of existence, for narrative is 'a primary act of mind transferred from art to life' (Hardy, 1977). It is a major means of thinking, communicating and constructing meaning for we are all storytellers (as the prominence of mobile phones testify), and thinking through story remains a universal ability which can be developed and extended. Yet storytelling is a learning tradition which remains somewhat untapped in the primary classroom. It builds on children's natural narrative competence and its spellbinding power can liberate their imaginations and motivate their engagement. Storytelling can be seen as a form of symbolic play, since stories are metaphors for children's concerns and lives which they borrow and transform. Children can acquire very advanced linguistic structures from their encounters with emotionally strong narratives (Fox, 1993). In orally retelling tales, children are free to embellish and exhibit their creative competence, which is often more difficult for them to demonstrate in writing.

Personal stories deserve a central role in the curriculum, for as children retell their life stories they exercise considerable influence over language and will organise the structure of the tale, making spontaneous choices about vocabulary, style, language and imagery. The work of Zipes (1993) and Rosen (1988) among others has shown the significance of autobiography and of individual, as well as collective memory, in the formation of identity. In honouring children's personal stories you can create strong relationships with your class, develop their narrative capacity and spoken fluency and enhance their sense of self and identity.

Traditional tales too should be given prominence. The work of Fox (1993), Grainger (1997) and Grugeon and Gardner (2000) has shown that such tales can play a key role in literacy learning and can in particular make a real contribution (Barrs and Cork, 2001; Frater, 2001; Grainger *et al*., 2004, 2005). Traditional tales were originally moulded for the ear and those with a strong oral orientation still retain considerable repetition, rhythm and sometimes rhyme. This often prompts more active audience engagement and encourages listeners to journey alongside the teller and taste the flavour and poetic resonance of the tale. Over time, children tacitly learn to use the oral patterns of such texts as well as the rich story language, which is both memorable and rhythmic in nature.

Oral storytellers, whether they are sharing personal or traditional tales, are language artists who make full use of their voice and perhaps gestures, props, visuals and songs to convey the essence of their tale. The core medium of this art form is the story itself, which tellers choose how to share using numerous skills to assist their telling as they create a style which suits the tenor and temperature of the narrative. Through telling and retelling tales of all kinds, children experience the fluency, flow and feel of their words, and can try out their own and others' tunes and receive a real response. Through telling and retelling tales, you can help children develop their verbal artistry, their ability to use language to create effects and to employ pause, pace, intonation, gesture and feeling in the process. Simultaneously, they will learn to respond to their audience and revisit and reshape tales through this social process (Grainger *et al.*, 2005). In retelling tales, learners release their potential to play with sounds and words, hear their own tunes, refine their skills and develop their communicative competence as oral language artists.

Activity

Share a personal story with a partner and see how when you have shared this tale with two or three other colleagues, the tale itself begins to be shaped and developed through the telling. Or alternatively try to retell a traditional story, preferably a little known one (for examples see Grainger et al., 2004). You may want to lean on a place you know well and retell the tale in the context of this new setting. Afterwards, reflect upon how much the place changed the story and how, as an oral language artist, you have woven something of yourself into the tale, not merely in terms of the scene, but the words which you use to recreate the tale or the manner or style of its telling.

Preparing to be storytellers

Children can develop their skills as tellers of tales in a variety of ways. If you employ storytelling conferences in preparation for an afternoon of tale telling (when perhaps classes share stories), you can help the young learners refine their skills and their fluency and ease as storytellers. Such conferences will involve small groups of children listening to extracts from each others' stories and responding reflectively to one another's telling, as the following examples from learners (aged seven) indicate:

> 'You were great at gestures, as each time the king came in I knew it was him cos of the crown thing you did.' (Rowan)

> 'I couldn't hear it all, you could make the wizard shout that might help.' (Jade)

> 'When you described the butterfly that was good but you keep saying "and then and then" and that makes it boring!'

In addition, if you offer children opportunities to work in A and B pairs (as tellers and listeners), to retell tales in small groups, or to take part in the whole-class story circle this will help develop their confidence and oral fluency. In all these contexts children can focus on improving particular aspects of their storytelling such as:

- **creative voice play (e.g. volume/intonation);**
- **gesture and body movement;**
- **pause and pace;**
- **facial expression/eye contact;**
- **visual aids and artefacts;**
- **framing opening sentences/musical introductions and endings;**
- **involving the audience.**

In supporting the development of children as storytellers in the classroom, you can use various strategies to enrich their story memories and recall of story structures. These can be modelled by the teacher in shared reading/writing and can be used in independent work. They include:

- *The three seeds of story.* **This indicates the beginning, middle and end of the tale. Pictures are drawn on three paper seeds to deconstruct a tale (or plan a new one), and are then watered by the storyteller's words in their retelling.**

- *Story mountains.* **This paper mountain reflects the trajectory of the story and is particularly useful for climactic stories. Symbols, pictures or words which represent key events in the tale are depicted on the mountain range.**

- *Skeletal summaries.* **These are keyword summaries which are listed on the body of a skeleton drawing. Significant phrases from the story can also be included.**

- *Emotions maps or graphs.* **These focus on the characters and involve the learners in recording in map or graph form a character's journey though the narrative. They are particularly helpful for retelling the story from a character's perspective.**

In using such strategies to recall the overall sequence of events, the storyteller becomes better acquainted with that sequence in the tale and is then freer to find the words to recreate the narrative (for further ideas of this nature see Grainger *et al.*, 2004). Drama is also a useful tool to support story recall and narrative exploration, and conventions such as role play, hot seating, interior monologues, decision alley or role on the wall can all be used to prompt retelling from a particular character's perspective. Classroom drama can also give rise to further storytelling while the class lives imaginatively within the world of the story.

Pause for thought

The many benefits from integrating oral storytelling into the curriculum include an increase in:

- *motivation, commitment and pleasure;*
- *artistic engagement and creativity;*
- *spoken language competence and confidence;*
- *fluency, intonation and use of paralinguistic features;*
- *active listening and image creation;*
- *a sense of audience and community;*
- *written vocabulary and use of literary conventions;*
- *applied knowledge of story structure and narrative patterns;*
- *inferential response to text.*

Drama

The oral artistry of the spoken word can be creatively employed in the context of play and drama. Imaginative play, whether in the role play area or in improvisational class-room drama, involves you and the children in making and shaping new worlds, investigating issues within them and returning to the real world with increased under-standing and insight. Such process drama invites children to exchange ideas and experiment with alternative perspectives and interpretations and raises questions rather than answers (O'Neill, 1995). Significantly, it also leaves room for ambiguity, since you'll be exploring the unknown together and using language spontaneously as you travel (Grainger, 2003).

Drama, like storytelling, draws on a complex web of different sign systems which includes facial expression, body language, intonation, gesture, mime, movement and space. These combine to communicate in sound, image and movement. As an inter-textual art form, it encompasses these 'dramatic literacies' (Nicholson, 2000) and has the potential to create imaginative and motivating contexts, which are experi-enced as real and provoke a variety of oral responses. In drama, children engage emotionally and this influences their spoken contribution which is often freer and attuned to the imagined context in which they find themselves. Process or story drama (Booth, 1996) is essentially oriented towards both creating and solving problems and talk is an essential part of its currency. The National Curriculum in England (DfES, 2000) describes the elements of speaking and listening as: speaking, listening, group discussion and interaction and drama. However, if drama is well planned and developed, then all four elements can be encompassed and children can develop their oral confidence and competence to play their way forwards creatively in a range of contexts.

In the fictional situations created in improvisational drama, authentic reasons to communicate emerge and you'll all be involved in discussing ideas, generating possible responses in role, co-operating with others and adapting your speech for different purposes and audiences. In this present tense context for literacy learning, the chil-dren and you will be involved in experimenting with vocabulary and with language styles and registers appropriate to their role and the imaginary scenario. The oppor-tunity to reflect on these choices also contributes to a growing command over the spoken word. You can access different registers and oral genres easily in drama and develop your lateral thinking too. Being creative is not purely an intellectual activity; feelings, intuitions and a playful imagination are an equally important part of the process and these come to the fore in drama and enable both purposeful and creative language to be generated.

Activity

Discuss with colleagues what you have seen in school under the banner of drama. Have you, for example, observed any of the following:

- *performances?*
- *visiting theatre in education groups?*

- *play script reading?*
- *role play areas?*
- *improvisational/process drama?*
- *puppetry or mask making and playing?*
- *costume/focus days, e.g. Victorian days?*

These various forms of drama can all support the oral artistry of the young, although the open-endedness and real-time dimension of process drama means that it is often the richest resource for developing young people's oral confidence and spoken creative contributions. If you are going to undertake process drama, you will want to harness a number of drama conventions to enrich both the creative spoken involvement of young learners and their comprehension and written composition. Conventions are tools for investigating meaning and represent a range of choices that can be flexibly used to frame and focus an investigation in the context of the text. Each also provokes particular kinds of talk and writing, which will influence your selection of these in the context of drama. Conventions work best if there is some element of ambiguity, uncertainty or tension inherent in the fictional scenario. They are not rigid structures, but can be combined and adapted to suit the dramatic exploration and trigger talk. Brief preparation time before each convention is often helpful in generating ideas, so the children are not pressured to take part in a hot seat, for example, before they have had the chance to think out possible questions with a partner. You'll need to develop a wide repertoire of drama conventions that can enrich children's oral artistry. Particularly useful will be working in the poetic mode which Neelands and Goode (1990: 6) describe as 'conventions which emphasize or create the symbolic potential of drama through highly selective use of language and gesture'. The following sample list may help you widen your repertoire of poetic and narrative conventions. For additional examples see Grainger and Cremin (2001).

Forum theatre (poetic). This is an improvisation performed by a few members of the class in the forum of the classroom, which then is discussed, revisited and developed. In its simplest form, an important situation is improvised and watched by the class, and the words and actions of those involved are commented upon (with the helpful mediation of the teacher). Then the same situation is reworked taking into account what has been said. It is most useful in a tense or significant situation.

Ritual or ceremony (poetic). The teacher and the class create some form of ceremony which is part of the drama to work out ways of marking significant events in the narrative. This slows the drama down and provokes a deepening sense of significance as well as reflection. For example, children as villagers might create a chant, a prayer or a dance to thank the gods for their beneficence. Ritual is often used to conclude work or to intensify the emotional tenor of the drama.

Small-group playmaking (poetic). In small groups, children discuss, plan and create a piece of prepared improvisation which expresses their understanding of an issue. It could be in the manner of a TV drama or documentary.

Decision alley. This is useful to examine conflicting interests or dilemmas and reveals the pros and cons of a particular decision. Two lines of children face each other and one child in role as a character walks slowly down the alley between them. As they progress, their thoughts or the sets of views for and against a particular course of action are voiced aloud by the rest of the class standing in the two lines. The character can be hot seated at the end of the alley, to ascertain their decision and its justification.

Freeze-frame. This convention is also known as 'creating tableaux', still images or statue making. Individually, in small groups or as a whole class, the children use their bodies to create an image of an event, an idea, a theme or a moment in time. This silent picture freezes the action, as do newspaper photographs, but can also portray a memory, a wish or an image from a dream, as well as represent abstract themes such as anger, jealousy or the truth. Freeze-frames can be brought to life, and subtitled with appropriate captions, written or spoken, and may have noises and sound effects added to them. In addition, the words or inner thoughts of members of the tableau can be voiced when the teacher touches children on the shoulder. Freeze-frames offer a useful way of capturing and conveying meaning, since groups can convey much more than they would be able to through words alone.

Hot seating. The teacher and/or a small group of children assume the role of one or more individuals from the drama and are questioned by the remainder of the class, who are *also* in role. The class needs to be forewarned and primed to think of questions. This is a useful probing technique which seeks to develop knowledge of a character's motives, attitudes and behaviour and increases awareness of the complex nature of human behaviour.

Improvisation: whole class or small group. The whole class, or a small group including the teacher in role, improvise together. This can be planned or spontaneous, 'formal', as in a whole-class meeting, e.g. a court scene, or informal, e.g. a market scene, a family at home. Whole-class role play reduces the pressure of being watched since everyone is corporately engaged and lives inside the moment, responding to each other spontaneously within the imaginary context.

Mantle of the expert. This involves children being given or adopting roles which necessarily include the expertise, authority, knowledge and skills of specialists. This knowledge may be recently acquired from classroom research, or may be bestowed imaginatively by the teacher in role, welcoming them as, for example, nurses or scientists. The status it gives the children allows them to significantly influence the drama. The teacher honours their expertise and ensures they can use it in the drama.

Overheard conversations. In small groups conversations between characters are improvised and a few 'overheard' by the class. This adds tension, offers information and enables a range of viewpoints to be heard. Key conversations from the past can also be created. The teacher as storyteller may later integrate these perspectives into the drama.

Thought-tracking. In this convention, the private thoughts of individuals are made public. This can be organised in various ways; the teacher can touch individuals on the shoulder during a freeze-frame or halt an improvisation and ask them to voice their thoughts. Alternatively, the class could simultaneously speak aloud their thoughts and fears in a particular situation. Or the teacher and children in role can give witness to the class and speak personally about recent events from a 'special' chair; members of the class can take turns in moving forward to stand behind the chair and express their thoughts from the character's perspective.

Teacher in role. This is the most powerful convention and involves the teacher engaging fully in the drama by taking various roles, e.g. leader, infiltrator, collaborator, messenger, vulnerable individual and so on. Through these, the teacher can support, extend and challenge the children's thinking from inside the drama. Every role has its own social status which gives access to different degrees of influence and power.

Writing in role. Different kinds of writing can emerge from the lived experience of the drama and can be written in role from the emotional stance and informed perspective of one of the characters – letters, diaries, messages, pamphlets, notes, even graffiti. Children often write with considerable urgency and passion in drama since they own the purpose and have a clearly imagined audience for their communication.

Improvisational process drama can be a powerful tool for enabling young writers to generate ideas, to rehearse their ideas orally and artistically and to shape the content of their writing. The spoken word can enrich the written in this context if you bridge effectively between the oral and the written. The last improvised scenario acts as a kind of dress rehearsal for the children's writing. The lived experience of the drama thus becomes a natural writing frame charged with the emotions and engagement of the imaginary scenario in which they have responded with energy and agency. As a consequence their writing in role has more voice, verve and conviction (Grainger et al., 2005). In addition to the potential of improvisational drama, the performance of drama can also contribute to children's oral artistry as they line their mouths with other people's words and experience the language of playwrights telling stories in this medium.

Pause for thought

Rooted in social interaction, improvisational drama is a powerful way to help children relate positively to each other, experience negotiation and gain confidence and self-esteem. Significantly, it also offers opportunities for children to use language creatively as they respond to the fictional situations in which they find themselves. Performance drama, or theatre as it is conventionally known, can also enable children to develop their oral artistry through trying out others' words and experiencing the power of language sculpted by talented others.

Teachers as language artists

The imaginative world of drama and the collaborative experience of oral storytelling are powerful language art forms which support the oral artistry of the spoken word. Both demand your full involvement as a fellow artist, working alongside your class and creatively using your own language to generate ideas, express yourself and interpret meaning. Your creative and artistic engagement in the language and literacy curriculum is central to ensure effective learning. Your ability to interest and inspire, communicate creatively and listen deserves attention and development. Your playfulness, openness and innovative bias also need to be nurtured and enriched if they are to contribute imaginatively to the construction of creative, competent and curious learners. You need to learn to tell stories yourself, to use rich imagery and varied intonation patterns to model the creative process, and you need to feel confident to take up roles in drama, using your words flexibly and imaginatively. An important feature of creativity, as Craft (2000) has observed, is being able and willing to express oneself. This will involve you in taking risks and being observed in this process. Wilson and Ball (1997) also found that risk-taking is a common characteristic of highly successful literacy teachers, not merely in relation to their artistic oral engagement, but also in their capacity to experiment and remain open to new ideas and strategies which may benefit the learner. This thoughtful playfulness is a characteristic of creative practice, and will involve you in exploring and developing possibilities in literacy and then testing and evaluating them with the children (NACCCE, 1999).

Research in the field of creativity highlights several other features of creative teachers, including a particularly learner-centred focus and an awareness of the personal oral stories of their young learners. Creative teachers tend to place the learners above the curriculum; the combination of a positive disposition towards creativity and person-centred teaching actively promotes pupils who learn and think for themselves (Fryer, 1996; Beetlestone, 1998; Craft, 2000). Such teachers respond to children's feelings, engage their interests, maintain their identity/autonomy and encourage their capacity to reflect critically (Jeffrey and Woods, 1997). 'Young people's creative abilities are most likely to be developed in an atmosphere in which your creative abilities are properly engaged' (NACCCE, 1999: 90), and recent studies indicate that when teachers are creatively engaged and lead by following, ensuring relevance and facilitating autonomy, then creativity and innovation are fostered (Barrs and Cork, 2001; Graham, 2001; Grainger et al., 2005).

As a potential practitioner you must at all costs avoid becoming a classroom operative who parcels out apparent curriculum knowledge in regularised chunks to passive recipients. Instead you need to use your voice and your imagination to conjure open invitations to learn and to negotiate the curriculum content (Grainger, 2003e). You need to recognise and develop your own creative potential as a language artist and value the creative dimensions of your own life, making creative connections between your personal response to experience and your teaching (Prentice, 2000: 15). In addition, you can learn to bring an author's voice to life evocatively and develop your own ear for language and awareness of the colour, movement and drama in words. If you can help children hear, notice and experience language emotionally, aesthetically and artistically, their voices will begin to ring with authenticity and individuality and carry a sense of their full participation and experiential engagement in the process of learning.

Through your own imaginative involvement, you can release your creative potential and enrich your confidence, commitment, knowledge and understanding of the oral artistry of the spoken word. In turn this will enable you to extend the children's development as oral language artists and as creative written language users. For part of learning to read and write involves children in learning to hear the tunes in texts (Barrs, 2000) and learning to use all the available resources to find the tunes and rhythms in their own voices. Extensive aural experience of language and the opportunity to explore their own oral artistry can contribute to the development of literate and creative individuals.

Oral artistry: storytelling and drama: a summary of key points

Oral artistry

— *The oral artistry of the spoken word is important to recognise and develop in the classroom; it can enrich children's confidence and competence as effective language users who employ their imaginations to find ways forward in collaboration with others. In the context of both storytelling and drama, as well as through performance poetry and in reading aloud, children can develop their fluency and ease as spoken language artists. Such artists play with words and meanings and take pleasure in the power of words and the emotional temperature of language. Such artistry will offer rich rewards in the context of their social and cultural lives and enable them to examine the potential of creative spoken words and actions.*

What can teachers do?

— *As artists in our classrooms too, telling tales or taking part in the imaginative world-making play frame of drama, we are freed from the traditional patterns of classroom interaction and are more personally and affectively involved, using our oral skills to the full and stretching our own language in involving contexts. As professionals we should listen for and notice children's creative and poetic language use, and build on their playful oral potential by providing plenty of opportunities for creative storytelling, for drama and other verbal art forms.*

— *The sound and savour of words need to be celebrated and experienced; we all deserve to find pleasure and delight in the oral artistry of the spoken word and develop our creative spoken potential.*

4 CREATIVE YOUNG READERS
PRUE GOODWIN

Introduction

> When you look at a painting
> let the dancing begin.
> Let the rhythm unlock
> the way your body rocks.
> Don't be shy, let your eyes jump in –
> Surprise the dancefloor of the painting.

Take a look at this verse from a poem by Grace Nichols (2004). As I read this poem, the exhortation to combine the sensations of sight and movement, together with the sense of hearing rhythmic music, motivate me to get up and dance. But how is that happening? How am I being inspired to dance, to gaze, to relish – to respond so creatively? The answer, by reading. To the outside observer I may be sitting in a crowded train with my nose in a book, but inside my head I am twirling and leaping, surrounded by colour and rhythm. The reading of the poem engages all my imaginative energy and through that engagement I am at one with the writer, constructing my own version of her meaning. No doubt my 'dancing' and my 'seeing' are different from those of Grace Nichols but, through her choice and combination of words, she has enabled me to experience a physical response through my imagination.

How do young readers acquire this particularly potent aspect of being a reader? And, perhaps a more important question, how can teachers ensure that pupils experience being readers in that way? This chapter argues that by involving children in thinking, talking and acting creatively, by engaging their imaginations through the sharing of powerful texts and by valuing their personal responses to literature they will become aware of the full potential of their own literacies as well as more proficient readers.

The power of reading

Although the poem 'When you look at a painting' is a particularly sensual piece of writing which elicits an equally sensual response, the process of reading would involve similar engagement from the reader no matter what the text being read. Reading is not a passive reception of what an author has written. There is a fusion of the ideas presented by an author and the linguistic, intellectual and emotional responses of the reader. No two readers will understand what they read in exactly the same way because everyone brings their own experience and expectations to each new text they read. As acknowledged in the Bullock Report (DES, 1975) when it presents definitions of reading:

> ... *reading is more than* a reconstruction of the author's meanings. *It is the perception of those meanings within* the total context of the relevant experiences of the reader — *a much more active and demanding process. Here the reader is required to engage in critical and creative thinking in order to relate what he reads to what he already knows; to evaluate the new knowledge in terms of the old and the old in terms of the new.* (DES, 1979: 79)

Readers encountering a new text will go through processes which enable them to determine what the words are, what the words mean and what ideas the meanings engender. This process takes place without any outward sign of what is happening in the minds of readers. Nor are the readers necessarily conscious of the process because they are absorbed in the meanings which are constantly shifting as they are being constructed. It will only be when they stop reading that they are conscious of having been entertained, informed, scared, amused or exhilarated by the experience. It is by reflecting on reading after the event that internal responses become explicit. The experience can feel so powerful that it seems odd that there has been no physical manifestation of it. However, the fact that there is nothing to see does not mean there is no 'product' resulting from the experience. It may not always be made apparent to others but '... while the act of reading may produce no physical outcome, it does produce an outcome of value — a changed person, with more knowledge or more emotional depth or both' (Holden, 2004: 25).

Pause for thought

Do you recognise the description of 'getting lost' in reading?

What were your experiences of reading when you were at primary school?

Did they ever include occasions when you can remember having strong, positive feelings about books that you read or that were read aloud to you? If you did what were the books?

Many adults have particularly strong ties to books or poems that moved or amused them when they were children. Which books from your childhood do you remember fondly? Could you choose a 'desert island' list of six books from your childhood?

About creativity

Creativity, as it is discussed in this chapter, involves ideas, invention, exploration, imagination and risk taking. It is about how we think, learn, have cognition and understanding of the world around us. It is concerned with the potential in everyone to generate imaginative ideas and to explore connections between seemingly unrelated pieces of knowledge. It is what Anna Craft (2001, 2002) calls 'little c creativity'.

... little c creativity ... focuses on the resourcefulness and agency of ordinary people. A 'democratic' notion, in that I propose it can be manifested by anyone (and not just a few), it refers to an ability to route-find, successfully charting new courses through everyday challenges. It is the sort of creativity, or 'agency', which guides route-finding and choices in everyday life. It involves being imaginative, being original/innovative, stepping at times outside of convention, going beyond the obvious, being self-aware of all of this in taking active, conscious, and intentional action in the world. (Craft, 2002: 56)

The processes and outcomes of creativity can be unexpected. Jerome Bruner (1962: 18) says 'An act that produces effective surprise — this I shall take as the hallmark of creative enterprise.' The 'surprise' occurs when unpredictable connections of otherwise unrelated bits of knowledge or experience spark new insights and understanding. Thinking and acting creatively involve a certain amount of insecurity, something that may seem inappropriate when struggling to learn a complex skill such as reading. However, from the earliest stages, learning to be a reader entails engagement with the whole process — what the words are, what the words mean and what ideas the meanings engender. Imaginative response articulated through discussion or represented through creative activity greatly enhances the ability to understand and explore a text beyond the literal level to discover many layers of meaning.

It is important that teachers plan opportunities for creative thinking and activity as part of the regular reading curriculum. Reading aloud to children from the works of excellent writers is one of the most important ways of captivating imaginations. Stretching creative interaction with what has been read can be brought about through open-ended discussion or through an engagement with the creative arts (music, art, drama and dance). The question arises, however, of whether it possible to spend time being creative with reading when a government-led curriculum is perceived as being didactic.

Creativity and the National Curriculum

In the National Curriculum for English, there has always been a requirement that children be encouraged to respond imaginatively to what they have read (DES, 1989; DfE, 1995). In the *Handbook for Primary Teachers in England* (DfEE, 1999c) this requirement was expanded to explain how 'respond imaginatively' could be achieved in primary classrooms:

respond imaginatively in different ways to what they read (for example, using the characters from a story in drama, writing poems based on ones they read, showing their understanding through art or music). (DfEE, 1999c: 47)

Since the most recent curriculum document in 1999 and the establishment of, firstly, the National Literacy Strategy (NLS) and, from 2003, the Primary National Strategy (PNS), education agencies have actively sought to encourage creativity through their publications and websites. For example, the QCA website **www.ncaction.org.uk** has a link to a section entitled *Creativity: Find it! Promote it!* which provides information, advice and descriptions of good practice of creative approaches across the curriculum. The PNS through its document *Excellence and Enjoyment* suggests that the best primary schools are 'creative and innovative in how they teach' (DfES, 2003). In August 2003, the Office for Standards in Education (OFSTED) produced an e-publication entitled *Expecting the unexpected* with the intention of encouraging schools to be more adventurous in their use of creativity across the curriculum. The report acknowledges the insecurity and unpredictability of creativity but urges teachers to accept that challenge:

> In successful teaching for creativity, teachers know not only what it is they are promoting but also how to create opportunities for this to happen. Usually this means providing pupils with challenges where there is no clear-cut solution and in which pupils can exert individual or group ownership. (OFSTED, 2003a: 8)

There is no lack of encouragement from politicians, or politically appointed educationalists, to be 'creative and innovative' in the ways that we teach and, although there may have been confusing messages in training, the approaches advocated by the NLS (particularly shared and guided reading) are founded on sound learning principles based on creative thinking and discussion. In fact, by following the NC requirements to 'respond imaginatively' and the NLS advice to have group discussions (guided reading), teachers should provide an environment well-disposed to the vulnerable nature of creativity.

Pause for thought

It hasn't always been standard practice to take account of the need for creative approaches in literacy learning. However, in recent years, since the publication of Excellence and Enjoyment (DfES, 2003), narrow ways of planning have been challenged and teachers are being encouraged to take more control of the curriculum. One way of doing this is to inject far more active and personal learning into literacy sessions. Ask children questions such as:

- *How does this story make you feel – excited, amused, sad, confused, etc.?*
- *Does this story/poem relate to your life?*
- *Does this story/poem make you want to draw, dance, sing, etc.?*

Be prepared for creative and personal responses. They are unpredictable, defy assessment and can sometimes take you completely by surprise. But that is one reason why they are so valuable. Allowing such free expression may feel insecure at first but levels of intellectual development can soar as a result – and that will be reflected in more formal literacy events (e.g. assessment tasks).

Getting beyond the literal

Most of the time, experienced readers are unaware of the linguistic processes that enable them to decode print because, for them, the whole procedure has long been automatic. Equally, they won't be conscious of how they are constructing the full meaning of the text, including those meanings which lie between the lines and those beyond the lines completely. As a reminder of what happens when we read, read the following extract from the story *The Librarian and the Robbers* by Margaret Mahy:

> One day Serena Laburnum, the beautiful librarian, was carried off by wicked robbers. She had just gone for a walk in the woods at the edge of the town, when the robbers came charging at her and carried her off.
> 'Why are you kidnapping me?' she asked coldly. 'I have no wealthy friends or relatives. Indeed I am an orphan with no real home but the library.'
> 'That's just it,' said the Robber Chief. 'The City Council will pay richly to have you restored. After all, everyone knows that the library does not work properly without you.'
> This was especially true because Miss Laburnum had the library keys.
> 'I think I ought to warn you,' she said, 'that I spent the weekend with a friend of mine who has four little boys. Everyone in the house had the dread disease of Raging Measles.'
> 'That's all right!' said the Robber Chief, sneering a bit. 'I've had them.'
>
> (Mahy, 1981: 53)

Answering a question on this passage could depend on a variety of things. It could depend only on your ability to read at a literal level: for example, what is the name of the librarian? The words you need to provide the answer are literally there in front of you. Or it could ask you to read beyond the literal: for example, what can you tell me about the character of Serena? Reading between the lines, she is quite calm and logical despite being kidnapped. This extract is so short that you may not have enough evidence to answer: do you think this will be a serious story or amusing? What do you think might happen? These questions call on all your previous literary experience of stories and your consequent expectations of this text. Other questions may not be appropriate in this instance: has reading this text moved you emotionally, made you ask yourself challenging questions, changed your thinking in any way? As these questions get more personal the answers reveal the depth of your understanding. In the case of every question it is likely that you looked back at the passage to verify your answer. Whatever level of meaning making a question demands, returning to the text is the means by which an answer will be found.

We access the literal meaning of a text by decoding print through a combination of syntactic information (grammar and language structure), graphic or visual information (letter shapes, punctuation marks, etc.), phonic information (sounds) and semantic information (literal meanings in context). Our previous experience of reading prompts expectations of a text based on our bibliographic knowledge (how books work/ purposes of texts) and particularly our knowledge of how stories work. Understanding meanings between and beyond the literal can include (to different intensities for different readers) internal imaging, questioning, inferring, predicting, commenting, using intertextual references and applying personal experience. What cannot be listed are the emotive responses any reader may or may not have. Yet, in addition to the linguistic decoding skills and the means of understanding sub-text, readers know that their personal feelings about what they read are valid and relevant to meaning making.

Personal response

How do teachers ensure that pupils learn the full range of skills, concepts and experiences that make them into a reader? The simple answer is by ensuring that they have plenty of opportunities to respond personally to what they read. Personal response goes way beyond the simple question: did you like it? The conventional book report offers little chance for genuine response and can actually discourage children who find the effort of writing the report cancels any pleasure to be gained from the reading. It is also difficult to cater for genuine response in written 'comprehension' exercises. Even when questions ask 'What do *you* think…?' there is usually a specific answer rather than the range of possibilities. Real comprehension will come when readers feel free to express their own feelings about and understanding of a text. To help children to do this, teachers must create opportunities that provide time to think, discuss, return to the text and respond in a variety of ways.

> *Examining the text to support and justify response means that we are a world away from simplistic notions of likes or dislikes. Of course, each reader will create their own meanings so that no two readers will read the same text in the same ways (and that is a challenging thought for any teacher) but 'to go back to the text to support … response' means the parts played by both the text and the reader are recognised and given status in the classroom. There is no difference between response and comprehension.* (Martin, in Goodwin, 2005: 39)

The following sections of this chapter offer ways that teachers have found successfully engage children in their reading and allow them to demonstrate comprehension through response.

Reading aloud to children

All readers – adults as well as children – love being read to, and listening to a story read aloud well will always be both a pleasure and a benefit. As soon as children are captivated by the story, their imaginations are at work. In the early stages, it is essential that children experience the total absorption that they will later get from being lost in a book. But at all stages of reading development, sharing the experience of a story enables children to understand more deeply and to tackle more complex ideas than they could alone. The end of a listening session is the time for teachers to introduce children to the pleasures of considering literary experiences with others – informally swapping opinions and chatting about feelings. Talking about books is a fundamental aspect of being a reader.

Pause for thought

Reading aloud is just one reason why all primary practitioners need to know a lot of children's books. Keeping up to date with the vast range of books available is not easy so it is a good idea to subscribe to a magazine and explore websites for advice (see reference list for further information). While keeping up with new books, don't forget the good old favourites that children have loved hearing read aloud to them for decades. For example:

- *Martin Waddell and Barbara Firth,* **Can't you sleep, Little Bear?** *Walker Books.*
- *Quentin Blake,* **Mr Magnolia.** *Red Fox.*
- *Shirley Hughes,* **Dogger.** *Red Fox.*
- *Michael Bond,* **A bear called Paddington.** *Collins.*
- *E. B. White,* **Charlotte's web.** *Puffin.*
- *Roald Dahl,* **Charlie and the chocolate factory.** *Puffin.*
- *Gene Kamp,* **The turbulent term of Tyke Tiler.** *Faber Children's Books.*

You will be most effective when reading aloud from books that you love. Children will pick up your enjoyment and enthusiasm.

Talking about reading

In his book *Tell me: children, reading and talk*, Aiden Chambers (1993) describes what he believes changes people from 'flat-earth into not just round-earth but intergalactic readers'. When discussing how he and his colleagues became such thoughtful and committed readers, they discovered that the greatest influence on them as youngsters had been the discourse they had had with experienced readers:

> It was in what other people told us about their reading, and what we told of our own, that we thought we had discovered the heart of the matter: a certain kind of booktalk gave us the information we needed, the energy, the impetus, the will to explore beyond familiar boundaries (...) We could all remember moments of booktalk that sent our reading another turn up the literary spiral. (Chambers, 1993: 14)

Chambers goes on to describe and promote book talk in every classroom as being the means by which teachers can similarly influence their pupils with reading. It is important to provide such contexts for talk about reading in school not just because talking about books is pleasurable but also because it enhances the ability to comprehend.

> The readiest way of working on understanding is often through talk, because the flexibility of speech makes it easy for us to try out new ways of arranging what we know, and easy too to change them if they seem inadequate. Of particular importance is the fact that we can talk to one another, collaborating and trying out our new ways of thinking. (Barnes, 1992: 125)

Creative readers will constantly find 'new ways of thinking' about the meanings they make from texts if the circumstances that encourage and sustain book talk exist. The open-ended discussions that take place can focus on all aspects of meaning making and will vary according to the age and experience of pupils. In order to establish competence in fully comprehending text, whatever their age, children should be encouraged to express personal opinions and to support their views by referring not only to the text but also to their own experience.

Book talk is essential for developing readers' understandings of the multi-layered mean-
ings of texts. The key to good book talk is good questioning that does not inhibit
response, but guides the reader to more considered understandings. (Hobsbaum,
Gamble and Reedy, 2002: 14)

Talking about books itself is a crucial part of being a reader. That is evident whether
we consider readers who choose to meet to share the experience of a selected
book or the informal comments made between individuals about a football report in
a newspaper. Among adults, the reason for talking about books is principally because
it is pleasurable; it increases levels of understanding and appreciation. Exchanging
opinions with others provokes deeper insights into what has been read and
encourages reflection and internal debate. The trading of thoughts about and
responses to books underpin shared and guided reading. Both approaches are based
on the belief that talking about a text enhances and develops understanding. Adult
book clubs, such as those replicated on TV shows such as *Richard & Judy* and *Oprah*
Winfrey, are examples of classroom-based group reading in the adult world. In organising group reading, teachers should aim to bring about as much reward in the
discussion about books as is experienced by members of adult book clubs.

There are many ways in which group reading can be organised but it is always based
around a shared text and free-flowing, purposeful discussion. The variety of approaches
include those which have been given specific names – for example, guided reading,
literature circles and reciprocal reading. Although these vary in purpose and presentation, each group approach is still based on shared text and talk. Literature circles
provide the closest experience to the sort of book talk identified by Chambers as
being influential in motivating young readers. Literature circles are student-led book
discussion groups which involve pupils making the choice of books, engaging in open,
natural conversations about books (Daniels, 2002) and having an enjoyable book talk
experience. Whatever the activity is called, it is within the context of group interaction
that children become reflective, analytical and opinionated readers, willing to extend
their thinking in creative and challenging ways.

Responding imaginatively

Imaginations are always at work as we listen to, read and when we discuss books but
there are few tangible results. More substantial evidence of the imagination at work
can be gained by seeking response through creative activities. Asking children to
respond to what they have read by inviting them to solve a problem, produce a piece
of artwork, compose some music or produce a piece of drama or dance enables
them to get beyond the literal meaning of a text and to gain deeper insights to the
meaning of a text. It also provides a context for discussion of abstract ideas. In addition
to the authentic need to return to the text in order to plan the activity in hand, the
creatively charged meeting of the imaginations of the writer and the reader can
spark exciting and innovative work.

Sharing meanings is a richly complex feature of human behaviour and literacy will not be
promoted by simply sticking to books and talk about books. The experience children
bring to school and group settings and the new experiences they find there must be re-

> enacted or tried out in many different symbolic ways – singing, dancing and music-making, drawing and painting materials, dressing up clothes and play artefacts, moulding and sculpting media and construction equipment and natural objects. These are the foundations of early literacy and not 'optional extras'. (Whitehead, 2004: 208)

And it is not purely in the early years that the interpretative powers of the creative arts should be employed as a routine part of literacy teaching.

> Helping children engage in the drama of reading, helping them become dramatist (rewriter of the text), director (interpreter of the text), actor (performer of the text), audience (actively responsive recipient of the text), even critic (commentator and explicator and scholarly student of the text), is how I think of our work as teachers of reading. (Chambers, 1993: 12)

Imaginative response is not limited to the creative arts. Pupils who may not enjoy a 'performance'-based activity, such as drama or painting, may feel more comfortable solving problems posed by a book or working on a computer to recreate a story. These approaches span the full primary age range. Some activities will take a few minutes within a literacy lesson, others may need several lessons dedicated to them. The following two examples of imaginative response describe a lesson with a class of six-year-olds and a project with three classes of nine-year-olds which took place over three days.

Pause for thought

The following descriptions of response activities with children of primary school age are intended to offer practical ideas that you can replicate. The books at the heart of these activities are super and work well in motivating children but it is not the books that make the learning successful – it is the engagement with text. Children's engagement with text is brought about through the sharing of a literary experience between teacher and pupils. Any book that you choose will 'work' just as well as long as you support the children's learning. How do you get started?

Personal and creative responses have to be modelled just like any other reading behaviour so, before expecting spontaneous response from children, ensure that you have led sessions that show children the range of possible responses. When you feel the children are confident enough to be challenged, take a step back in the process and let them start to make the decisions without your input.

Preparing for response activities

- *Select the text you want to share. You may select a book or poem that you recognise has tremendous potential for particular sorts of response (e.g. discussion, music-making, problem-solving or drawing).*
- *Plan how you will share it and how you will get the children to think more deeply about it.*
- *Prepare open-ended questions to set ideas going.*
- *Include time for the children to think, talk and plan.*
- *Have materials ready for use.*

Remember this is not a product-led activity. The learning outcome is related to the deeper understanding and appreciation of a text – not whether there is a good drawing, musical or dramatic performance. However, children love sharing their work and it is always uplifting to celebrate any artistic or other results that are produced.

Making connections with the Tooth Fairy

At the beginning of their second year in the infant school many children are losing their milk teeth. Tooth fairies are of immediate concern. With that in mind, the choice of *Dear Tooth Fairy* by Alan Durrant was a good choice to engage every child's interest in the book. The story is about Holly, who does not want to give her tooth away and so leaves some plastic Dracula fangs for the Tooth Fairy instead. We are informed on the front cover of the book that it 'Contains many real fairy gifts and letters!' – and so it does; every other page has an envelope to open and a message to read. The Tooth Fairy leaves a note, Holly replies and so the book goes on until Holly is convinced that leaving her tooth is a good idea. At the end of the book, Holly receives her coin. The focus of the session was on the reading of the story and messages and talking about different text types. Alongside a dramatic sharing of the book, there were a variety of activities that happened before, during and after the reading. These included:

Singing (before reading)	The teacher had prepared words to the tune of 'Matchmaker, matchmaker': Tooth Fairy, Tooth Fairy tell me the truth, Will you give me a pound for my tooth?
Movement (during reading)	Wriggling shoulders when the Tooth Fairy describes 'tingling in the tips of her wings'.
Drawing and colouring (after reading)	The book shows that there are many different sorts of tooth fairies. The children were invited to draw their own fairy.
Problem-solving/ design and technology (after reading)	The Tooth Fairy gives Holly a riddle-teller (folded paper square). In groups the children were helped to make one.
Music (after reading)	In groups, a teaching assistant helped the children to compose a theme to illustrate the flight from Fairyland to Holly's bedroom.

Finally, in keeping with the theme of the book, everyone wrote a thank you letter from Holly on a Post-it note (the right size for a fairy letter).

All the activities took place during one lesson. The extras (drawing, moving, singing, writing, etc.) took place in minutes. Not all the children completed everything they wanted to do in the time, so some activities spilled into 'choosing time'. Meanwhile, other Tooth Fairy stories were made available in the book corner – notably the lovely *Dave and the Tooth Fairy* and *Toyin Fay*, both by Verna Allette Wilkins – for children to read to themselves.

Transforming texts

Three classes of nine-year-olds were introduced to two texts – *Ex Poser*, a short story by Paul Jennings, and *Once upon an ordinary school day* a picture book by Colin MacNaughton and Satoshi Kitamura. *Ex Poser* is a first-person narrative in which a boy, David, tries to expose two classmates as being boyfriend and girlfriend. David's mate Boffin makes a lie detector to try to catch the victims out. *Once upon an ordinary school day* tells a tale, in word and image, of how an inventive teacher inspires his class by setting their imaginations free through listening to music. Both are school-based stories set in classrooms similar to those the children worked in every day.

The children were told that they were going to transform the texts by interpreting them through either music, movement, application of ICT or art. The three classes were divided into four groups, and asked to decide which text they would use, whether they would work as one big group, in small groups or as individuals. Each group was led by a teacher whose role was to encourage, support and facilitate the children's creative ideas.

In this project, although there were adults with each group, the intention was to see how many interpretations the children would come up with through their own ideas.

Music	Separate groups: • Wrote, composed and sang a song. • Wrote and accompanied a rap. • Composed a 'question and answer' tune on guitar and recorder to represent a lie detector. • Composed an instrumental piece to re-tell the picture book story.
Dance	• Worked as a whole group on a re-telling of the picture book through mime and movement.
ICT	Separate groups: • Retold the stories through video, illustrated recordings and PowerPoint presentations.
Art and DT	Separate groups: • Did impressionistic pictures to illustrate feelings (as in the picture book). • Designed and built lie detectors using boxes and scrap materials. Batteries were installed to make sounds or lighting effects. • Drew cartoon versions of the short story. • Painted portraits of characters. • Made masks and props to help them dress up as characters.

As could have been predicted, the outcomes were varied in content and quality. However, as this was a literacy project, the learning outcome was judged on the depth of interaction with, and deeper understanding of, the text, not the product or performance. From the point of view of the National Curriculum for English, there were many other positive outcomes in speaking and listening ('talking effectively as members of a group') and writing (most groups wrote draft plans and several wrote scripts, lyrics and annotated diagrams). It is also reasonable to assume that the creative arts, ICT and design benefited from the project as well.

Creative classrooms

Creativity can be unpredictable, anarchic, boundary-breaking and insecure but it is also playful, invigorating and highly pleasurable. In the primary classroom, the creative and innovative teacher will have a long-lasting effect on her pupils' learning in all subjects, but especially in literacy, where the ability to be creative is an essential element of both reading and writing.

Indicators of a creative classroom according to the QCA website (2004) are as follows:

When pupils are thinking and behaving creatively in the classroom, you are likely to see them:

- **questioning and challenging;**
- **making connections and seeing relationships;**
- **envisaging what might be;**
- **exploring ideas, keeping options open;**
- **reflecting critically on ideas, actions and outcomes.**

This list works equally well as a list of what should happen during book talk, group reading or response activities. Teachers must establish an environment where pupils feel safe to try things out, to take risks and to value novel ideas. In order to encourage artistic activity, it is not necessary for teachers to be skilled in the arts themselves. All it takes to provide the conditions for creativity in the classroom is for teachers to be open minded, flexible and prepared to take a few risks – to organise a classroom where teachers and learners:

- **relax and enjoy their learning;**
- **are curious and questioning;**
- **encourage and support effort;**
- **are intrinsically motivated, persistent and spurred on by challenge.**

The most difficult thing to organise is time. But time to engage the imagination will not be time wasted. As Ted Hughes says: '… imagination, with its delicate wiring of perceptions, is our most valuable piece of practical equipment. It is the control panel for everything we think and do, so it ought to be education's first concern' (1988: 36).

Creative young readers:

a summary of key points

- *When understanding a text, readers go beyond both decoding and comprehension into personal, emotional and creative response to what they are reading. Understanding involves a combination of decoding skills, reading beyond the literal, the engagement of the imagination and the experience of emotion.*

- *It is personal response which enables readers to fully understand.*

- *Children need to have the experience of being a reader, in its broadest sense, modelled alongside the more functional aspects of learning to read.*

- *The best way of learning literacy skills – both functional and affective – is through engagement with literature.*

- *The best context for learning is through positive engagement with a book or poem. Enjoyment should not be viewed as a chance by-product of reading but as an essential element which, because it is very rewarding, will motivate and inspire young learners.*

- *Effective ways of enabling children to get beneath the surface of a text include:*

  - *reading aloud;*
  - *talking about what has been read in discussion, book talk sessions and reading groups;*
  - *responding imaginatively through problem-solving, the creative arts or ICT tasks.*

- *All primary teachers need a developing knowledge of children's books. There are many sources of support to help keep up to date with books or to assist teachers in identifying particular sorts of texts.*

- *The sharing of literary experience should be a source of pleasure and enlightenment for both teachers and pupils.*

Useful websites

Literature Circles: **www.literaturecircles.com**

Office for Standards in Education (2003) *Expecting the unexpected: developing creativity in primary and secondary schools* HMI 1612. E-publication downloadable from: **www.ofsted.gov.uk**

QCA, *Creativity: Find it, promote it*. See: **www.ncaction.org.uk/creativity/**

Keeping up with children's books

Books for Keeps
1 Effingham Road, London SE12 8NZ
Tel: 020 8852 4953
E-mail: **booksforkeeps@btinternet.com**
Website: **www.booksforkeeps.co.uk**

Carousel
The Saturn Centre
54–76 Bissell Street, Birmingham B5 7HX
Tel: 0121 622 7458

E-mail: **carousel.guide@virgin.net**
Website: **www.carouselguide.co.uk**

Reading Zone: a new website about books for children from birth to Key Stage 3.
See **www.readingzone.co.uk**

Achuka UK: a magazine to keep adults up to date with children's publishing.
See: **www.achuka.co.uk**

Acknowledgements

Many thanks to the teachers and pupils of Onslow Infants School, Guildford, and Tillingbourne Junior School, Shalford, for their work on response activities.

5 WRITING CREATIVELY
DEBRA MYHILL

Introduction

The principle of creativity expressed through writing is close to the heart of most teachers of English, both in the primary and secondary sectors. And yet both 'creativity' and 'creative writing' are loosely defined terms, used liberally, but probably with little genuine shared understanding. In this chapter, I will explore what it means to write creatively in the light of both psychological and educational perspectives on creativity and on writing, and I will consider teaching strategies which will support young writers in gaining the confidence and understanding to write creatively.

Defining creativity

Runco (2004) notes just how difficult it is to define creativity, because it is a complex concept with various very differing ways of being manifested, from the solving of a difficult problem to the creation of a work of art. Moreover, this complexity is compounded by the fact that creativity can be attributed not just to outcomes, such as works of art, but also to people deemed creative personalities, and to processes. For example, Sternberg (1988) distinguishes between *process* and *product* creativity. Product creativity is the creation of a work which is original, innovative and important, and few people are genuinely creative in this sense; process creativity is applying knowledge inventively to a current situation and is common, in varying degrees, to all people. Csikszentmihalyi (1996) describes the process of being creative in terms of 'flow', when an individual is fully absorbed and engaged by the task and the thinking it demands.

However, common to many psychological definitions of creativity are the concepts of flexibility, divergence, originality and an ability to synthesise ideas. Guilford, one of the earliest psychologists investigating creativity (1950, 1967), detailed the following factors as likely to be evident in a creative person:

- **a sensitivity to problems;**
- **fluency: the ability to produce a large number of ideas quickly;**
- **an ability to produce novel ideas;**
- **flexibility of mind;**
- **a synthesising and adapting ability;**
- **adeptness at the reorganising of ideas;**
- **competence at evaluating results.**

These characteristics are essentially cognitive, and some distance from the associations of creativity with inspiration, or what Csikszentmihalyi (1999) calls, with suspicion, the 'aha experience', that moment of sudden insight or understanding. Csikszentmihalyi's reservations about conceptualising creativity in terms of moments of inspiration are echoed by the NACCCE (1999) report on creativity in education. The report argues that 'creativity is not simply a matter of letting go': rather, genuine creative work 'relies on knowledge, control of materials and command of ideas' and involves not just innovation but also knowledge and skills.

From the perspective of this book, and specifically this chapter, two key questions to emerge from the research literature on creativity are: can anyone be creative, and can creativity be learned and developed? There has been a significant amount of research into identifying and measuring creative potential, particularly by Torrance (1962, 1963, 1979; Torrance and Myers, 1971) including tests which attempt to assess creativity and heuristic techniques which attempt to develop creativity. But this is an issue which divides. Runco (2004) argues that everyone has the capacity to be creative, and Sternberg's discrimination between product and process creativity asserts that while only a minority will produce widely acclaimed creative products, anyone can engage in creative processes. In an interview debate (1999), Csikszentmihalyi and Epstein articulate these conflicting viewpoints. Epstein argues that creativity can and should be taught, while Csikszentmihalyi argues that only a minority of people can be deemed creative in each generation. For Csikszentmihalyi, creativity involves cultural judgements about what is valued: 'The judgment of others is essential for us to be able to call an idea creative, to distinguish it from delusion.' This idea that creativity is not exclusively about the individual but is culturally determined is echoed by Amabile (1983) who demonstrated how the recognition of creativity was strongly influenced by social and cultural processes. It is easy to see how this might be true if you think about people's responses to the modern art in the Tate Gallery, or whether the novels of Barbara Cartland are creative and worthy of study.

Pause for thought

- *Do you think of yourself as a creative person? What aspects of your personality or way of working do you think are creative?*
- *Talk to three or four of your fellow trainees: what would be their instant definition of creativity?*
- *Do you and your peers believe creativity is a characteristic of some people or a potentiality in all people?*

Creativity in writing

The term 'creative writing' was once commonplace, describing the kind of imaginative and personal writing which took place in English, and there are many teachers of literacy and English in both primary and secondary who still use the term. Yet the phrase does not occur anywhere in the National Curriculum for English or in the National Literacy Strategy. In part, this may be because creative writing is rather unclear in terms of its intended audience, its purpose and the form it should take.

The phrase is also associated with a particular style and era of teaching, when stimuli were heavily used to generate creative writing and when, allegedly, anything written was acceptable. The Bullock Report (DES, 1975) was critical of creative writing, which was valued for its spontaneity and precocious language, rather than for any genuine ability to communicate powerful feelings in words:

> *It usually means in actuality, colourful, or fanciful language, not 'ordinary', using 'vivid imagery'. It is often false, artificially stimulated and pumped up by the teacher or written to an unconscious model which he has given to the children. It is very often divorced from real feeling.' (DES, 1975: 11.3)*

Perhaps because of a sense that the idea of 'creative writing' has been discredited, the term 'original writing' is sometimes used, including at GCSE, where a piece of original writing is submitted as a coursework component. But this is no less problematic. On one hand, most pieces of writing are original in that they are a new and different combination of words, sentences and ideas from anything that has gone before. Every shopping list I write is wholly unique and original, but few would argue for its creative genius. Alternatively, you could consider writing as creative and original depending upon its effect on the reader. But divergence and originality which are characteristics of creativity, as noted above, are frequently not appreciated by readers: James Joyce's *Ulysses* commands fewer enthusiastic readers than Barbara Cartland's romances.

It is possibly more helpful to think of writing creatively as being about the process of writing rather than about the writing outcomes – although the discussion about whether some types of writing are more intrinsically creative than others is a valuable one to consider. There are many who would argue that the act of writing is a creative, generative, meaning-making activity, not just when the writing is labelled as 'creative writing'. Emig (1988) conceptualises writing as a 'creative process in which meanings are made through the active and continued involvement of the writer with the unfolding text.' This slightly romantic view of the writing process falls into what Hayes and Flower (1980) described pejoratively as the 'inspiration paradigm', a paradigm which they saw as part of a mythology about the creativity of the writing process and which they damned as, in some cases, 'pure bunk'. More recently, however, researchers and writers have offered a more complex view of the act of writing as involving interrelated and mutually complementary skills, one component of which is creative thinking. Sharples (1999) sees a writer as 'not only a creative thinker and problem solver, but also a designer', generating ideas, juggling with task constraints and drawing upon the creative and linguistic resources available. Kellogg's (1994) psychologist's perspective argues that writing draws on critical thinking, the ability to make judgements and creative thinking, the ability to create and communicate ideas, a view which is strongly echoed by children's writer, Tim Bowler (2002):

> *Why is writing so tricky? Because it requires mastery of two conflicting skills: a creative skill and a critical skill. The former is of the imagination, the latter of the intellect, and they come from different brain hemispheres. To write well, we have to employ both to maximum effect.*

For those of us concerned with teaching writing, it is Sharples, Kellogg and Bowler who offer the most helpful ways to think about writing, and which point to writing classrooms where the imagination, the intellect and the struggle with words and ideas are all equally important facets of writing creatively.

Pause for thought

- **Do you think we should think of creativity in writing in terms of the kinds of writing produced or in terms of the writing process children engage in?**
- **Are some kinds of writing more 'creative' than others? For example, is a poem, more creative than an argument? Justify your answer!**

The writing process

Given just how central writing is to education, you might be surprised to find out that research into the psychological processes involved in writing are remarkably recent, and this is very much a developing field of research – a complete contrast with learning to read, about which there is a vast amount of research. The first rigorous attempt to describe the thinking and mental processes we go through in tackling a writing task was undertaken by Hayes and Flower in 1980, who devised a model of the writing process. Their observations with students during and after the writing process highlighted that the processes involved in writing are recursive and intertwined: in other words, it is not simply a step-by-step linear process. They describe the writing process as having three elements: planning, translating and evaluating. *Planning* is not quite what we might think it is from the way we use the word in school: planning refers to the retrieval and selection of ideas, or generation of ideas, and the sorting and organising of these ideas to select those relevant to the task. This is when the imagination is at its most fertile. Much of this happens in the head not on paper, though some elements of planning will include capturing ideas on paper. *Translating* refers to the process of moving from ideas to sentences and text: in essence, it is the drafting stage, and is essentially a language-based stage, shaping ideas into a written composition. Finally, *evaluating* involves all the editing and revision elements of composing writing: re-reading, changing words, and cutting and changing larger chunks of the text.

To emphasise that these three elements are not linear, Hayes and Flower include the idea of a *monitor* in their model, which switches attention backwards and forwards between these elements. Sometimes, you might be aware of this monitor at work when you write – when you are trying to think of the right word to describe something, and you are rejecting the words your brain is suggesting, your monitor is switching attention like a ping-pong ball between planning and evaluating. Or you might have written three or four paragraphs of a story and realise you need more ideas about the main character's appearance: here the monitor switches attention from translating (writing the paragraphs) to evaluating (realising you need more ideas), back to planning (thinking up new descriptions of your character's appearance). The writer's brain is a clever thing!

Yet despite this ability of our brains to do so much almost simultaneously, we all have limits. If we try to do too much at once, we overload our brain and cannot cope, and writing is a highly demanding cognitive process. One very real problem for children learning to write and for weak writers is that they devote so much 'brain power' to some aspects of writing that they have no mental energy left for other aspects. Psychologists talk about 'cognitive load', which is how much we are asking the brain to do at once: most of us reading this book would find it easy to write a paragraph about ourselves without pausing too much to think about it. We are fluent writers. But children learning to write have to cope with handwriting and all the demands of shaping letters on paper; they have to think about how to spell words; they have to think about where full stops and capital letters should go – and all this at the same time as trying to communicate the ideas in their heads. This is a real problem for young writers and something which can hinder creativity because all the attention is on more obvious writing problems. When I write text messages on my mobile phone, I suffer from just this kind of cognitive overload, because I am hopelessly inept at the process: I look at each number on the keypad to find the letter I want; I consciously count how many clicks I've made to get the right letter; I keep looking at the display to check the right word is there; and I am very slow! I also avoid long words, use no punctuation (because I still don't know how you do this) and the thought of writing a long message is too daunting so I make them short and to the point. There is little room for creativity in my text messages. If we want to help children to write creatively, we need to plan our teaching and support with an understanding of the different elements in the writing process, and create space for creative thinking and the imagination by reducing cognitive overload.

Figure 5.1, with apologies to Hayes and Flower, is a simplified version of the writing process which attempts to illustrate some of the sub-components of writing and to emphasise their interrelatedness. The following three sections explore each of these sub-components in more detail in the context of the primary classroom, but if you would like to read more about the writing process, follow up the references to Hayes and Flower (1980), Berninger et al. (1996) and Bereiter and Scardamalia (1987) in the References at the end of the book.

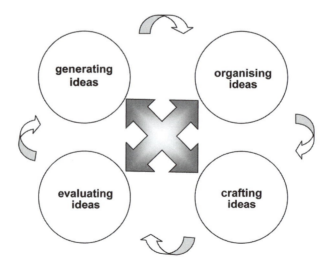

Figure 5.1. The writing process – a recursive process.

'I don't know what to write!' – generating ideas

The imagination is the distinguishing characteristic of man as a progressive being.
(Coleridge – *The Education of Children*)

Writing creatively is fundamentally about communication and the expression of ideas, feeling, opinions and arguments, so it is easy to see why generating ideas is an important sub-component of the writing process. The frustration of 'writer's block' is symptomatic of this stage rather than of the organising, crafting and evaluating stages, and the blank page can be an intimidating thing. Collins and Gentner (1980) divide the act of writing into two phases, *idea production* (generating) and *text production* (organising, crafting and evaluating). Idea production is a free-ranging, non-linear activity: it is unpredictable, resistant to control and inconsistent. In this phase, the conscious and the unconscious mind interrelate as words and images crystallise. I am sure you have wondered where a particular idea came from: cognitive psychologists will tell you that you have probed in your long-term memory till you found what you needed, then dragged these ideas into your working memory. Psychologists developing creativity theory suggest very similar notions, though the vocabulary is often different with more references to the unconscious, to inspiration and to the act of creation. So Koestler (1964) argues that we can create when we let go of familiar routines and habits, which restrict the imagination and our generative powers – the moment of discovery 'often means the uncovering of something which has always been there but was hidden from the eyes by the blinkers of habit'. Seeing things differently, 'a placing of things in new perspective' (Bruner, 1979) or associating together things that are conventionally separate are central to the mental processes of generation, and of course metaphor and simile do just this.

In the classroom, this means that we need to ensure that we devote time to supporting the haphazard process of generating the communicative ideas which will form the basis for writing. Most teachers are already familiar with a host of imaginative strategies which offer a range of stimuli or starting points for writing through the use of props and artifacts, toys, drama, pictures or a poem or story read as a trigger for more ideas. Valuable as these are, and excellent for creating an impulse to write, on their own they may not be sufficient to support children in the process of creating and capturing what they want to write about. In planning for teaching at this stage, you could usefully think about three further strategies which will strengthen the impact of the stimulus or starting point used.

1. *Free the mind to create*. Bearing in mind the idea of cognitive load described earlier, we can help children at this point by trying to free up as much of their mental capacity for the process of generation. In particular, this involves removing the fear of evaluation and reducing the need for writing at this stage.

2. *Offer choice*. Topic choice can be a motivational factor which allows creativity to occur. Despite the anecdotal view that boys dislike writing narrative and prefer non-fiction, there is very little hard evidence that this is true. But there is growing

evidence that boys enjoy the creative freedom that story or imaginative writing offer (see Flutter, 2000; Myhill, 2001; Grainger T, 2003; and Goouch and Lambirth, 2003).

3. *Capture initial ideas using holding forms.* A holding form helps to pin down the messy process of generation after there has been a period of creative activity; it acts as a bridge between the freeflow of generation and the movement towards the writing task.

Classroom strategies to support the generation of ideas

- Deliberately avoid telling children what kind of writing they will have to do so that they are not constrained in idea production by the task demand. Knowing that you will be writing a story about a surprise present can act as a dampener as you think simultaneously about the plot as well as about generating core ideas.

- Stress the importance of quantity rather than quality. All ideas are potentially good ideas as weak ideas can spark off better ones and earlier ideas can generate later ones – often the most unusual or divergent thinking occurs when you have exhausted the more obvious responses. It's worth remembering that children may need support in understanding that quality is not the prime consideration at this stage as quality is such a focus in most areas of school endeavour. One significant inhibitor to creative thinking is the marker in the head who rejects emerging ideas before they have even come to birth.

- Use talk to reduce cognitive load: for example, thought showering, talking to peers about ideas, explaining ideas to the class. This acts as an oral rehearsal of thoughts later to be written down.

- The process of writing in fluent writers can itself generate ideas – we do not need to know everything we intend to communicate before we start writing. The advice here would be 'just write!'. For younger, more novice writers who have not yet automatised the transcription processes, this will be less useful.

- When you are specifying the form or text type for a piece of writing, offer children a choice about the topic content. For example, everyone could be writing an instructional text, but individuals could choose the activity they want to provide instructions for.

- Listen hard to children's requests to write about or do something different from that you had intended. Is it really important that they stick with your guidelines or can they still learn about writing through the choice they have made?

- Use a repertoire of holding forms to help children capture and 'hold' their ideas after the initial flow of ideas. Holding forms you could try include lists, tables, diagrams, spider charts, sketches – indeed anything which simply captures thoughts and does not attempt to impose any order on them. You could also try an oral holding form, such as taping initial ideas.

- Free writing, where children simply write continuously without stopping or evaluating, can be a holding form with more able writers.

- **Look back at some of your planning for writing: identify a point where you offer a starting point for writing and adapt the planning to specifically include some of the ideas above.**

'I don't know how to say it!' – organising and crafting

Every line, every phrase, may pass the ordeal of deliberation and deliberate choice. (Coleridge, *Biographia Literaria*, p. 611)

Collins and Gentner's (1980) distinction between idea production and text production is a useful one from the classroom perspective, as the two different processes require different kinds of teaching attention. Unlike idea production or creative generation, text production is the imposition of linguistic order upon ideas. In Hayes and Flower's terms, text production is the planning and translating stage, where shape and coherence are given to amorphous, incoherent and emergent thoughts and ideas. For immature writers, failing to see the distinction between idea and text production can be a problem, and can cause stumbling blocks to progress. Older writers may have the insight to see that writing involves both – the 12-year-old boy who complained, after having had to write an argument about animal testing, that 'This test is wrong because I don't know anything about animal testing so therefore could not show my argument skill', showing an awareness of the need to both have access to *what* to write and *how* to write it in order to be successful.

In essence, the organising and crafting stages involve selecting and ordering material at text and paragraph level, and making choices about words, phrases and sentence structures. For children who are learning to write their ability to organise and craft will be strongly related to their developmental stage. Bereiter and Scardamalia (1987) believed that most young writers under the age of ten were in what they called the 'knowledge-telling' phase, where writing was a chain of associations and one sentence led to the next sentence. The only macro-structure this kind of writing has is completion of what the child wanted to say. In contrast, more mature writers are 'knowledge-transformers', able to manipulate their ideas and structure their writing to suit different purposes and audiences.

The aim of teaching children to understand how to shape and craft their ideas should be to help them understand that the effectiveness of what they want to say is influenced by how they say it, that form and content interact to create meaning. The NACCCE report (1999) on creativity in schools drew attention to this interaction of form and meaning in all creative enterprises: 'The look, sound and feel of work in the arts is inseparable not only from what it means, but from how it means.' In practice, this means encouraging experimentation and playing with language, not teaching rules for effectiveness, and playful experimentation with effect can begin well ahead of the ability to reproduce those features in writing. So, for example, Early Years children can play with alliteration and repetition, mirroring the language patterns found in many children's picture books, and children at every level can experiment with word choice. Again, talk is a valuable medium for supporting children's understanding of some of the choices available to them: use oral rehearsal to help children develop an ear for the sound of written sentences rather than spoken sentences.

Classroom strategies to support organising and crafting

- *Oral rehearsal – the magic pen.* This is a special pen that can think and talk as well as write. Set up a writing task and in groups of three or four with one magic pen per group – the children use the magic pen to orally rehearse their sentences. The magic pen is given to one child who tells the rest of the group what sentence the magic pen is telling her to write, and the rest of the group listen to the sentence. Then the magic pen is passed around the group so that each child can speak the sentence the pen is saying.

- *Oral rehearsal – designers.* Collate together as a class some key vocabulary related to the writing task: this should include nouns and verbs (for more able writers perhaps it could also include some adverbs and some subordinators?). In pairs, children design the opening sentences for their piece of writing by choosing some of the key words and adding the words they need to make a good sentence. When appropriate, stop the class and ask three or four children to orally rehearse their sentences for others to hear.

- *Graphic organisers.* Help children to develop macro-structures for writing texts by using graphic organisers or advance organisers which map out a broad route through the piece of writing. Examples of graphic organisers include storyboards for narrative, flow charts for instruction texts, argument trees (with main branches for 'big ideas' and side branches for smaller, related ideas).

- *Shared writing.* Use a shared writing time to model to the class some of the ways in which you have crafted and shaped a piece of writing, making your thinking and choices transparent.

- *Whodunnit?* Find a selection of examples of the passive from real texts, perhaps taken from texts used in class recently. They should include some passives which include the by-agent (who did it) and some which omit the by-agent. Play a quick detective game where they sort the examples into mysteries solved and mysteries unsolved. Pull the game together by highlighting the two different ways the passive can be used by telling 'whodunnit' or by concealing 'whodunnit'.

Pause for thought

- **The National Literacy Strategy has introduced a more explicit attention to grammar in relation to writing, but it is important that children fully understand how making grammar choices can affect their writing. This is more important than the grammar terms themselves. Observe a class being taught some feature of grammar, or teach a literacy lesson yourself addressing grammar. Then talk to the children about their understanding of how this might help their writing.**

- *Your own subject knowledge of how texts work is important if you want to draw attention to this in the classroom. Take adjectives, and write yourself a 'Teacher's aide-memoire' of all the different ways adjectives are used in different texts.*

'I don't know if it's any good!' – evaluating

For all writers, of all ages and all abilities, being able to determine the quality of what you have written is a hard task, not least because of the personal investment you have made in the task. But being able to evaluate what you have written is part of writing creatively, and indeed evaluation is a key part of all creative endeavours. Indeed, you could say that it is the presence of evaluative ability which distinguishes between a genuinely creative enterprise and an indiscriminate 'anything goes' enterprise. The NACCCE report (1999) notes that 'there is always a stage where critical appraisal is necessary'. However, being critical is a facility which requires nurturing, and it is a mistake to think that only mature, able writers are ready to develop skills of evaluation.

In the classroom, there has always been a tendency to make evaluation the final stage of the writing process, but the more we can build the recursiveness of the writing process into our teaching, the better. Evaluation can occur at every point in the writing process, not simply at the end. So, for example, after generating ideas, there is usually a need to select the best ideas, which involves evaluation; after organising your instructions into a flow chart to support sequencing, there is a need to check the sequence is correct, which involves evaluation. We should capitalise on all these opportunities to foster the skills of reflection upon writing. Perhaps the word evaluation is too often used synonymously with assessment, whereas in terms of developing writing, we are more concerned to develop judgement and the ability to make discriminating choices.

Developing critical judgement is largely a collaborative, social activity, involving realising how others respond to our writing and constructing shared understandings. Nixon and Topping (2001) found that carefully structured peer interaction had a qualitative impact on children's writing. They used paired writing, with each pair made up of a Year 6 pupil and a reception class pupil. The paired writing sessions were very focused and close relationships developed. Interestingly, the Year 6 pupils were selected as having themselves been slow to develop literacy skills, and were intended to benefit from the tutoring experience. In Holland, teachers and researchers (van den Bergh and Rijlaarsdam, 2001) have been experimenting with observational learning techniques, which help writers understand the needs of their readers. They divided children into groups and gave one group several pieces of writing and asked them to judge which was the best; another group observed this process and devised a list of the criteria they thought were being used to make these judgements. Both these strategies encourage children to reflect on their writing, but it is also valuable to develop metacognitive thinking about the process of writing, so that children become more aware of what they do as they write and are thus better able to cope with problems that arise.

Classroom strategies to support evaluation of writing

- Avoid always putting evaluation at the end of the writing process; encourage children to see evaluation as expressing judgements and making choices, not marking their writing. Introduce evaluation points, relevant to the learning objectives of the lesson, at different stages in the writing. For example, when moving from having created a holding form (perhaps a spider diagram) to selecting and organising ideas you could ask children to underline their four most vivid images or their four best arguments.

- Be sensitive about when to introduce an evaluation point: you may have planned an evaluation activity, but if it is evident that there is a creative 'flow' and children are absorbed in their writing, then don't interrupt it. Remember that evaluation at the wrong time can hinder creative generation.

- Develop evaluation strategies where no writing is required: in particular, using talk to discuss choices made and their effectiveness. This could be a plenary point where one child's work is shared and discussed by the whole class.

- Develop children's confidence in peer evaluation: to work well peer evaluation takes time and needs teaching support. Give children prompts, questions and clear focuses for peer evaluation so they develop a way of thinking about writing which will help them evaluate their own and each other's work.

- Use guided writing to help smaller groups evaluate their writing, using questioning and discussion very carefully to scaffold and support their understanding of how to judge their writing.

- Metacognition. Try to make the processes of writing more visible to children as writers. It is a mistake to think this is only possible for older, more mature writers – Early Years children are fully capable of beginning to think about and reflect upon the writing process at their own level. For older writers, one particularly helpful to distinction to make is the difference between holding forms, such as thought showers or spider diagrams, which capture and pin down random, freeflowing ideas, and graphic organisers, such as concept maps, which begin to impose order, structure and shape onto those initial ideas.

- Metacognition. Develop children's thinking about writing processes by using strategies such as the thinking hat. Put your thinking hat on – this is a special hat that helps you to think *about* what you are doing. Thinking hat questions (choose to match task) include: What did you do when you got stuck? Where do you get your ideas from? What did you find difficult about rehearsing your sentences? Why are your sentences like writing not like talk?

Writing creatively:

a summary of key points

Rather than offering you a prose or bullet point summary of the chapter, I thought it might be more helpful to express the thinking in this chapter in a table which makes connections between Guilford's characteristics of creativity and the classroom implications these suggest for writing creatively.

Guilford's creative characteristics	Classroom implications for writing creatively
A sensitivity to problems	Encourage talk about the writing process so that problems become a time of learning rather than barriers to writing.
Fluency: the ability to produce a large number of ideas quickly.	Encourage the confidence to generate ideas without evaluating them as they emerge.
An ability to produce novel ideas.	Encourage risk-taking and experimentation, and enjoy the funny, the unusual and the quirky ideas. Not all novel ideas for writing are good ideas, but some will be.
Flexibility of mind	Encourage looking at writing from different perspectives and allow divergent ideas to be valued.
A synthesising and adapting ability	Encourage playful experimentation with words, phrases and ideas, and particularly the use of effective metaphor.
Adeptness at reorganising of ideas	Encourage the use of devices such as graphic organisers, or on-screen writing, to develop awareness of organisational and reorganisational possibilities in writing.
Competence at evaluating results	Encourage awareness of linguistic choices and possibilities for crafting writing to develop a metalanguage for evaluating writing.

You must be disciplined, you must be free; you must allow time, you can write effectively to strict deadlines; you must edit, you can get sincerity and freshness from instant jottings ... Writing poetry is not necessarily easy and teaching it demands sensitivity, understanding and skill on the part of the teacher. These things don't come without a willingness to become involved and to invest time and effort. (Dunn, et al., 1987: 30)

Introduction

The purpose of this chapter is to try to help you to think through your own views about poetry in order for you to understand the underlying potential for creative thinking offered by poetry in education. In doing so, it presents a creative approach to teaching poetry in the primary school, while offering a critique of current curricular recommendations. The creative approach described is linked to creativity theory, and practical suggestions for creative poetry teaching are made. The chapter closes by presenting a summary of key points to bear in mind when embarking on a poetry topic or project with primary school children.

The problems with poetry

The chances are that the time you have spent studying poetry on your initial teacher training course is less than that devoted to other genres within the primary English curriculum. The reasons for this are not clear: we can only speculate why this might be. Ironically it is probably not because poetry is considered to be lacking in value or importance by those who train you. The reasons are more complex than that, and have to do with poetry's place in the culture at large, upon which formal schooling is only one influence among many.

The status of poetry teaching is still unclear, even though poetry has undergone a change of late, from being a 'Cinderella' subject (Benton, 1978: 114), taught ad hoc according to primary teachers' enthusiasms and/or anxieties, to a compulsory element in the National Curriculum (NC) (DES, 1990; DfE, 1995; DfEE/QCA, 1999a) orders and National Literacy Strategy (NLS) recommendations (DfEE, 1998). One of the problems with this unclear status is that there is not a consensus as to the merits of such recommendations. Some have welcomed poetry's inclusion in the NLS because the Strategy helps children access 'sophisticated formal aspects of language' (Coulson, 1999: 8; Kerr, 2002: 25), while others see the prescribed material of recent orders as anathema to the very qualities poetry teaching should promote (Carter, 1998).

Another reason for this uncertainty is that poetry arouses very strongly held beliefs in those who teach and write about it. For example, conflicting claims are made about the methods of teaching it to children (Hughes, 1967; Rosen, 1989; Brownjohn, 1994; Pirrie, 1994). Teachers lacking confidence in teaching it (Benton, 1986; O'Hara, 1988; Wade and Sidaway, 1990) therefore have a wide range of material to access to give them ideas, but each of these is underpinned with very different notions of what poetry is. These are often different to the views of poetry in the NLS and other documentation.

Finally, you might want to consider poetry's place within current National Testing arrangements. Poetry is the only kind of writing taught in primary schools which has so far not appeared in National Test papers at Key Stages 1 and 2. This dates back to the first version (1989) of the English National Curriculum, when Cox said that poetry was too difficult to 'map onto levels' for it to be formally tested. While this has saved poetry, perhaps, from being taught in an instructional way, there is also anecdotal evidence emerging (Henry, 2001) that some Year 6 teachers now avoid teaching poetry writing until after their classes' May tests. This leaves the status of poetry in an unclear position, 'above' testing procedures on the one hand, but not 'recognised' by them either.

Pause for thought

Your views on the nature of poetry

If you were asked to write down your views on the nature of poetry, what would you say? Some possible answers might include:

- *It is about important experiences.*
- *These experiences are so important to us that we want to preserve them.*
- *We preserve them in a way that makes them memorable to some degree.*
- *The manner – the form and language – in which the poem is written is as integral to its meaning as the content.*

Depending on your own experience you might emphasise some aspects of poetry more than others. Which of these experiences are ones which have formed an inclusive or wide-angled view of poetry, and which have not?

A working definition of poetry

'Poetry' is one of the terms we use in our culture without having a very good idea of what it means. We are happy to translate the concept of it to other areas of our lives, labelling, for example, 'poetic films', 'poetic novels' and 'poetic views of the countryside'; but, if pushed, we are often at a loss to know how properly to define it for ourselves.

Poetry is one of those concepts, like art, that we feel we recognise when we see it. Like definitions about 'art' and 'beauty', poetry is perhaps more easily defined by what it is not. Poetry, more than any other verbal art, tells us what it is not as soon as we see it on the page: prose. This is one of the most recognisable characteristics of poetry for children, according to Tarleton (1983). It is what Strauss (1993: 3) has called the 'hedged-off area'. In this way, anything calling itself a poem is a poem (Armitage, 2002).

This, however, tells us nothing much about music, rhythm, rhyme, memorability or language. Neither does it tell us much about how the form of a poem is very concentrated. As Emma, aged 10, says (cited in DES, 1987: iv): 'I think with a poem, it's very important that you can have it all packed in, full of all the things you wanted to say … I think that's what attracts a reader, what it sounds like, the way it's written, the sort of flow of words'. We may say, then, that poetry is a form in its own right in which form, feeling and language are intertwined to such a concentrated degree as to make them inseparable from meaning.

To this we may also add Auden's idea of poetry as 'memorable speech' (in Mendelson, 1996: 105). This is useful because it reconnects us with poetry's origins as a spoken rather than written form. This is a particularly valuable idea to take into the classroom, for, as Rosen says (1989), it opens up all kinds of possibilities as to what poetry might be about, which forms it might adopt and who it might be for. If we accept this as an important characteristic of poetry, it would follow that one of poetry's functions may be to remain in a state of constant renewal and negotiation with the reader as to what these possibilities might include.

A poem, then, has a different form from prose and has lots of meaning 'packed in[to]' it. Although the first poems were very long and told stories, we are more used to poems being short in our contemporary culture, and of performing, as Emma would recognise, some sort of function with words which makes meaning and form, finally, indivisible from one another. (For a diagrammatic representation of these concepts, see Figure 6.1.)

What are the aims of teaching poetry?

As I indicate above there is little consensus on teaching methods between the four major writers in the postwar period on poetry in primary schools (Hughes, 1967; Rosen, 1989; Brownjohn, 1994; Pirrie, 1994) . Paradoxically, however, they use very similar language when describing the aims of such teaching. From these descriptions we might ascertain two main aims for teaching poetry to children. We might call these language values and numinous values.

In practice these are intertwined, but it is also possible to see one leading onto the other. In the first category the four writers above emphasise the importance of poetry's ability to offer children 'freedom', 'release', 'empowerment' and the opportunity to 'find a voice' for themselves. The theory underpinning this runs as follows: by engaging with poems through reading and writing, and by paying 'a special kind of attention' (Britton, 1982: 12) to language used in this uniquely concentrated way, children can discover and control its power to say things, in Rosen's phrase, which 'matter' (1997: 3) to themselves. Through the process of empathising with voices, cultures, forms and experience which are not one's own, this leads on to the second of these values, namely the desire and ability to consider their world, values and place within it. In this way poetry teaching has at its heart the liberal-humanist aim of 'opening up a conversation … based on personal reflection' (Rosen, 1989: 26).

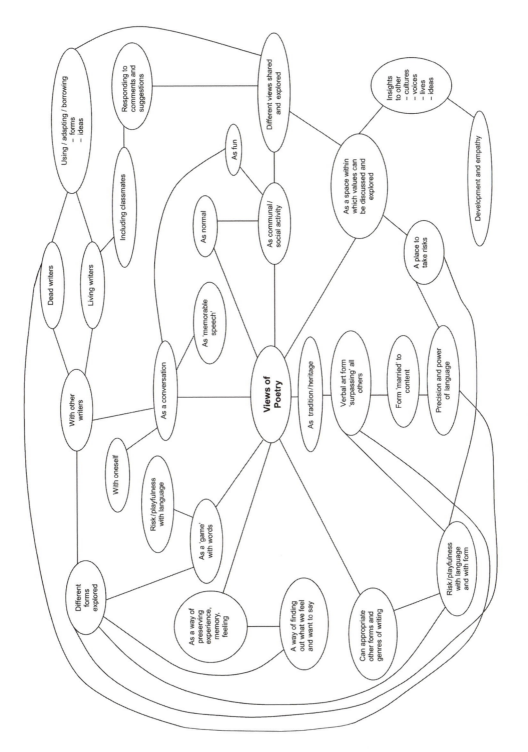

Figure 6.1: Different views of poetry

Poetry is therefore a genre where language, form and feeling are intertwined in a uniquely concentrated way. To teach poetry therefore, is to open up a space where these things are reflected on. This process has been described by Nobel Laureate Seamus Heaney: 'Poetry holds attention for a space, functions not as distraction but as pure concentration, a focus where our power to concentrate is concentrated back on ourselves' (1988: 108). As we shall see, adapting this view of the purposes of poetry in education has important consequences for how we see creativity relating to it.

Pause for thought

How can we describe poetry by children?

Can children write poetry? What distinguishes it from poetry by adults? What are the similarities in your view, and the main differences? How does poetry by children enlarge or enhance your view of the possibilities of poetry as a genre? You might like to consider the view of Morag Styles, one of the most respected poetry teachers and anthologists in the UK. How does her definition match your own?

I call [children] poets because the type of writing I am about to discuss uses economic language, is memorable, has a strong sense of rhythm (though sometimes it is the natural rhythms of speech), is shaped into lines and provokes an emotional response in the reader. *(Styles, 1992:74)*

The NLS model of poetry

Contained in Table 6.1 (page 76) is a summary of poetry to be studied by children at Key Stage 2. There are many things to commend in the NLS range of poetry writing by children. Its recommendations are thorough in terms of content covered and in terms of progression, with more demanding poetry writing forms offered as children grow older. They are an attempt to hold in equilibrium aspects of composition which are common to writing of all kinds (drafting, polishing and editing). You might like to compare these recommendations with Styles's vision of poetry, above.

Pause for thought

The NLS also supports some creativity theory well in that it helps make decisions about writing explicit, including Resnick's 'executive processes' (1987), and the 'review of knowledge, direction of attention and marshalling of resources' (Copley, 2001: 44). The problem with the NLS is not in the theory underpinning its strategies, therefore.

It is that its view of poetry writing is very much form-driven. In other words, the progress in poetry writing which the NLS describes is centred on children progressing through a series of adult-made forms or 'types' of poetry, not on the demands on thinking and learning involved in writing poems in these forms. For example, in Year 4 Term 3 the range of forms to be studied includes: haiku, cinquain, couplets, list, thin poems, alphabets, conversations, monologues, syllabics, prayers, epitaphs, songs, rhyming forms and free verse. This, by any standard, is a huge range for children and their teachers to cover. Leaving aside arguments about the desirability and possibility of covering such a range in so short a space of time, one is left asking how these forms actually relate to each other in terms of learning.

Another criticism one could make of these recommendations is that there is not enough mention of writing poems from personal experience or from personal feelings (Year 4, Term 1 and Year 5, Term 1 only), both of which one would expect to see featured more in this genre of writing especially. These are the only hints in the Strategy regarding poetry composition which suggest that the point of teaching poetry might be about something other than form and structure, the preservation of feelings or experience, for example.

How are these aims different from the aims discussed above? What are the implications for practice of relying on a form-driven view of poetry? If one were to rely on these recommendations alone, what would happen to children's learning about, and perceptions of, poetry?

What is poetry's role in developing creativity?

Most of the theory about what it means to be a creative practitioner of poetry has been written by poets themselves in their attempt to explain the demands of their craft. There is a large literature on this subject. In the fraction referred to below, there is, even in such a diverse group of poets, an understanding of poetry as a form of 'serious playfulness', which relies upon flexible and open-minded thinking and a preparedness to take risks (Hughes, 1967; Heaney, 1988; Koch, 1991, 1999; Ash, in Crawford et al., 1995; Gunn, in Herbert and Hollis, 2000; O'Hara, 2003; Paterson, 2004).

Underpinning much poetic practice since Modernism, and in a summary of the above, has been the credos of two American giants of the form, Ezra Pound and Robert Frost:

- **Pound's dictum was that poets should strive to 'make it new'.**
- **Frost insisted that every poem was a 'fresh look and a fresh listen'.**

Poetry's role in developing children's creativity is nothing less, therefore, than the challenge to see and record the world with new eyes, as it were. Poetry is uniquely placed to encourage this kind of thinking thanks to the techniques of simile and metaphor.

The challenge of developing these habits of mind in children might be to rely, therefore, on the kind of flexible thinking noted by Dunn et al. (1987) in the quotation at the start of this chapter and which Andreasen and Powers (1974) described as 'over-

Year 3 Term 1	**Range of poetry studied:** poems based on observation and the senses; shape poems.	**Writing composition** 12 to collect suitable words and phrases, in order to write poems and short descriptions; design simple patterns with words, use repetitive phrases; write imaginative comparisons 13 to invent calligrams and a range of shape poems, selecting appropriate words and careful presentation; build up class collections
Year 3 Term 2	**Range of poetry studied:** oral and performance poetry from different cultures.	**Writing composition** 11 to write new or extended verses for performance based on models of 'performance' and oral poetry read, e.g. rhythms, repetition;
Year 3 Term 3	**Range of poetry studied:** humorous poetry, poetry that plays with language, word puzzles, puns, riddles.	**Writing composition** 15 to write poetry that uses sound to create effects, e.g. onomatopoeia, alliteration, distinctive rhythms
Year 4 Term 1	**Range of poetry studied:** poems based on common themes, e.g. space, school, animals, families, feelings, viewpoints.	**Writing composition** 14 to write poems based on personal or imagined experience, linked to poems read. List brief phrases and words, experiment by trimming or extending sentences; experiment with powerful and expressive verbs
Year 4 Term 2	**Range of poetry studied:** classic and modern poetry, including poems from different cultures and times.	**Writing composition** 11 to write poetry based on the structure and/or style of poems read, e.g. taking account of vocabulary, archaic expressions, patterns of rhyme, choruses, similes 13 to write own examples of descriptive, expressive language based on those read. Link to work on adjectives and similes;
Year 4 Term 3	**Range of poetry studied:** range of poetry in different forms, e.g. haiku, cinquain, couplets, list, thin poems, alphabets, conversations, monologues, syllabics, prayers, epitaphs, songs, rhyming forms and free verse.	**Writing composition** 14 to write poems, experimenting with different styles and structures. Discuss if and why different forms are more suitable than others 15 to produce polished poetry through revision, e.g. deleting words, adding words, changing words, reorganising words and lines, experimenting with figurative language
Year 5 Term 1	**Range of poetry studied:** poems by significant children's writers; concrete poetry.	**Writing composition** 16 to convey feelings, reflections or moods in a poem through the careful choice of words and phrases 17 to write metaphors from original ideas or from similes
Year 5 Term 2	**Range of poetry studied:** longer classic poetry, including narrative poetry.	**Writing composition** 12 to use the structures of poems read to write extensions based on these, e.g. additional verses, or substituting own words and ideas
Year 5 Term 3	**Range of poetry studied:** poems from a variety of cultures and traditions; choral and performance poetry.	**Writing composition** 11 to use performance poems as models to write and to produce poetry in polished forms through revising, redrafting and presentation
Year 6 Term 1	**Range of poetry studied:** classic poetry by long-established authors including study of a Shakespeare play.	**Writing composition** 10 to write own poems experimenting with active verbs and personification; produce revised poems for reading aloud individually
Year 6 Term 2	**Range of poetry studied:** range of poetic forms, e.g. kennings, limericks, riddles, cinquain, tanka, poems written in other forms (as adverts, letters, diary entries, conversations), free verse, nonsense verse.	**Writing composition** 12 to study in depth one genre and produce an extended piece of similar writing, e.g. for inclusion in a class anthology; to plan, revise, re-draft this and bring to presentational standard, e.g. layout, paragraphing, accuracy of punctuation and spelling, handwriting/printing;
Year 6 Term 3	**Range of poetry studied:** comparison of work by significant children's poets: (a) work by same author; (b) different authors' treatment of same theme(s).	**Writing composition** 13 to write a sequence of poems linked by theme or form, e.g. a haiku calendar

Table 6.1: Summary of range of poetry to be covered at Key Stage 2

inclusive', in which 'ideas coded as separate by most people [are] treated as belonging together' (Cropley, 2001: 38). In practice this means that we can, as teachers, promote different metaphors about poetry, for example that it is a 'game' and that it is also part of 'tradition', without one necessarily cancelling the other out.

Pause for thought

Creativity and poetry: a checklist

Poetry can contribute to children's creativity by:

- *encouraging a new way of seeing and recording the world (not relying on cliché);*
- *encouraging a risk-taking approach: with language (e.g. imagery) as well as with form (trying out new forms);*
- *encouraging a problem-solving approach (thinking of new ways to proceed when you are stuck);*
- *encouraging over-inclusive thinking – being open to:*
  - *different models of poetry*
  - *different views of poetry*
  - *different approaches to writing*
  - *the fact that one's opinions/views can change;*
- *encouraging the view that to be better at something you need to practise it, and that on some occasions your practice will be more successful than on others.*

Activity

How can poetry be taught creatively?
To demonstrate 'over-inclusive thinking' you might aim at creating what Rosen calls a 'poetry-writing-friendly' classroom, where 'poems flourish in an atmosphere of sympathetic sharing' (1997: 4–5).

As you start a poetry project/topic in school make a poster with the following messages. Note how your class's responses change over time (see Figure 6.2). Set these out to the children at the outset of the project, taking care to remind them, where appropriate, as the project develops.

- *responses (written and oral) to poems read in class cannot be wrong;*
- *anything can be the source of a poem or can be material for a poem;*
- *comments will be made on poems by the teacher and by children – these are intended to be helpful and children are at liberty to ignore them;*
- *a poem written by a child belongs to a child, and decisions about the form and language of their poems ultimately rest with them.*

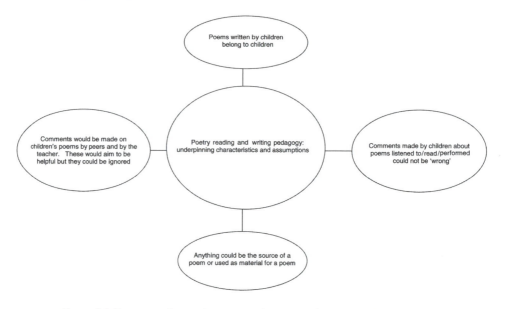

Figure 6.2 Poetry reading and writing pedagogy: underpinning characteristics and assumptions.

You may find the following behaviour taking place:

- children finding poems for themselves and requesting them to be read as well as sharing and performing them;
- children requesting favourite poems again;
- children bringing in poems written at home;
- children bringing in poems read at home;
- children of different abilities sharing each other's written work during the writing process and opening it up for comment;
- children using poems from their own reading as models to base poems on;
- children possessing and articulating an expanded view of what poetry can be.

Can you teach poetry uncreatively?

The answer to this question is that you can. You have to be aware that, in spite of good intentions and openness to new ideas, teaching poetry can be as uncreative an act as any other. You might want to consider how creatively you teach the reading and writing of poetry to gauge your own preparedness to try different approaches in the classroom.

Reading

- When you read a poem with your class, what are your first instincts about what you should be doing with it?

- Are you encouraging responses from the children to the poem as a whole, or are you focusing straight away on aspects of technique and form?

- Try to avoid going on what Benton and Fox (1985) described as 'metaphor hunts and simile chases' for the sake of it. If we take seriously Charles Causely's dictum that a poem is not an object, fixed in time with a single immovable meaning, but first and foremost a living organism (cited in Balaam and Merrick, 1988), then we need to treat children's responses to it with respect and enthusiasm.

- Try poet and former teacher Wendy Cope's idea (in Wilson with Hughes, 1998) of restricting yourself to asking one question per poem, and letting the children's responses to it guide the way you discuss it in class (see Figure 6.3).

Writing

- When you are working with a new poetic form with your class, do you attempt to teach it as you would non-fiction or fiction, by modelling it through shared writing and demonstration? Do you allow the children to talk through their sentences/phrases first, as they would in other genres?

- Do you see the imperative as being 'fulfilling the demands of the form', or do you see writing poems like a series of negotiations between the impulse to 'genuinely say what [you] genuinely need to say' (Sansom, 1994: 20) and the form of the poem?

- What matters to you more: that, say, the haikus your class writes all have the required number of syllables in each line, or that they encapsulate and provoke a moment of reflection and revelation through visual imagery?

- Try to create metaphors with your class to describe the marshalled creative process that is making a poem. US poet and critic Stephen Dunn has described it as like playing basketball (2001: 46). This is not as fanciful as it sounds: not passing to the open player, he says, is like holding onto lines in poems which the poem has no place for. Both are self-indulgent. What other metaphors can you come up with to describe the making of a poem?

Pause for thought

Annotate a favourite poem or one well known to you.

- *Are there different responses which can be brought to it?*
- *What kinds of questions can you develop about it?*
- *Can you find ways in which the poem might open up a discussion with your class about its subject matter?*
- *Does the poem widen children's sense of what is possible within a poem?*
- *Are there any cross-curricular links to made with the poem?*

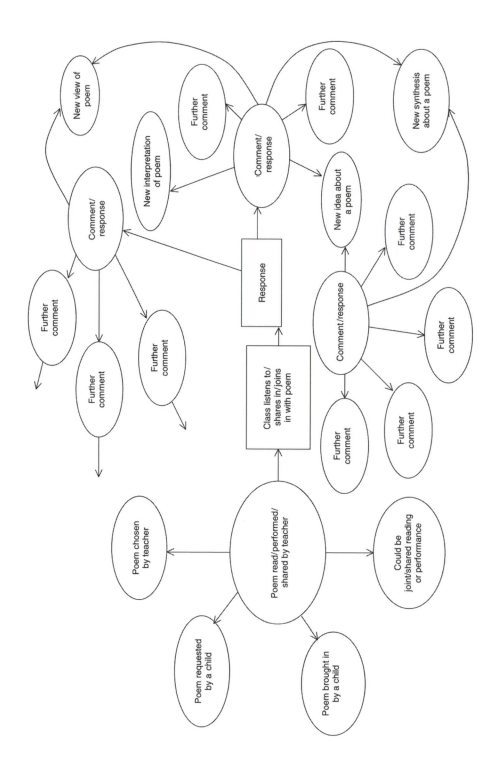

Figure 6.3 Poetry reading, sharing and discussing.

How can you teach your children to be creative poets?

Poet and teacher Kenneth Koch said the following about teaching children to write poems: 'I may be inspired to write a poem by walking past a bakery, listening to a piece of music, falling in love, or reading a poem, but none of this happens to anyone at nine o'clock in the morning at PS 61. You have to make something like it happen there' (Koch, 1996: 156). What is important to remember here is that, in spite of the many potential hindrances to children writing poems, Koch believed it could be done. Central to teaching children to write poems is a belief in poetry as a process of creative discovery. As Dunn says to his writing students: 'Your poem effectively begins at the first moment you've surprised or startled yourself. Throw away everything that preceded that moment, and begin with that moment' (2001: 137). Seeing the making of poems as something fluid and open-ended, such as a game, journey or 'step taken into the unknown' (Dunn, 2001: 142) within which surprise and revelation take place as opposed to a fixed set of rules to be adhered to, is one of the most important things you can do for your class as you teach them poetry.

What follows is not a perfect list of instructions which, if applied, will 'produce' perfect poetry pedagogy, much less perfect poems by the children you teach. What it might do is open up a few possibilities for how you might choose to teach it at certain times. It is offered not as a 'solution', but in the hope that it might prompt new poetry teaching ideas of your own. Finally, it is important to remember that once a poetry idea has been started on by a child or group of children, it should then belong to that child and they have control of it (see Figure 6.4).

Some creative ideas for children writing poems

1. Playing a word-game

FURNITURE GAME

This is an exercise from Brownjohn (1994). Well known for generating metaphoric writing, the exercise requires children to describe a famous person in terms of food, objects, colours, places, seasons, furniture, modes of transport, etc. It is a very useful exercise for getting children away from lifeless descriptions along the lines of 'He has brown hair, he has blue eyes, he is nice', etc. and making them think in terms of images instead. For example, the Queen becomes a headscarf, a muddy Land-Rover, binoculars trained on horses and so on. There should be one line per idea. The children read their poems at the end of the lesson. The class has to guess (like a riddle) who has been written about.

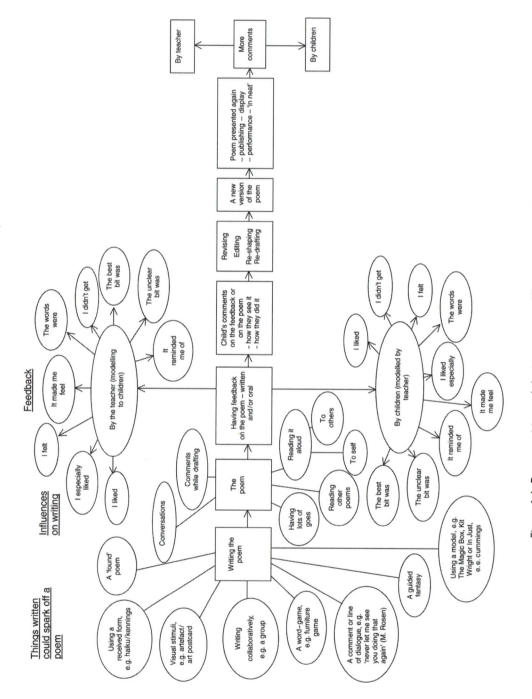

Figure 6.4: Poetry writing and sharing sequence (illumination to verification).

PLAYING WITH SHAPES

Look at words which can be played around with to create shape poems. Try: 'tree', 'tunnel', 'umbrella', 'mountain'. In pairs, ask children to write a certain word in as many ways as they can. Model one or two methods first. 'Grasshopper' is an excellent example:

(from Klassen and Struthers, 1995).

2. Writing collaboratively (with a partner or in a group)

Using the writing game on questions and answers described by Brownjohn in *To Rhyme or Not to Rhyme?* (1994), ask the children to think of 'big picture' open questions that need answering: 'Where does God come from?'; 'What's inside a cloud?'; 'Why is thunder cross?' They can be on any theme, or a variety. A good source of these is *Why do the stars come out at night?* by Annalena McAffee (Red Fox). Model to the children with shared writing the kind of question you think works best, and ask them to suggest them to you. Children then work in pairs (not necessarily grouped by ability), where they write a question down for each other, swap papers, then write an answer; they then swap papers again, and do another question, and so on, until they have a good list. A good target to aim for is 10 lines (five questions and five answers). The resulting writing can then be manipulated to create new poems. Words can be changed, lines moved around, themes developed. If no themes emerge, use just one line as a starting point for a new poem. This is a very good exercise to show how all writing can be 'valuable' even if it is not used in the final product.

3. Using a comment or line of dialogue

You can ask children to experiment with just one phrase from a poem, e.g. 'Never let me see you doing that again' (Mike Rosen) which might look like:

Never let me
see you
doing that
again

or:

NEVER
let me
see you
doing
that
AGAIN

or:

Never
    let me
        see you
            doing that
                again

These could be modelled on the board.

The possibilities are endless. The original (in *The Hypnotiser*) goes:

Never
let
me
see
you
doing
that
again

Share and discuss different versions; pay attention to how layout affects the emphasis. This can lead on to the next exercise.

CHIVVY (MICHAEL ROSEN)

This is a really good poem for showing children that you can put down one idea per line and that these lines don't have to have matching lengths or rhythms or rhymes or indeed have any rhymes at all. It is also very good for encouraging what I call the scavenging aspect of poetry, i.e. that it can borrow from all kinds of speech and talk. An extension to set children could be: make a 'What Politicians Say' poem; or a football managers poem, or a dinner ladies poem, or a sisters poem. This is a very good exercise for getting children to write about themselves honestly.

4. Looking at an artefact or art postcard

Each child has one postcard to look at (art cards work best, figurative or abstract). They have to write a description of the card by imagining they are looking into a world never seen before. They have to list the rules/laws of that world. From this piece of writing they then make a poem which implies, but does not state directly, the rules they have invented. Another approach is to ask questions as in 'Guided Fantasy' (see below), some with 'real' answers ('What are the main colours?', 'What do they remind you of?') others with imaginary answers ('What time is it in the picture?', 'What is just to the left of the picture?', 'What noises can you hear?'), which children use to make poems by quarrying their answers later on.

5. Using a received form

HAIKU

This is a good exercise to help children see that poems are about concision and precision and do not have to rhyme. A good source of haiku is *In Tune with Yourself* (Dunn *et al.*, 1987). The concept here is to try to get the children to write about the essence of something and capture it in as few words as possible. I tell them syllable counts are important but not so important as getting the 'snapshot' of the experience, object, person or place. Try to emphasise that haiku is a reflection on an experience, so often has a lyrical feel to it. Describe and explain these terms. Model one of your own on the blackboard. The aim here is to get them writing less, not more. This can lead into the next exercise.

KENNINGS

Like haiku, kennings are brilliant for teaching brevity and a kind of 'less is more' approach. Rooted in Anglo-Saxon poetry, a kenning is two words fused together with a hyphen to make a new noun, for example: swan-road = river; spear-din (Anglo-Saxon) = battle; skull-splitter = sword/axe, and so on. The two words can be noun/noun, noun/verb, verb/noun, adjective, colour/noun/verb, and can be used to make a list describing an object, emotion, quality or animal, in any combination. A good source of kennings by children is *The Poetry Book for Primary Schools* (Wilson and Hughes, 1998).

6. Guided Fantasy

'Guided Fantasy' is any lesson in which the teacher/tutor guides the participants through a series of questions to which they write responses, one at a time. Once they have finished writing their answers they have many lines on the page from which to edit and draft a new poem. This is a good approach for children who lack confidence, as it gives them material to work with, helps scaffold their thinking and takes away the pressure of 'the blank page'.

Questions often include the following:

> You are in a place you remember from a while ago; what do you see?
> You hear music: what is it? does what you see change?
> There's an object in your hand: describe it; what is it like?
> There's a smell in the air – what is it? What does it remind you of?
> You come to a door; it could be an exit or an entrance; what do you feel as you go up to it?
> You go through the door and something happens; what do you feel and think?

The children read through their material, then write down the name of the feeling they described going through the door. This will form the basis of the final poem. Without naming it directly the children have to write a poem describing their feeling. This is done metaphorically, with lines like 'It says things like … '; 'It dreams of … '; 'It cannot believe in … '; and so on. The riddling guessing game aspect at the end children like. This can lead into the next exercise.

FEELINGS

Similar to 'guided fantasy': process writing. Children think of a feeling. Then they draw up a list of questions which the feeling then answers in an assumed voice. Children swap books so they are answering someone else's questions to make their own feeling speak the poem. This is a very good exercise for getting metaphorical writing. Reading at end and guessing are aspects children like.

7. Finding a 'found' poem

This is an idea borrowed from King (1998). The children each receive a copy of a piece of prose. The idea is to quarry from this certain phrases and lines which can be used in the same order to make a poem. I tell them the poem can be nonsense and not true, but that they have to use the words in the same order as they appear on the paper. It has the advantage of having lots of unusual vocabulary for the children to play around with. This can lead into the next exercise.

CUT UPS

This is a follow-up to the 'found' poems idea. In many ways this exercise is the same concept, only instead of one piece of unbroken text the children are given packets of words found from newspaper headlines. In groups they have to assemble as many as they can from each packet into short poems. I tell them the poems do not have to make sense.

8. Using a model (a poem you have read or heard)

THE MAGIC BOX

This is based on another model poem, by Kit Wright. Children are given their own copy of the poem on an A4 sheet. The poem is read out and discussed. The children are encouraged to look at the richness of the language, the way opposites are included, as well as sounds, sights, smells and textures. It is suggested as a model for use by children for their own poems. Stanzas may be modelled on the board in shared writing, in order to encourage children to 'chunk' meaning, as they would in paragraphs for prose. The poem can be about the 'magic' box, or anything they like.

IN-JUST

This is an exercise developed by Tatiana Wilson and described in Wilson and Hughes (1998). The purpose is to use the poem as a model using some of e.e.cummings's tech-niques (words joined together, kennings, repetitions). The poem writing is only attempted after a full discussion of the poem has taken place. The children are also shown a poem by a child written using this as a model (or if you do not have one, one by yourself).

Poetry, Children and Creativity:

a summary of key points

Poetry's unclear status

—— *Poetry enjoys mixed status in the curriculum. On the one hand it enjoys high status as a revered verbal art-form; on the other, some teachers are unsure how to teach it, as it does not appear in National Tests.*

Definitions of poetry

—— *Children appreciate that poetry is different from prose, but need to apprehend that it is poetry's unique concentration of language, feeling and form which make it so powerful.*

—— *To this we can add the idea of poetry as 'memorable speech', which opens up the idea of poetry as being both grounded in experience and about things which matter to us.*

Aims of poetry teaching

—— *We can list the aims of poetry teaching as focusing on language values and numinous values: by focussing on the concentration of language, form and feeling a space is opened up in which we can consider our world, our own values, and their place in it.*

—— *Poetry by children is itself able to do this. To hold this view of children's writing is to challenge the view of poetry in recent recommendations.*

Poetry's role in developing children's creativity

—— *Engaging with poetry challenges children to see the world freshly and to record it in new ways. To take on this challenge requires a preparedness to take risks and to think flexibly.*

The challenge of teaching poetry creatively

—— *This challenge centres on how poetry reading and writing are taught:*
  – by treating poems as living organisms, not fixed objects;
  – by encouraging children to say what they genuinely want to say.

You can teach children to become creative poets

—— *By maintaining open-ended views of poetry and what it can achieve.*

—— *By treating the writing of poems as a process of discovery.*

Introduction

Creativity is not a word that often springs to mind when we think of science. Science is more often thought of as a body of certain and unchanging knowledge. This narrow view does not acknowledge the tentative nature of scientific theories and the creativity of scientific discoveries which broaden our understanding of the universe, changing the way we think and the way we view the world. This narrow view can be seen through the pictures of scientists as drawn by children (see Figure 7.1), where scientists are white, male and white-coated, although the addition of 'thought bubbles', exclamation marks and the use of words such as 'Eureka!' indicate an element of invention, discovery and innovation if not creativity. The reason for this seeming anomaly is that creativity is not only difficult to define and used synonymously (Childs, 1986) with words such as originality, but also has different meanings in science and technology than in the arts.

This chapter will require you to think through these and other preconceptions about science and science teaching in order to answer these questions:

- **What is creativity in science education?**
- **Why is creativity in science education important?**
- **Why is it difficult to be a creative science teacher?**
- **How can we be more creative in our science teaching?**

Figure 7.1: A stereotypical picture of a scientist (Johnston, 1996: 33)

Pause for thought

What picture comes into your mind when you think of science?

How would you draw a picture of a scientist?

Do you think the stereotypical image of science and scientists is outdated?

It is necessary to extend our understanding of creativity in order to see how science can be creative and we should include creativity of thinking and problem-solving (de Bono, 1992), as well as discovery and innovation. Creativity is not exclusively an artistic attribute (Prentice, 2000) and is described in dictionaries (Macdonald, 1972) as concerned with bringing into being or making something new, a definition that can be applied to science with ease. Beetlestone's (1998) six-part definition of creativity:

- *learning*
- *representation*
- *productivity*
- *originality*
- *thinking creatively/problem-solving*
- *universe/creation-nature*

can be applied to science and acknowledges the multifaceted and all-encompassing nature of creativity in science.

If we look at historical science, we can see innovation, discovery and creative thinking in science and the scientific process and creative scientists as risk-takers. Leonardo da Vinci is considered to be one of the greatest artists and scientists, producing significant works of art and scientific ideas which have been used to support understanding (e.g. human anatomy) and technological advances (e.g. aircraft design). Newton, Archimedes and Curie demonstrated creativity of thought which led to improved understanding of our world (e.g. Newton extended understanding of gravitational force and light) and technological advances (e.g. Archimedes' ideas led to the use of levers to help lift heavy objects and Curie's discoveries led to radiotherapy). Other scientists such as Darwin and Galileo took great risks in communicating their ideas to a world that was unwilling and unready to accept them, and faced public humiliation and incarceration.

Our science education has an important influence on our perception and understanding of science. Differences in understanding appear to result from societal emphasis (OFSTED, 2003), views of the world (Kahn, 1999) and science education (Johnston *et al.*, 1998). Sometimes primary science education has a biological and geographical emphasis (Finland, Bosnia) with chemistry, physics and mathematics being taught as secondary sciences, is mainly knowledge-based and curriculum-focused (England post-National Curriculum, Macedonia and Japan), or is skills-based and child-centred (England pre-National Curriculum).

Activity

Learning about scientists and their discoveries can help develop a better understanding about the nature of science and scientific discoveries.

- *Try learning about Leonardo da Vinci through reading extracts from his notebooks and explore gravitational force by making paper helicopters (see Figure 7.2). Explore what happens when you use different types of paper/card or different sizes or add extra paperclips or fold the wings the opposite way.*

- *Read the story of Darwin's voyage on the Beagle and sort pictures of animals or collections of plants according to observable features. Look at teeth, skull shapes, leaf shape or seeds and think what this tells us about the animal/plant.*

- *Retell the story of Archimedes and then explore how different objects affect the water level of a tank of water (Johnston and Gray, 1999). Does the weight or size make a difference?*

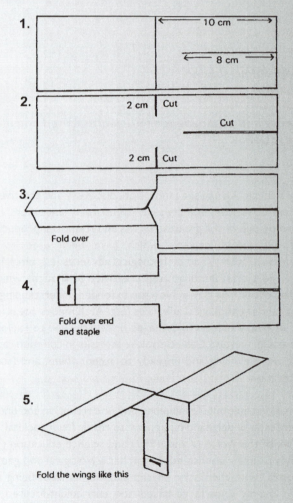

Figure 7.2: Making a paper helicopter

What is creativity in science education?

Creative science education is a complex interrelationship between science and education made difficult because of the different natures of science and education. Science education in our present national curriculum (DfEE, 1999c) has focused on factual learning, reflecting views of science as a body of empirical, non-political knowledge. Education is felt to reflect changes in society and views, is inherently political and values all knowledge and understanding and is therefore less static in its development than science. Science education sits somewhat uncomfortably between science and education and is viewed differently depending on whether it is viewed, initially, from a science or education strength. Where science is the stronger partner, then progress in science education can be slowed by the empirical view of the nature of science.

Making connections is considered (Duffy, 1998) to be an important aspect of creativity and creativity in science education involves making connections between aspects of learning across the curriculum (DfES, 2003). In this way science education will not focus solely on the acquisition of limited scientific knowledge, but involve the development of scientific understanding, skills and attitudes, integrating other subjects through real-life contexts so that knowledge and skills can be applied in real situations – that is, the development of scientific literacy.

Creative science education involves practitioners with subject and pedagogical knowledge in adapting their teaching to suit the learning objectives, children and context. Creative science education does not follow rigidly imposed methodologies such as implied by the introduction of some primary strategies (DfEE, 1998, 1999d). Such changes in education are thought to have affected pedagogical practice (Cullingford, 1996; Johnston, 2002) and reduced the practical component of much science teaching (ASE, 1999) so that many science lessons are not structured sufficiently to effectively develop scientific learning objectives. Creative science education is active and child-centred, involving individual problem-solving and exploration and not more passive learning approaches which published schemes, CD ROMs and schemes of work (e.g. QCA, 2000) appear to advocate. Creative science practitioners make their own decisions about teaching styles and learning experiences, producing novel ideas for achieving objectives to the benefit of the children's learning (QCA, 2003; DfES, 2003). They are enthusiastic about science education and balance the needs of the whole curriculum with those of children's creative development (Boden, 2001). Excellent science practitioners have been identified (Fraser and Tobin, 1993) as those who manage their classrooms effectively, use teaching strategies which focus on the children's understanding, provide learning environments which suit the children's learning preferences, have a strong content knowledge and encourage children's involvement in classroom discussions and activities.

Pause for thought

Look at Figure 7.3 and decide what you think is good teaching and learning in science.

TRADITIONALIST
Emphasis on authority, dissemination, imparting knowledge and training skills

Highly structured teacher-led instruction/ demonstration	Teacher-led exploration
Structured teacher-led instruction/ demonstration	Structured teacher-led exploration

POSITIVIST

Pursuit of knowledge as a truth

CONSTRUCTIVIST
Constructing understanding from experience

Exploration

Debate/discussion/argumentation

Discovery

POSTMODERNIST
Emphasis on engaging with issues/ideas and challenging interpretations

Figure 7. 3: How pedagogical approaches fit into the constructivist/positivist and traditionalist/postmodernist continua (Longbottom, 1999)

Pedagogical approaches in science can fall along two continua, constructivist/ positivist and traditionalist/postmodernist (Longbottom, 1999) as seen in Figure 7.3.

Highly structured teacher-led approaches are ones in which the teacher imparts scientific knowledge, demonstrates concepts and instructs pupils in the use of equipment. These approaches fall within the traditionalist/positivist sector and are the least creative type of approaches. More creative are teacher-led explorations, where the teacher sets up and structures explorations and investigations to enable pupils to construct their own scientific conceptions and develop skills. These fall into the traditionalist/constructivist sector. Even more creative science education involves exploration and discovery where teachers guide pupils and support the construction of understandings through scientific challenge and discourse. These types of approaches fall into the constructivist/post-modernist sector. Other creative approaches engage pupils in the discussion and argumentation of scientific understanding and abstract ideas and these fall into the positivist/ postmodernist sector.

Student and teacher views of creativity in science education

In one piece of research (Johnston and Ahtee, 2005), I compared 98 student teachers' attitudes towards teaching physics activities with their attitudes towards teaching their mother tongue (English), mathematics and science using a previously validated semantic differential questionnaire with 20 bipolar adjective pairs (Ahtee and Rikkinen, 1995; Ahtee and Tella, 1995). The semantic differential (SD) is a method of observing and measuring the connotative meaning of concepts (Osgood *et al.*, 1967). The scoring adopted was +2, +1, 0, −1, −2 with high positive scores signifying a positive attitude. The bipolar adjectives were grouped in four broad categories with five pairs in each:

- *level of difficulty* (**easy/difficult, self-evident/abstract, commonplace/mystical, simple/complicated, productive/trivial**);
- *level of interest and involvement* (**interesting/boring, gripping/undesirable, active/passive, social/individual, practical/theoretical**);
- *perceived nature* (**free/compulsory, open/closed, creative/non-creative, cheerful/sad, broadening/constricting**);
- *perceived value* (**valuable/worthless, profound/superficial, wise/foolish, selfish/ unselfish, sublime/ridiculous**).

Activity

Decide for yourself which of the bipolar adjectives (as above) you feel describes science.

Compare your results with those of the students in Figure 7.4.

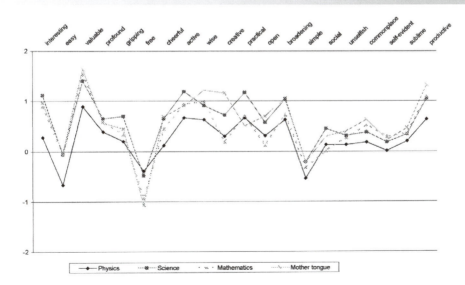

Figure 7.4: Student teachers' attitudes to the teaching of science, physics, English (mother tongue) and mathematics (Johnston and Ahtee (2005))

The results, as shown in Figure 7.4, show that science education is viewed as less creative than English teaching, but physics education is not viewed as creative and mathematics (sometimes referred to as the purest of sciences) is considered to be the least creative educational subject.

I once asked experienced teachers (Johnston, 2003) to explore their perception of science education by asking them to identify how it fitted into the constructivist/positivist and traditionalist/post-modernist continua described earlier and shown in Figure 7.3 (Longbottom, 1999). This indicated that teachers had a more creative perception of science education, with recognition of its multifaceted nature and the importance of scientific learning relevant to everyday life. These findings, however, were in contrast to those of science teachers in previous studies (Lederman and Zeidler 1987) although more akin to the multifaceted views found to be held by chemistry teachers in Koulaidis and Ogborn's study (1989) and generalist primary teachers (Johnston et al., 1998). However, I was unsure whether these views were reflected in the science that is taught in school and so in a further piece of research, student teachers' espoused philosophical views of primary science teaching were compared with their planning and practice.

The student group involved ten science specialist initial teacher training students at the beginning of their second year of undergraduate work. At the start of a module on the science curriculum, the students were asked to identify their pedagogical views on science education by identifying where they felt science education fitted into the two continua shown in Figure 7.3. Of the ten students involved, five placed science teaching and learning at the centre of the continua; four students felt that science teaching and learning was firmly in the constructivist/post modernist sector and one student felt that it was very slightly in the positivist/traditionalist sector. There followed some teaching on good practice in science teaching and learning and individual planning of science teaching. Finally, student interaction with 30 Year 3 children, while engaged in the 'discovery learning approach', was observed. Observations of their practice identified their approaches as falling into four out of five categories, from highly creative guided discovery to highly structured teacher-led imposition of knowledge:

1. *Guided discovery and exploration* (0 students). Children are allowed to explore independently, with guidance from the teacher, by way of appropriate interaction such as incidental questions (DES, 1967: DfES, 2003).

2. *Teacher-led exploration* (4 students). Children are led through an exploration, with almost complete teacher involvement.

3. *Structured teacher-led exploration* (3 students). Children are led through an exploration, with teacher instructions and complete teacher involvement.

4. *Structured teacher-led imposition* (1 student). Children are directly taught knowledge through instruction, questioning and practical activity.

5. *Highly structured teacher-led imposition* (2 students). Children are directly taught knowledge through instruction, questioning and teacher demonstration.

The results for the comparison between the student teachers' espoused views, planning and practice can be seen in Table 7.1 and show that there is very little correlation between their espoused views, planning and practice. This may indicate a tension between espoused beliefs on the nature of science education and the implicit message within the science National Curriculum, which emphasises science as 'knowledge consisting of relationships between self-evident variables that are related in regular law-like ways' (Monk and Dillon. 2000: 80) – in other words, science as empiricism. This is not a new phenomena, as research has found (Fensham, 2001; Taber, 2002) that the wealth of knowledge on constructivist science teaching has not had a significant effect on the content of science education. However, this tension can only have a negative impact on creative teaching and learning, as new practitioners struggle to come to terms with the ideological rhetoric of creative science education and pragmatic classroom reality.

Table 7. 1. The relationship between the student teachers' views on science education, planning and practice (Johnston, 2003)

Student	Views	Planning	Practice
1	Central	Exploratory (C/PM)	Structured teacher-led exploration with a focus on knowledge (T/C)
2	Central	Structured teacher-led (T/P)	Highly structured, teacher-led with a focus on knowledge (T/P)
3	Traditionalist/ Positivist (T/P)	Exploratory (C/PM)	Structured teacher-led exploration with a focus on knowledge (T/C)
4	Central	Structured teacher-led exploratory (T/C)	Teacher-led exploration with a focus on knowledge (T/C)
5	Constructivist/ Postmodernist (C/PM)	Structured exploratory (T/C)	Teacher-led exploration with a focus on knowledge (T/C)
6	Central	Structured teacher-led (T/P)	Highly structured, teacher-led with a focus on knowledge (T/P)
7	Constructivist/ Postmodernist (C/PM)	Exploratory group work with teacher cue cards (T/C)	Teacher-led exploration with a focus on knowledge (T/C)
8	Constructivist/ Postmodernist (C/PM)	Structured teacher-led with some problem-solving (T/P)	Teacher-led exploration with a focus on knowledge (T/C)
9	Constructivist/ Postmodernist (C/PM)	Structured teacher-led (T/P)	Structured teacher-led with a focus on knowledge (T/P)
10	Central	Teacher-led experiment (T/P)	Structured teacher-led exploration with a focus on knowledge (T/C)

Key	T/C	=	Traditionalist/Constructivist	C/PM	=	Constructivist/Postmodernist
	PM/P	=	Post-modernist/Positivist	T/P	=	Traditionalist/Positivist

Problem-solving activities can help learners of all ages develop scientific understandings as well as understandings of the nature of science. One such problem can be to design and make a one-minute timer – a series of energy transfers which take one minute from start to finish. For example, lighting a candle can burn through a thread and release a ramp down which a ball bearing will roll. This may roll down a maze and then be attracted to a magnet pushing a needle into a balloon which bursts. This variation of a mousetrap game can be undertaken by learners of all ages, as they will apply and build on their initial knowledge and produce a timer which demonstrates their understanding of different types of energy transfers (light, heat, mechanical, kinetic, magnetic and sound).

Why is creativity in science education important?

While there have been disputes among psychologists as to whether creativity is a characteristic of the highly intelligent (Munn, 1966; Childs, 1986), it is also considered to be a potential in all of us which needs encouragement and motivation to flourish (Medawar, 1969). Creative science education will involve planning for and responding to creative pupil ideas and this has been found (QCA, 2003) to develop curiosity, motivation, self-esteem and academic achievement, as well as having a positive effect on adult life skills. Creative children are more likely to be creative adults who can solve problems, take risks and be motivated to continue to learn; as W. B. Yeats identified, 'education is not the filling of a pail but the lighting of a fire'.

Pause for thought

Creative science educational experiences have three essential elements: they should be practical, memorable and interactive. The importance of practical exploratory approaches in scientific development is well established and can be seen in many learning models in science (see Karplus, 1977; Renner, 1982; Cosgrove and Osborne, 1985), including the constructivist approach (Scott, 1987) which has become increasingly popular in science education. Practical science will develop important scientific skills and generic cognitive skills such as problem-solving and thinking skills. Scientific thinking skills can be developed by:

- *challenging children's ideas, by getting them to test out their hypotheses;*
- *setting problems for them to solve;*
- *discussing their ideas and comparing with the ideas of others;*
- *encouraging them to make causal links.*

Through practical activities and discussion of ideas (Costello, 2000: 87) children develop thinking in science in the Early Years (Keogh and Naylor, 2000) and when older (Jones, 2000). Through explorations, problem-solving and discussions children begin to explain their ideas, think hypothetically (de Bóo, 1999) and make causal links between phenomena and their hypothetical ideas. They can also identify their metacognitive processes, that is how they solved problems or the thinking behind their interpretations and hypotheses (Fisher, 2003).

Consider how thinking skills can be developed within the QCA (2000) schemes of work. How can you add challenge to the activities?

I once asked Key Stage I children to explore a collection of toys in a toy box, after reading *Kipper's Toybox* (Inkpen, 1992). They explored the toys and were encouraged to play with them, exploring how they worked. The children were then encouraged to sort the toys according to their properties, putting them into sorting hoops. All the spinning toys were put into one hoop, all the magnetic toys in another, pushing toys in another and jumping toys in another. A magnetic gyroscope which spins on a metal frame with two metal rails caused a few problems as this was both a spinner and magnetic. One child decided that we could place the gyroscope between the spinning and magnetic hoops, so that it touched both. Another child suggested that we could separate the two parts of the gyroscope and put the spinning part in the spinning hoop and the metal frame in the magnetic hoop (although it was not itself magnetic). A third child suggested an alternative solution, by overlapping the hoops so that there was another section for magnetic spinning toys. This was a good example of children developing and using their thinking skills to solve simple problems.

Memorable science education supports the development of important motivating attitudes (Johnston, 1996), such as curiosity, which is essential in harnessing children's interest, encouraging them to take risks, make scientific discoveries and construct scientific understandings. Attitudes can usually be observed in some kind of behaviour and the importance of the resulting behaviours is thought to affect development in science (DfEE, 1999a; Bricheno et. al., 2001). Attitudes can be:

- **generic, that is those needed throughout education (co-operation and perseverance);**
- **scientific, that is those that are important in science education (respect for evidence and tentativeness);**
- **affective or emotional (enthusiasm);**
- **cognitive (curiosity, respect for evidence, thoughtfulness, reflection, tentativeness, questioning);**
- **social or behavioural (co-operation, collaboration, tolerance, flexibility, independence, perseverance, leadership, responsibility, tenaciousness).**

Creative science education can help to develop many of these attitudes, by motivating children to want to explore and discover, encouraging them to work co-operatively and supporting their cognitive development.

Children need to interact with their environment, their peers and supportive adults in creative science experiences. Creative science learning environments will encourage cognitive development: 'encompassing milieus, in which the messages of learning and work are manifest and inviting' (Gardner, 1991: 204). Interacting with others will encourage them to consider the ideas of others and develop thinking skills. Interaction with supportive adults can challenge ideas and interpretations, with the role of the adult being to facilitate learning rather than impart knowledge, recognising that creative science education is an active rather than a passive experience in which an adult supports children in the development of skills and understandings which can later be applied in other contexts and everyday life.

Why is it difficult to be a creative science teacher?

Creative science teaching and learning is thought to pose problems particularly regarding time, coverage, control, safety and achievement of learning objectives. In practice, creative science can effectively address all these issues and make learning fun for both practitioner and child.

The science curriculum contains an enormous amount of material and one pedagogical solution is to impart knowledge, as this takes less time than exploration, discovery or investigation. The difficulty of covering the curriculum, together with the understandable fear of a whole class practically exploring and investigating in science, sometimes leads to the type of teaching approaches advocated in literacy and numeracy. This means that some science lessons become whole-class demonstrations which impart knowledge to children en masse. For teachers who are lacking in confidence in science and inexperienced in teaching this approach to science education appears to be an effective way to manage the demands of the curriculum and maintain good levels of behaviour, controlling children's learning and ensuring safety. In fact, such an approach leads to poor quality learning. Effective science learning occurs through teaching approaches which engage and interest children (Hidi and Harackiewicz, 2000), approaches which are practical, developing skills alongside understandings and paying attention to detail rather than coverage, and where practitioners facilitate individual or small group learning, bearing in mind individual learning abilities and styles (Gardner, 1983).

The very large demands of the science curriculum can be effectively covered by practically focusing on small aspects of conceptual understanding rather than knowledge and in a context which children can relate to. Practical work (explorations, investigations, problem-solving and guided discovery) will support the development of scientific skills (Sc1 of the National Curriculum) which cannot be achieved in a non-practical way. The focus on conceptual understanding will help children to apply their understanding in new contexts and support their understanding in other scientific concepts. Effective and creative science education does take time for children to explore, investigate and discover new ideas. It does involve giving children time and encouragement to support their explorations and discoveries and also support their behaviour. Behaviour is improved by child-centred, creative scientific activities; in fact we can have greater control over behaviour and learning by being less controlling.

Whole-class directed scientific learning does not allow children to develop their own understanding, implying that all children need the same experiences and that the practitioner knows exactly what is best for each learner. In fact, children's development is more effective when they are motivated to learn, take ownership over their own learning and work with practitioners to develop knowledge, understanding, skills and attitudes.

Within the primary strategy, creative science education becomes a reality by:

- *Making learning vivid and real, by developing understanding through enquiry, creativity, e-learning and group problem-solving;*
- *Making learning an enjoyable and challenging experience, by stimulating learning through matching teaching to learning styles and preferences;*
- *Enriching the learning experience, by developing learning skills across the curriculum.*

(DfES, 2003: 29)

For many practitioners the problem is how to incorporate the features of effective creative science education, but maintain the rigour and focus on key objectives for development and learning. Scientific concepts, knowledge and skills are static and unchanging so that creative science activities are almost impossible to deliver. We need to remember that many aspects of science will be new for children and have the potential to inspire them. We can also be creative in our teaching, especially when we become confident ourselves in scientific understanding. Every teacher has the potential for creativity, in the same way that every child has. Too often our creativity in science education is adversely affected by our lack of scientific understanding and we are unable to use our creativity in our teaching.

Pause for thought

Do creative children need creative teachers?

If we lack creativity in our teaching, we will structure and control all aspects of learning and restrict any creativity on the part of children. They will be unable to take alternative viewpoints, solve problems or challenge interpretations and their understandings are likely to be less sophisticated. If we allow children some freedom to explore their own ideas and value their alternative views of the world, then we support creativity and learning. (See PSR, 2004, which focused on creativity and science education.)

How can we be more creative in our science teaching?

Effective, creative science teaching and learning can be best achieved by providing motivating exploratory and investigatory experiences for children. One form of creative science involves structured exploratory discovery learning (Johnston, 2004). Discovery learning (DES, 1967) was popular in the 1960s and 1970s, although over time it was seen to involve children playing without purpose or learning objectives and did not take into account existing conceptual ideas of the world they had developed from birth. This definition has been updated for modern teaching and so an exploratory discovery approach is one where:

- *the child is central to the learning;*
- *children explore and discover things about the world around them, which stem from their own initial curiosity;*

- *children construct their own understandings through exploration and from the experience of discovery, as well as develop important skills and attitudes;*
- *teachers support and encourage children to ensure that their explorations and discoveries are meaningful to them;*
- *teachers utilize knowledge about the children as learners (e.g. Gardner, 1983) and pedagogical theory and practice to provide an excellent learning environment.*

(Johnston, 2004: 21–2).

An example of a creative discovery approach is a potions lesson (after Harry Potter, Rowling, 1997; see Johnston, 2005), which I have carried out with children from Year 2 to Year 6. This begins as a fairly formal lesson with me wearing an academic gown and in role as a Hogwart's supply teacher. During the lesson, the children predict and investigate what will happen if they mix small amounts of substances with water in clear plastic beakers. The substances include unidentified solids (salt, sugar, cornflour, talcum powder, bicarbonate of soda and plaster of Paris) and liquids (white vinegar, detergent, lemonade, cooking oil, lemon juice and colour change bubble bath). Through investigation the children will experience dissolving (salt and sugar), solutions (cornflour, bicarbonate of soda, lemon juice), density (talcum powder, oil and plaster of Paris) and colour change (bubble bath). Later, the lesson becomes more exploratory with children discovering what happens when they mix different substances together in different proportions (vinegar and bicarbonate of soda fizz, plaster of Paris and water produce heat) and they can even write instructions for their potion and identify what effects it will have through an advertisement or jingle. In this way children are developing scientific skills (observation, prediction and hypothesis) and understanding (the way materials change when mixed) through a creative, cross-curricular activity that will motivate them.

Problem-solving is another example of creative science and can vary from the small challenges given to children while they explore or play to specific problems that involve the use of scientific skills and knowledge, sometimes in a technological context. While young children play in the sand or water or discover materials through a potion exploration, the practitioner can challenge them by asking questions:

- **What will happen if you add water to the sand?**
- **How can you make a water spout?**
- **How can you make the potion change colour/fizz/...?**

Activity

Design a ball-sorter where balls of different sizes and made of different materials (polystyrene balls, marbles, ball bearings, golf balls, table tennis balls, tennis balls, etc.) have to be sorted by a machine made out of a large cardboard box and other junk materials.

Criteria for sorting can include size, density, mass, magnetism, etc.

You can also do this activity with children. They are expected to work together in small groups to make accurate, original machines which sort the balls in a number of different ways. At the end of the activity, the machines can be tested and certificates given to groups for originality of design, accuracy of sorting, number of different ways of sorting and group collaboration skills. In this way children are developing skills in designing and making (DT) as well as planning (Sc1) and knowledge and understanding of forces (Sc4) and materials (Sc3). You can make sure that each group receives a certificate and this can be an added motivational factor.

For younger children, play areas such as a garden centre or bakery (see de Bóo, 2004) can lead to scientific learning about plant growth or materials and properties in a cross-curricular way. In these play experiences, children can develop their own under-standings at a rate and in a way that is appropriate. Some children will learn best when interacting with other children, while others will be much more solitary in their play but still make good developmental progress.

What is creativity in science education?:

a summary of key points

____ *Creativity is not a description that is generally attributed to science.*
____ *Historically, creativity is an essential factor in the scientific discoveries of many famous scientists, such as Darwin, Leonardo da Vinci and Archimedes.*
____ *Science education sits in a difficult position between more creative education and less creative and less flexible science.*
____ *Creative science educational experiences should be practical, memorable and interactive.*
____ *Children need creative teachers to be creative learners.*
____ *Creative science teaching involves challenging and changing approaches and adapting teaching to suit learners.*
____ *The problems of including creative science activities in teaching are time, coverage, control, safety and achievement. However, the benefits in terms of future development outweigh the problems.*

I am interested in mathematics only as a creative art. (Hardy, 1941)

Introduction

The purpose of this chapter is to prompt you into thinking through your views and attitudes towards mathematics so that you can begin to understand and develop its potential for creative teaching and learning in primary schools. Specifically it will address three questions:

1. Is mathematics a creative subject?

2. Is creative mathematics only for the most able?

3. What does it mean to teach mathematics creatively?

The problem with mathematics

'Creative mathematics' appears for many to be a contradiction in terms. Mathematics has a reputation for being either right or wrong: where can the creativity be in that? Yet mathematicians discuss the elegance in proofs and the creative patterns in algebra and fractals. The majority of people learning and teaching mathematics don't ever get to study at the level where creativity would appear to really get started. We may feel like the following summary from King (1992), that mathematics is to be endured:

> *All of us have endured a certain amount of classroom mathematics. We lasted, not because we believed mathematics worthwhile, nor because, like some collection of pre-vailing Darwinian creatures, we found the environment favourable. We endured because there was no other choice. Long ago someone had decided for us that mathematics was important ... so we were compelled into a school classroom fronted with grey chalk-boards and spread with hard seats... the room in which we sat was a dark and oppressive chamber and we thought of it then and now as Herman Melville thought of the Encandatas: only in a fallen world could such a place exist.* (King, 1992: 15)

Our views of mathematics are also coloured by the fact that is it often seen as a utilitarian subject. Mathematics taught at school is a basic skill and needed for the real world. Yet how much mathematics do we use in our real lives? Most of us might say we use measures, aspects of number and estimating in everyday activities. We might see problem-solving as part of mathematics and therefore an aspect we might use in our lives outside education. We may even see problem-solving as creative if there are a number of solutions to a given problem.

Pause for thought

Before looking at the issue of creativity within mathematics in detail it would be worth considering your own perspective on this issue. Do you think mathematics is a creative subject? Is creativity situated in specific topics within mathematics or is it possible to see creativity throughout mathematics?

The case for creativity in mathematics

Mathematicians' view of their work is often framed in the use of specific mathematical vocabulary and therefore unless we speak the language of mathematics fluently it can appear inaccessible. The following quotation from King (1992) demonstrates something of that difficulty and a view of mathematics that may be very different to our own:

> It is a continuing controversy in mathematical circles as to whether new mathematics is created or discovered... The idea that mathematics, as a physical world seems to exist, independent of human thought and activity is a notion at least as old as the philosophy of Plato ... a second view claims that mathematical structures are created and that they have no existence independent of the person that created them. This notion meshes well with the nature of modern pure mathematics. (King, 1992:41)

Society's view of mathematics, however, tends to focus on arithmetic and correct answers to calculations. Mathematics is seen as providing the evidence for other subjects, the proof that things are true if you can prove them mathematically.

The following, about the American poet Robert Frost, is a good parallel with mathematics in that it shows us how a subject or phenomenon is itself a way of looking and serves a wider purpose than the strictly utilitarian. You may know that Frost lived in the farming area of Vermont and was inspired to write poetry through the imagery of the farmers' daily activities:

> He understood, as do all true artists, that it is metaphor and symbol, and not plain reality, that is memorable and significant. Mathematicians, like poets, see value in metaphor and analogy. The lines they draw are made, not only of words, but of graceful symbols: summations and integrals, infinities turning on themselves like self-swallowing snakes, and fractals like snowflakes that, as you blink your eye, turn to lunar landscapes. Mathematicians write their poetry with mathematics. (King, 1992: 11)

Mathematicians see their subject as having a poetic quality as well as the potential for ambiguity and interpretation. How does this fit with current views of creativity?

The challenge to teach mathematics creatively

Mathematics by its nature is often seen as a visual subject with symbols written on a page. However, Tall *et al.* (2001) would suggest that learners need to move towards the abstraction of mathematics to become flexible in their approaches, particularly to calculation, in order to become successful mathematicians. They focus on the child's attention during actions on objects when calculating. Often 5 + 3 can be seen as an array of objects which children imagine in order to combine the quantities. For some children seeing arithmetic in terms of mental images of objects persists and this prevents them from moving into the higher realms of mathematics. These children rely heavily on counting strategies, which increase the possibility for errors with increasing number size. The higher achievers seem to focus more on the symbolism itself. They utilise known facts and move away from counting strategies more quickly, seeing the relationship between numbers. These skills enable the children to be able to engage more easily with the creative opportunities in mathematics. The ability to visualise in the abstract is a key skill in success in mathematics and not just in relation to number. It is a clear prerequisite skill for success in geometry. Creative activities in mathematics should give learners an opportunity to explore the possibilities, working in ways that motivate and engage their interest.

This means looking beyond the structure of the Numeracy Strategy three-part lesson and differentiation through use of three levels of tasks often in the form of work-sheets in the main activity phase of the lesson.

To address this, activities will be used to show how creativity can be enhanced through visual, verbal and kinaesthetic approaches. These link to areas discussed in relation to learning styles which have gained prominence in recent years. The activities outlined in responses to the key questions for this chapter can be classified as enhancing either visual, verbal or kinaesthetic creative activity, in some cases more than one.

Current definitions of creativity

The DfEE (1999a) report on creativity provides a definition, which is broken down into four characteristics. Creative thinking or behaving creatively can be seen as imagina-tive, purposeful, original and of value. If we look at mathematics we can see that thinking mathematically can be purposeful and of value as we can solve problems with mathematical skills and knowledge. We value calculations and measuring where accuracy is important for safety or economy. The imaginative and original behaviours in mathematics appear at first to be more difficult to access. We might see children creating original methods of solving problems, repeating patterns or creating games.

Young children thinking creatively

Young children are fascinated by words and playing with rhyming, often making up new words when they do this with counting rhymes and counting words. These are areas that we might cite as creative activities within the subject of English or literacy. If you listen to children playing they will invent words for quantities as part of playing with language for a specific purpose. Mathematics can be seen as a language that we learn how to speak. We also learn that precise language can be used to describe situa-tions, events or to classify. Two-year-old Alex was overheard trying some of these things out as he was talking to his toys. 'Tigger has a tail ... Alex has no tail'. This small boy was playing with his classification of objects including self, all part of

beginning to think mathematically. This would have been a source of celebration for his parents, were it not two o'clock in the morning.

For young children it may be simple connections between the mathematical skills they are learning and the situations they find themselves in. An example of this is a small girl Ellen of about three who was asked by her mother if there were enough drinks for her mother, her brother and herself. Ellen proceeded to count 1, 2 and then instead of saying three she said 'me' and then decided that there were enough drinks for everyone. Ellen was making her own original connections between her counting skills and the need to use one-to-one correspondence to find out if there were enough drinks for everyone. QCA (2004) describes how you can spot creativity and gives as examples making connections and seeing relationships in mathematics. Ellen is clearly demonstrating a very early start to making connections in order to solve a problem.

Pause for thought

Wilson and Briggs (2002) looked at more able children's approaches to solving mathematical problems for example:

a and b are whole numbers. What could they be?

$$a \div b = 4.125$$

One child Zoe took time to make sense of the problem from the outset, using her insight to plan a strategic response. She took control of the task, exploited connections and relationships, producing an elegant solution. After thinking for some time, she voiced that she saw the problem as 'See how many times you have to do the 4.125 to make a whole number. Zoe recognised the relationship:

$$4.125 \times b = a$$

This enabled her to develop the strategy of multiplying 4.125 to make a whole number. But rather than trying numbers randomly, she exploited what she knew about decimals in order to obtain:

$$4.125 \times 2 = 8.25$$
$$8.25 \times 2 = 16.5$$
$$16.5 \times 2 = 33$$

This is an example of a creative approach using the elegance of the mathematics as well as her previous knowledge.

Is creative mathematics only for the most able?

Since the 1980s there has been a developing focus of attention on children who are 'gifted and talented'; this has to be linked to numerous additional programmes for these children. One key issue for teachers is how to identify and support these particular learners. Porter (2005) describes some of the difficulties of identification with young children. She suggests that teachers tend to under-identify both the gifted children who appear to engage with activities very slowly and those who are creative and do not conform. At the same time it is possible to overestimate the abilities of children who engage with tasks readily, cooperate easily and, perhaps more tellingly, conform to the expectations of adults.

Although Porter's work is focusing on gifted children generally she raises specific issues in relation to mathematics and particularly in relation to children with learning difficulties. We do not associate 'giftedness' with any difficulties yet Porter (2005) clearly sets out examples of children with a gift in one or more areas of the curriculum but who appear to have difficulties in others. This has significant implications for a stance which allows access to creative mathematics only to the most able. Children with the difficulties Porter describes may well be denied access to the opportunities to be creative in their strongest area. Porter describes the difficulties for teachers to be able to identify these children as more able as their difficulties may mask their true abilities. To avoid this situation teachers need to ensure all children have access to creative activities in mathematics; only this will allow them to show their real abilities and offer teachers different situations in which to accurately assess their potential.

Engaging all learners with the potential for enjoying and therefore seeing the creativity possible within the subject is a key challenge for teachers. Robinson and Koshy (2004) suggest that we look at school mathematics as partitioned into three elements: procedures, application and elegance. They see the way forward for increasing the creativity in mathematics by providing opportunities for children to learn all three elements in order to introduce children to the 'more beautiful aspects of mathematics'.

This would seem to be backed up by the intentions behind the National Curriculum, which include recommendations for mathematics to be seen as a creative subject. DfES/QCA (1999) states that 'Mathematics is a creative discipline. It can stimulate moments of pleasure and wonder when a pupil solves a problem for the first time, discovers a more elegant solution to that problem, or suddenly sees hidden connections' (14). These are not recommendations for a few; we are looking at an entitlement for all children to be able to engage with mathematics as a creative subject and this is where the role of the teacher in facilitating access to this approach to mathematics is paramount.

What does it mean to teach mathematics creatively?

The National Numeracy Strategy (NNS), commonly described as the 'numeracy hour', began its implementation in schools in September 1999, complementing the introduction of the literacy hour during the previous year. Martin Hughes (1999) describes the strategy as 'undoubtedly the most prescriptive approach to primary mathematics ever developed in this country' (4). Has this changed the way we think of teaching mathematics? Definitely. Does it mean that there we see less creativity in teaching mathematics? Possibly.

Activity

Can you think of someone you consider teaches creatively? Does this include their teaching of mathematics? What are the key elements of their teaching that make it creative? Try to list these elements for yourself.

Pause for thought

These are difficult questions and could suggest that you are looking for continuous evidence of flare and imagination. The issue with this interpretation is that a high level of imaginative teaching can be a clear aspiration but can be hard to sustain across all topics/subjects and may even set unrealistic expectations. This is not to say that this shouldn't be the aim of teaching mathematics. However, we need to consider that many people teaching mathematics in the early years and primary age range do not hold positive feelings about the subject. These feelings about mathematics are likely to affect the approaches to teaching the subject to children.

The NNS has made significant changes to approaches to teaching mathematics. The first area of change is the emphasis on numeracy as opposed to mathematics, and a clear focus on numeracy skills for everyday life. The second is the structure of the lesson into three clear parts. For some teachers this is a narrowing of the flexibility in approach and organisation of the lessons that was apparently there before. A conversation with a colleague from a school which had recently been inspected led to a discussion about creative teaching and in which subjects it occurred. (This was a school which had been very successful with its inspection, and many of the lessons had been graded highly.) His perception of the lessons that were graded at the highest levels was that the teachers were taking some risks with lesson formats and the activities selected. Interestingly, the perception was that none of these lessons were within the core curriculum. The power of the inspection in this case was perhaps limiting the creativity among this group of teachers, though the discussion extended beyond the inspection period to patterns of teaching which had begun to emerge. The influence of a structure to the lessons, particularly in mathematics, was apparent for this school. It was felt that, somehow, the ability to structure lessons flexibly had become emblematic of the school's development work on creativity, teaching and learning.

A problem-solving approach

One way of working on enhancing a creative and more open approach of teaching mathematics is to offer children problems which provide suitable entry points to children of a wide range of ability and therefore can be used within any class, not a specific class for the most able. Briggs (2000) argued this particularly in relation to the Early Years and in response to moving away from the use of worksheets within the main activity phase of numeracy lessons. The focus should be on making good learning opportunities for children. Below is a suggested checklist for deciding upon what makes a really 'good' task.

Pause for thought

Is my activity:

- *accessible to all;*
- *possible to extend;*
- *possible to narrow;*
- *enjoyable?*

Does it offer/present:

- *a practical starting point;*
- *oppportunities for mathematical discussion;*
- *a reason for children to record their ideas;*
- *opportunities for repetition without becoming meaningless both for teachers and children;*
- *clarity of underlying mathematics?*

Activity

Think about activities you use in your classroom. How do they compare to this list? Can you find an activity that fits all of these criteria? How might you use an activity that fits all of these criteria in a mathematics lesson?

Open tasks for children

The teacher can also use open task materials in flexible ways that respond to the needs and previous experience of the learners. Organisations like NRICH provide resources, which support the most able, but this is within the context of a broad interpretation and view of enrichment, not within a context of provision which simply targets the most able. Good enrichment education is good education for all. Good mathematics education should incorporate an approach that is an enriching and stimulating experience for all children – and, some would argue, the teacher. Mathematics education should stimulate teachers' continued development and interest in learning. NRICH suggest that this approach should include content opportunities designed to:

- **develop and use problem-solving strategies;**
- **encourage mathematical thinking;**
- **include historical cultural contexts;**
- **offer opportunities for mathematical extension.**

Therefore this enrichment is not simply learning facts and demonstrating skills. Mathematical skills and knowledge can be precursors to, and also outcomes of, an enrichment curriculum.

The aim of an enrichment curriculum is to support:

- **a problem-solving approach;**
- **improving pupil attitudes;**
- **a growing appreciation of mathematics;**
- **the development of conceptual structures (adapted from Ernest, 2000).**

This sounds as though to teach mathematics creatively you need to alter your teaching radically. I would argue that the smallest things can change the teaching and learning for the children and make a lesson successful for them as learners. Thinking creatively about mathematics teaching is about starting from what you know and adding to it.

Creative mathematics teaching in practice

An example of this was observed in a trainee teacher's mathematics lesson with a Year 3 class who were working on multiplying by 10. This is an area where there are lots of opportunities for children to acquire misconceptions, the most obvious being that if I multiply by 10 I just add a zero. This works for whole numbers but doesn't make any difference to the number if over-generalised and applied to decimals. The creativity in this lesson was in the modelling of what happens to numbers when multiplied by ten. The trainee had set up three large hoops on the floor for the whole class to see marked as hundreds, tens and ones. Children were asked to come out to the front and hold a digit card standing in the tens and ones hoop to make the number 14. Another child was asked to join them but stand initially a little way from the hoops holding a zero or nought. This child became 'naughty nought'.

The trainee with the children then modelled what happened when the zero was added to the original number pushing (gently) the digits along the hoops to increase their place value. This was completed after they had undertaken discussion about multiplying by 10 and what happened to the numbers with some children clearly spotting a generalisable pattern of adding a zero. The trainee felt it was important for the children to see and understand what was actually happening to the number. Digital pictures were taken by one of the class to form a display after the lesson to remind children of what had happened to the digits to form a new number after the intervention of 'naughty nought'. This was a creative, simple but effective model for all the children in the class regardless of ability. This approach begins to make links for the children between aspects of mathematics which is a key finding from the study into effective teachers of numeracy (Askew *et al.*, 1997).

The need to engage children in their learning is a topic of discussion in many countries in relation to mathematics. In Germany Meissner (2000) describes a project entitled 'We build a village' which concentrated on geometry to further concepts of both plane and three-dimensional geometry in primary schools. In this module for primary grades (aged about 8–10 years) the children worked with about 35 different solids made of styrofoam, wood, paper-nets or plastic. The activities for the children were diverse and consisted of: sorting and classifying, folding, drawing, cutting, constructing nets, using plasticine, and building solids and houses with these models. At the end of the module (of about seven lessons) the children had built their own village with a grocery store, a church, a school and other houses, as well as a creek, streets and parking areas. This kind of topic approach to teaching and learning is moving back into the primary curriculum with the introduction of the ideas from the Primary Strategy (DfES, 2003) and the subsequent continuing professional development materials. This is enabling teachers to look again at the ways they are constructing the learning to engage children with mathematics and learn to become creative mathematicians.

Other approaches to being creative with mathematics teaching can be seen in the use of children's current interests to motivate and stimulate curiosity. Briggs *et al.* (2002) is an example of an approach drawing upon the current interest created by the phenomenon of the Harry Potter books. All the activities described in the article are based around the theme of ideas from the wizarding books. The object of the creative approach is to enliven and enrich the mathematics lesson and to offer children a stimulus that they might then go on to develop by themselves. The activities also allow teachers to make connections for the children between aspects of mathematics (Askew *et al.*, 1997).

Activity

Think about the interests of the children you teach. As with the above example of Harry Potter, you might want to make a connection with a book you are studying or reading with the class. You might also want to think about the environment near to the school: are there particular natural features or local buildings which offer mathematical possibilities? Can you construct activities that will engage their interest with mathematics and help them to appreciate the creative opportunities within the subject? See if you can find out about the approaches to teaching implemented as a result of the Primary Strategy. What effect has this had on teaching mathematics creatively?

Creative mathematics:

a summary of key points

Cross (2004) has written passionately about the important questions in mathematics teaching which, for her, centred on: How do we engage children in their own learning? How do we engage them with mathematics and encourage them to want to know more? Her article also included a key quotation from the non-statutory guidance written to accompany the first version of the National Curriculum in 1989. It states that:

— *Mathematics is not only taught because it is useful. It should be a source of delight and wonder, offering pupils intellectual excitement and an appreciation of its essential creativity.* (NCC, 1989).

— *Teaching mathematics in this way makes demands on us as teachers, especially if we have not had good experiences of mathematics teaching as learners. This requires us to:*

- *reappraise our preconceptions of mathematics as having no creative potential;*
- *look beyond the structure of the three-part lesson promoted in the NNS to ensure that children's interests in mathematics are engaged and sustained;*
- *ensure that we develop ways of teaching which encourage problem-solving and open tasks, so that children's visual, auditory and kinaesthetic modes of learning are catered for;*
- *study closely the development of children of all abilities in our classes so that we do not fall into the trap of providing creative activities only for the most able, or as extension activities to raise the level of challenge for those pupils who finish activities quickly.*

Further reading

Craft, A., Dyer, G., Dugal, J., Jeffrey, R. and Lyons, T. (1997) *Can You Teach Creativity?* Nottingham: Ed Now Books.

Craft, A. (2000) *Creativity Across the Primary Curriculum*, London: Routledge.

Fisher, R. and Williams, M. (eds) (2004) *Unlocking Creativity: Teaching Across the Curriculum*. London: David Fulton.

QCA (2004) Creativity: Find it! Promote it! Promoting children's creative thinking and behaviours across the curriculum at Key Stages 1, 2 and 3. Suffolk: QCA Publications.

Uptitis, R., Phillips, E. and Higginson, W. (1997) *Creative Mathematics: Exploring Children's Understanding*. New York: Routledge.

Useful websites

www.enrich.maths.org
www.qca.org.uk

9 CHILDREN, CREATIVITY AND PHYSICAL EDUCATION
SUE CHEDZOY

Introduction

The purpose of this chapter is to try to help you to think through your own view of physical education (PE) and to recognise the potential of the subject for enabling children to be creative through movement, either alone or with others. Practical suggestions are made and the creative approach is underpinned with creative theory (Fryer, 1996; Steinberg et al., 1997; Beetlestone, 1998; DfEE, 1999; Craft, 2000; Aires et al., 2004) and good practice in the subject (Schools Council and Assessment Authority (SCAA), 1997; Hopper et al., 2000; Bailey and Macfadyen, 2000; DfES/DCMS, 2005).

The problem with PE

For those of you who remember your lessons in PE as unpleasant experiences on the hockey or rugby fields, being freezing cold and wearing unflattering kit, not being able to vault a horse in the gymnasium while being observed by the rest of the class or struggling around a 1500-metre track, creativity and physical education may not seem to be naturally well matched. It has to be said that many people have been put off the subject by a few teachers who adopted very didactic teaching styles, favoured the naturally gifted and focused on the activity rather than the child. Some of these teachers were generally insensitive to the individual needs of their pupils and failed to inspire in them a love and appreciation of physical activity.

Pause for thought

If you were to write down your views about PE, what would you say?

Some possible answers might include:

- *It's about keeping fit and fitness is important for a healthy lifestyle.*
- *Healthy lifestyles combat illnesses such as heart disease and diabetes.*
- *It's a range of competitive, creative and challenge-type activities.*
- *It's only popular with sporty people.*
- *Everybody can be good at PE.*
- *It's different from other lessons.*

Depending on your own experiences you might emphasise some aspects more than others. When you have completed this exercise turn to Figure 9.1 to see how others have described PE.

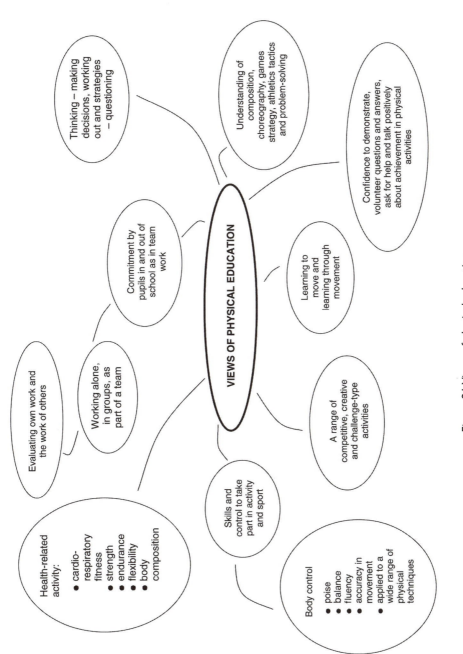

Figure 9.1 Views of physical education.

Creativity in physical education throughout this century

In the early days of the development of the subject there were hardly any opportunities for pupils to be creative. At the beginning of the century there was a concern that the nation's youth were unfit for joining the armed forces and the government introduced programmes of physical training into elementary schools, based on military drill. In these programmes there was no room for creativity; in gymnastics, for example, children were expected to respond to commands such as 'Atten-tion!' or 'Class – attention! Stand – easy!' or 'Stand at – ease!' (Board of Education, 1933).

In the 1940s the Ministry of Education took over responsibility for physical education from the Ministry of Health and the subject became more child-centred. Certainly the guidance for primary school teachers in the 1950s (Ministry of Education 1953 a and 1953b) recognised the need to relate to children's creative potential within the physical education programme in primary schools. The Plowden Report had an impact on the curriculum which followed and in the early 1970s the government issued a document relating to the physical education curriculum in primary schools named 'Movement' (Department of Education and Science, 1972). This document gave very little specific guidance to teachers on how to foster creativity but it was expected that modern educational dance and gymnastics were taught which encouraged a lot of exploration by children with very little structure.

In the National Curriculum for Physical Education (DES/WO, 1991) the teaching profession was guided towards involving children in the processes of planning, performing and evaluating their ideas and performances. It was intended that the process would underpin what children learn and do in physical education, changing the emphasis from a 'product (activity) based curriculum to a process (learning) based curriculum' (Murdock, 2005). This made more explicit the way in which we should encourage children to be more involved in, for example, composing dances, creating original sequences in gymnastics and water-based activities, working out tactics and strategies in games and athletics activities and creating adventures in the outdoors. The very nature of the subject is about doing and so performance has always been at the heart of PE, but the concept of pupils planning and evaluating their work and the work of others had never been made so explicit in past guidance for teachers. This process relates well to the model of learning in other art forms in the primary curriculum such as music, art and drama which involve the processes of composing, making and appreciating.

What does high-quality PE look like today?

When pupils are experiencing high-quality physical education they appear to enjoy the subject, seldom miss physical education lessons, always bring their kit and encourage others to take part. They know and understand what they are trying to achieve and how to go about doing it. They know how to think for different activities, for example composition in gymnastics activities, choreography in dance, games strategy, athletics tactics and problem-solving.

Pause for thought

What does this mean in practice?

How can you help children to think for different activities?

- *What skills do you need to teach them to help them to be able to choreograph a simple dance or gymnastics sequence ?*
- *What skills do they need to devise a games strategy?*
- *What skills do they need to be able to adopt a tactical approach to games or athletics?*
- *What skills do they need to solve problems in outdoor and adventurous activities and other areas of PE?*

Children who receive high-quality PE know how to evaluate their own and others' work in a variety of activities. They recognise the contribution that physical education can make to a balanced, healthy, active lifestyle and how success in aspects of the subject might affect their feelings about themselves.

Children who are experiencing high-quality PE have confidence in their ability. They are not afraid to show others what they can do, they volunteer questions and answers, ask for help and talk positively about their achievements, whatever their level of attainment. They explore and experiment with new activities without worrying about failing. Those who are more confident in an aspect of the subject are happy to help others.

Pause for thought

In order to be creative in PE children need to be and feel safe, that is both safe in the physical environment and safe to take risks.

- *How can you help children to feel safe and secure in their physical space?*
- *What kind of ethos do you need to develop with your class to enable children to feel confident to explore and experiment in PE?*
- *How can you help children in your class to value and receive others' efforts and performances in PE with sensitivity?*

Through high-quality PE children are able to demonstrate improved skills and control, poise and balance. They are able to apply and adapt a wide range of skills and techniques effectively and have developed stamina, suppleness and strength to keep them going. Children experience a range of competitive, creative and challenging activities both individually and as part of a group in high-quality PE programmes. They think about what they are doing and make appropriate decisions for themselves. They work independently and ask questions so that they can organise themselves and make progress. They devise ideas and strategies to help them to improve their performance. Children experiencing a high-quality PE programme show a desire to improve and achieve in relation to their own abilities; they are prepared to take time to practise and refine their performance and welcome the advice of others (DfES, 2004).

Physical education in the National Curriculum (DfEE/QCA, 1999d) requires children to be taught dance, game activities and gymnastics activities every year throughout Key Stages 1 and 2, as well as athletics activities, outdoor adventurous activities and swimming at Key Stages 2. The four strands of the Physical Education National Curriculum include:

- **acquiring and developing skills;**
- **selecting and applying skills and compositional ideas;**
- **evaluating and improving performance;**
- **knowledge and understanding of fitness and health.**

The Attainment Target for Physical Education contains eight level descriptions with an additional description for exceptional performance. These are central to planning in physical education and, as Gower (2005) reminds us, can be broken down into four aspects: a gradual increase in the complexity of the sequence of movement; an improvement in the demonstrated performance qualities; greater independence in the learning context; and a gradual challenge to the level of cognitive skills required. throughout the level descriptions.

Activity

Look at the National Curriculum for Physical Education (DfES/QCA) (1999d).

Look at each of the level descriptions for physical education. Look for the references to planning, performing and evaluating in each of the levels. Choose one of those levels and, using your experience of teaching an aspect of physical education (for example, dance at level 4), describe what you would expect a child to be able to do.

This has implications for the way you help children in their learning in all aspects of PE. You need to give them plenty of opportunities to be creative, to have opportunities to plan for themselves and to help them to develop a language with which to describe their own and others' work so that they are able to evaluate progress against given criteria.

Pause for thought

- *What kind of environment do you think you need to foster in your classroom to enable children to be creative in PE?*
- *How can you help children to feel free to explore and experiment in the different aspects of PE?*
- *What knowledge, skills and understanding do children need as tools for creativity in this subject?*
- *How can you encourage other children in your class to value the originality of opinion, response to a task or different interpretation to a given task?*

All aspects of the National Curriculum for Physical Education lend themselves to developing and celebrating children's creativity. You as a teacher have the key to opening this up. First of all you need to value the subject and feel reasonably confident in your own subject knowledge. You do not need to feel that you are an expert in all areas of activity but you do need to feel secure in setting up a safe physical environment (see BAALPE, 2004) and have a basic understanding about how children learn in and through physical education. You also need to help children to develop the vocabulary in movement so that they are able to use their skills to form their individual movement patterns.

Pause for thought

Select one of the areas in the National Curriculum for Physical Education. Design a work card to give to a group of children to help them to devise an original dance, game, gymnastic, athletic, swimming or outdoor and adventurous activity.

- *What space will be available to them?*
- *What equipment will be available to them?*
- *How long will the activity need to last?*
- *What guidance will be required with regard to safety?*
- *Are there any cross-curricular links you would like the children to include?*
- *How can the activity be linked in some way to previous work to enable the children to use previously acquired skills?*

Creativity in athletic activities

Athletic activities in the primary school involve running, jumping and throwing activities. At this stage of children's development it is important that they have success in these activities so that they feel good about themselves and recognise that, with practice, they are all capable of improving their performance. It is important that children are given time and plenty of opportunity to explore and experiment with different actions related to athletics, and that there is a fine balance between cooperative and competitive activity within the programme.

During the warm-ups for athletic activities children can experiment with different ways of running and can work alone, in pairs or small groups to make up and create their own running activities (Bray, 1992). Examples might include: asking the children to devise a warm-up in a grid which involves running in different directions: forwards, backwards, to the left, to the right and diagonally; creating a maze to run through around or over using hoops, bean bags, skipping ropes or low hurdles. Ask children to work in small groups and go on a journey in a single file: the first person in the line chooses the way of running, i.e. small steps, cross steps, large strides, variety of way and the rest of the group follow. The leader decides on the route, and on a signal the person at the back jogs to the front and creates the running pattern and pathway.

An example of larger-scale planning in athletics activities was described by Hornsby (1991) where children in Year 2 in a first school were set the problem-solving exercise of planning the Sports Day for the whole school. The children selected the activities, gave them names, created their own record sheets, wrote and sent the invitations, planned and prepared the refreshments, and had a wonderful time learning across the curriculum (Chedzoy, 2000).

Creativity in dance activities

Dance as a performing art seems to be the most obvious area of activity in the Physical Education National Curriculum to contribute to children's creativity and I am sure that if you have studied dance in your initial training you are aware of the potential for developing children's creativity through the activity. Dance provides opportunities for artistic and aesthetic education, and experiences in which children can develop emotionally and learn to express moods and ideas symbolically. Dance can also help children to develop rhythmic and musical sensitivity and a knowledge and understanding of the art form. Dance education can also contribute to children's understanding of traditional dance forms from different times and places.

In dance you will encourage children to compose dances by exploring and improvising, making decisions and solving problems . Give them opportunities to share their ideas with others through practical demonstration or discussion. This will help them to shape and refine movement phrases to form dances. Through performance children will develop physical skill and a repertoire of actions to travel, turn, jump and perform gestures to perform a set dance, express an idea, tell a story or communicate a mood. You need to give children time and opportunity to view dances, to appreciate their meaning, actions and qualitative and spatial features (Chedzoy, 1996).

There is such a wide range of stimuli for developing dance. These include other curriculum areas such as music, history, geography and art. Starting points for developing dance could be poems, stories, photographs, paintings, posters with different colours, text shapes and contrasts. Television adverts or film clips containing professional dance works may also be used to inspire children to create their own dances.

Even when teaching folk dancing you can encourage children to adopt a creative approach. For example, teach the children some basic moves and figures such as do-si-do, arches, right-hand, left-hand star, promenade, and ask them to compose their own circle or line dance in small groups using some of these figures involving meeting and parting.

Creativity in games activities

A high-quality games programme in the primary school will enable children to become confident and competent in a variety of invasion games, net/wall games and striking and fielding games.

Some people feel that all games teaching needs to be governed by the rules and regulations of the major game, or even their mini versions such as high-five netball, uni-hoc, five-a-side football, pop lacrosse, tag rugby or short tennis. If you watch children playing games in the park or on the playground you will often see that they make up their own structures and rules – jumpers for goals and boundaries and carefully nego-tiated rules to help the game flow. Rules that are negotiated and agreed by the group are more likely to be adhered to by children – which for you as a teacher makes things easier with regard to organisation. All governing bodies of sport advocate small-sided games for children of primary school age and if you are able to rely on chil-dren in your class playing games to their own rules you do not have to referee or umpire to help keep order in the group.

You might also consider adopting a creative approach to helping children understand the principles involved in the tactics and strategies of games. For example, ask children to work in pairs to make up a game involving aiming at a target.

All ball games require the accurate sending of a ball/shuttlecock into space or to a goal or target. Focusing on this skill in an innovative way can be fun and also helps the chil-dren to understand the basic principles of play. Ask the children to select their own target from a range of equipment. The targets could be markings on the ground, wall or fences, such as circles, faces, animal shapes or rocket shapes, or children could draw their own targets with playground chalk. Posts, trees, skittles and hoops also make suitable targets. Ask the children to choose their own equipment to send to the target. This could be a small or large ball, a bean bag, a rubber quoit, or a unihoc stick and ball. Ask the children to decide on their own area of play and agree on any rules before play begins. Will there be a method of scoring? If so, how will the score be recorded?

At the end of the session ask the children to show and share their ideas with others. Ask the children to evaluate their games. Ask questions such as: 'Is it easier to hit a target when you are close or far away? Is it easier to hit a big target or a small target? Is it easier to hit a target with a small ball or a big ball? Ask the children to give their game a name and ask them to write it up using the computer so it can be played by others at a later date (Chedzoy, 2000).

Any basic skills which you have taught the children can be used to help them to be creative in devising their own version of practices and small-sided games. Visit **www.ncaction.org.uk/creativity/whatis.htm** to see an example of this approach with a Year 8 class: 'Like hockey but different'. The same principles apply to games in the primary school and you might be surprised how competent children are at creating their own games, demonstrating the tactics and techniques required for understanding and playing invasion, striking/fielding and net games.

Creativity in gymnastics activities

Gymnastics activities is an area of the curriculum which can be a worry to newly qualified teachers with all the inherent concerns about safety and progression. Once you have more experience you will be comforted by the fact that children are in fact your best resource in this area of the curriculum. Their responses to your challenges will be rich and varied and if you can 'capture the moment' with good observational skills and ask children to show others in the class their movements you will enable children to increase their 'movement vocabulary' so that they have more ideas with which to create longer and more complex sequences. The most popular form of gymnastics taught in primary schools is educational or informal gymnastics (Reynolds, 2000). This approach is also sometimes described as curriculum gymnastics (Williams, 1997). In this form of gymnastics the pupil works at his/her own level within a framework set by the teacher. This is rather different from formal gymnastics in which the child has to perform stylised vaults and other prescribed gymnastic agilities. There are many good books to guide you through a progressive programme of curriculum gymnastics activities (Underwood, 1991; Benn and Benn, 1992; Williams, 1997; Devon LEA, 2002).

Creativity is at the heart of curriculum gymnastics. You are asking children to find different ways of travelling, jumping, balancing, turning, swinging, hanging, climbing and transferring weight from one area of the body to another. If you create a climate of mutual trust and encourage children to sensitively evaluate their own and others' work they will enjoy creating their own original pieces of work. It is an area of the curriculum which should be accessible to all, regardless of physical shape or athletic ability. In assessing children's ability in this area of activity, as in other areas of the physical education curriculum, credit should be given for the child's ability to compose sequences and appreciate the aesthetic qualities of performance as well as for the performance itself.

Creativity in outdoor and adventurous activities

The primary focus of teaching Outdoor and Adventurous Activities is to teach problem-solving skills, to focus on process, to learn to co-operate and to learn from group mistakes while participating. In a significant majority of Outdoor and Adventurous Activities, the skills, knowledge and understanding are almost immaterial to the primary focus, and do not significantly feature even as a secondary focus. (Martin, 2000)

Outdoor and adventurous activities are defined as problem-solving activities which can be planned in and around the school environment, using existing facilities and taught to the whole class by their class teacher. This is opposed to outdoor pursuits and outdoor education which tend to need specialist facilities and specialist tuition.

No two solutions to problems set for children will be identical as children will need to co-operate with others, make decisions and work together to test themselves in a variety of situations, and the outcomes will always vary accordingly. Different forms of orienteering such as cross-country, score orienteering and line orienteering contain elements of navigation, decision making and physical activity. (McNeill *et al.*, 1987; McNeill *et al.*, 1992; Chedzoy, 2000). Trails such as obstacle trails and string trails can present children with the challenge of making connections and seeing relationships. You can be imaginative in stimulating children's interest in their surroundings by taking photographs of features in the school and school grounds such as flowers, trees, shrubs, walls, murals and pond life and then backing these onto a firm fabric, giving each a number and setting up a trail for the children to follow. Another way of organising a trail is to create a texture trail, then give the children a base map, a wax crayon and a large sheet of paper with clues for the texture children should look for at given locations. Children then chase off to find them and make a rubbing of the texture, for example bark, brickwork, leaf or netting. You could encourage children to create their own texture trails.

Creativity in swimming

Try not to always think of swimming in the primary school as only teaching children in straight lines to learn and refine the prescribed swimming strokes. Of course you will wish children to develop water confidence and efficiency in moving through the water and to be able to fulfil the requirements of the National Curriculum for Physical Education which, by the end of Key Stage 2, requires them be able to swim at least 25 metres and have a good knowledge and understanding of safe practice in and around water. However, children can have a great deal of fun and develop confidence in the water if you can think of interesting ways to help them to be creative in these lessons. In fact it's worth remembering that most activities which can be planned, performed and evaluated on land can also be enjoyed in the water. This can make things easier for you as a teacher as you can help your children to transfer some of the ideas developed in the hall or on the field to be further explored in the water!

For children who are not confident in the water these activities will need to take place in shallow water in which children are able to move with their flotation aids.

Use music – this might be over a sound system in a public pool or a suitably insulated deck if used pool-side, or use percussion to stimulate the movement. Ask the children to travel with big steps, little steps, high knees, forwards, backwards and sideways. Their way of travelling is planned by them and they can choose the arm actions to go with their stepping pattern. Ask the children to think about different still shapes and perform them – wide, narrow, twisted, curled. Ask the children to think of characters – how would they move in the water? Find different ways of turning, spinning and rolling around in the water.

For stronger swimmers ask them to create different swimming patterns joining front and back swimming strokes with a turn, spin or roll. Ask the children to make gestures in small groups to create Mexican waves (i.e. one performs a simple action which is repeated by the rest of the group one after the other). Make patterns with the water, sprinkling, swishing, splashing (not at each other!) and whirling using different body parts, i.e. fingers, toes, elbows or knees. Suggest that the children make up their own patterns, for example picking up water in their hands and letting it fall through their fingers making patterns at different levels. Ask partners to share and join patterns together. You can ask the children to work in small groups together making circle patterns just as you might do in a folk dance so that the children compose their own patterns, for example holding hands, travelling four steps to the right, followed by four steps to the left, walking together into the middle and lifting hands high to repeat. The task you might set them could be to 'make up a pattern together' which involves everybody working in unison (all doing the same thing at the same time) which involves travelling (stepping, marching, swimming) meeting and parting.

Children, creativity and physical education:
a summary of key points

Physical education's development as a subject:

⟶ You need to understand the processes involved in teaching physical education today so that you can enable children to plan, perform and evaluate across the range of activities in the physical education curriculum.

Your views about physical education:

⟶ You need to have a clearly defined philosophy about the value of Physical Education and recognise the potential for fostering creativity across the whole of the physical education curriculum at Key Stages 1 and 2.

You need to recognise what high-quality physical education looks like:

⟶ You need to be able facilitate creativity by helping children to think for and through different activities.
⟶ You need to help children to develop skills of evaluation and a language with which they can evaluate their own and others' work.

You need to create a safe environment in which children feel free and confident to take risks, explore and experiment and to create innovative and original episodes in and through movement.

⟶ This requires you to pay particular attention to the physical space and facilities.
⟶ It also requires you to foster a climate of mutual respect where all children feel free to share and demonstrate their work without fear of failure or ridicule.

Website

www.ncaction.org.uk/creativity/whatis.htm

10 CREATIVE AND IMAGINATIVE PRIMARY ART AND DESIGN

PAUL KEY

Introduction

The purpose of this chapter is to encourage you to think about yourself as a creative and imaginative teacher of art and design. In addition we will consider how this approach to teaching will contribute to children's experiences in art and design, making them more meaningful and purposeful, as well as inventive and imaginative. The intention is to help you see art and design in more ambitious ways, in flexible ways, and in trusting ways. This may well improve the way that art and design is taught. In doing so, art and design can become the exciting and rewarding subject it has the potential to be, rather than the ill-conceived and lifeless subject it can become.

This creative approach to teaching and learning is set in the context of the National Curriculum 2000 (DfEE/QCA, 1999e), and the National Advisory Committee on Creative and Cultural Education (NACCCE, 1999) model of creativity.

Being creative and imaginative

The broader implications of the Primary Strategy, *Excellence and enjoyment* (DfES, 2003), have invigorated the need for creative and inventive work in primary schools.

The NACCCE (1999) publication *All Our futures: creativity, culture and education* appeared during a period of government drive to raise standards in mathematics and English with the introduction of the Primary Literacy and Numeracy Strategies (DfEE, 1998, 1999d). Although the initial impact of the NACCCE report was reduced with the emphasis on numeracy and literacy, it is certainly relevant now as we consider creative and imaginative art and design.

In this important document, creativity is considered as a mode for learning, which involves 'imaginative activity fashioned so as to produce outcomes that are both original and of value' (NACCCE, 1999: 29). The document continues to describe how it sees the relationship between 'imagination', 'purpose', 'originality' and 'value', in both *generative* and *evaluative* terms; 'helping young children to understand and manage this interaction between generative and evaluative thinking is a pivotal task of creative education' (1999: 31).

The relationship between making (generative) and evaluating (evaluative) is a process echoed consistently in curriculum models for art and design, including the National Curriculum Council, Arts in Schools Project (1990) and the current National Curriculum 2000 (DfEE/QCA, 1999e).

Using **imagination** involves:	Being **original** can be:
Alternative outcomes The unconventional Non-routine Generating originality Combining existing ideas Reinterpreting Making analogous relationships	Individual: in relation to previous work Relative: in relation to a peer group Historic: it can be uniquely original
Pursuing **purposes** involves:	Judging **value** involves:
Being actively engaged Applied imagination Being deliberate Solving a problem Changing from initial intentions	An evaluative mode of thought Judgement and analysis Individuals and groups Trying out ideas Critical thinking Immediate response or longer periods of reflection

Figure 10.1 The NACCCE model of creativity

Teachers need to help children gain control of the processes inherent in creative activity. This is not only the case in art and design but also across the curriculum. It is useful to remember that in whatever subject creative work appears there will be notable periods of engagement: of *focus*, *withdrawal* and *breakthrough* (NACCCE, 1999).

Using the NACCCE model and considering the periods of engagement, we can begin to envisage a teacher, a curriculum and pupils, working in a productive and evaluative way. We can imagine an atmosphere of *playful and purposeful experimentation*. We can imagine periods of focus, withdrawal and breakthrough. Equally we can see some of the tensions which will exist in terms of assessment or accountability, in monitoring and in progression. However, to work in a playful and purposeful way and to encourage pupils to do the same, we need to do things differently. To do so requires an appraisal of existing practices in art, and in primary school art and design.

What do creative artists do?

We can picture creative artists as being imaginative people, working with a sense of purpose and producing things that are original. We can imagine artists experiencing periods of focus, of withdrawal and of breakthrough. The results of their efforts appear as a diverse collection of images and artefacts and this diversity is not only evident within particular cultures, but also across cultures and across time.

We could spend a considerable amount of time debating how the images and artefacts come to be *art*, or even what the value of art might be: for pleasure, for the expression of emotions or for knowledge and understanding (Graham, 1997), or as a critique of these. Alternatively we can focus on what it is that artists do, and why people give their time, often their whole lives, to making art.

They appear to do so for a range of reasons and as a result their art serves different purposes for individuals and for social groups (see Figure 10.2).

Artists:

Ascribe meaning
Ascribe status
Catalyse social change
Enhance and decorate
Interpret
Make myths
Produce propaganda
Record history
Provide sociotherapy
Tell stories
Teach

Figure 10.2 Roles of artists (Chalmers, 1996: 35)

If we look at the list in Figure 10.2, we can see there are opportunities for teachers and pupils to embrace some of the roles in their own work, and to develop an alternative way of looking at the work of artists, craftspeople and designers, 'encouraging us to see the multicultural common functions of art' (Chalmers, 1996:38).

Pause for thought

Refer to Figure 10.1, the NACCCE model of creativity.

- *Have you observed any art and design lessons which have elements of the NACCCE model of creativity?*
- *Did you observe time and space for pupils to focus, withdraw and breakthrough?*
- *Could you identify a sense of playful and purposeful experimentation?*
- *Do you consider there to be barriers to individual, original and purposeful art and design activities?*
- *What opportunities can you think of to encourage individual, original and purposeful art and design activities?*

Refer to Figure 10.2, the roles of artists.

- *When you think about or look at the work of creative artists, do you think of it in terms of emotion, of pleasure, of expression, or of knowledge or understanding?*
- *What paintings, or buildings, or pieces of jewellery, or graffiti, or sculpture or film would you choose as examples of emotion, or pleasure, or expression, or of knowledge or understanding?*
- *Looking at the list of words which indicate what artists do, can you think of, or find, examples of practice to match the 'roles'?*
- *Think about the art works that are presented to children, how do they fit in this broader view of practice? What are the restrictions on choice? How can you overcome these restrictions?*

Primary school art and design: versions of the same scene

The National Curriculum 2000 (DfEE/QCA, 1999e) details a positive approach to primary art and design, involving exploration, investigation and making, review and revision, and development. It states: 'Teaching should ensure that investigating and making includes exploring and developing ideas and evaluating and developing work' (120).

This encouraging statement is then extended through the programme of study and includes: imagination, investigation, exploration and adaptation of personal ideas. It is suggested that this fairly open approach to learning in art and design be supported by knowledge and understanding in three areas:

1. The visual elements: line, colour, tone, pattern, shape, space and form, and how these can be combined and organised for different purposes.

2. Materials and processes: drawing, painting, printmaking, collage, digital media, textiles, and sculpture, and how these can be matched to ideas and intentions.

3. Artists, craftspeople and designers working in different times and cultures, in a variety of genres, styles and traditions.

(DfEE/QCA, 1999e: 120)

Unfortunately in practice the emphasis is often placed on what can be taught, rather than on what can, or might be, learnt (Steers, 2003). Consequently planning and teaching are implemented in very predictable ways. These narrow interpretations can often result in:

- **an emphasis on particular examples of art, by pupils and adults;**
- **an emphasis on the visual elements (line, colour, tone, pattern, shape, space and form), which become isolated from meaning or purpose;**
- **little consideration of presentation or audience;**
- **limited exploration of personal themes;**
- **limited exploration of drawing to invent, explore or imagine, as evident in children's *self-initiated* imagery (Adams, 2003; Anning and Ring, 2004) to develop personal themes.**

This has led to a particular look and feel to primary school art and design.

Despite its inclusion in the National Curriculum, art and design is often considered and presented as a marginal subject (Prentice, 1999). Consequently art and design in primary schools has felt it necessary to revise and reposition itself on a number of occasions. It has done so through theory, through practice, through publications, through exhibitions, and through the tireless energy of individual advocates. This has led to a number of well documented versions of art education and school art.

There are versions which emphasise the subject, versions which emphasise the individual, versions which emphasise society, versions which emphasise the cultural significance of art. There are versions which champion expression, others which venture for social change through the democratic process of education, and in our case art education, and others which promote the development of skill and technique. For the purpose of this chapter we don't need to rehearse these extensively, although further study will reveal a very interesting history of art education (Efland, 1990; Thistlewood, 1992; Macdonald, 2004).

A series of changes can be traced in art education's history. This process of change and renewal is claimed to be the 'lifeblood' of art education (Steers, 2003), to be encouraged and not suppressed. Art and design educators are certainly grateful there has been no national strategy for art and design or for creativity. However, the apparent need to revise the rationale for art can be seen as either a consequence of the need for change, or in some way the *symptom* of continued change. That is to say *change* becomes the orthodoxy for a subject that claims to avoid orthodoxy in its quest for difference and originality.

Either way, the picture is confused. Understandably practice becomes informed by a number of 'bits' taken from alternative versions. Occasionally practice is coherent and well conceived, and the results are interesting and varied, but at other times it is ill-conceived and restrictive.

In his examination of the influences on primary art and design teaching Prentice (1999) suggests that existing practice is based on the following poorly defined concepts of skill acquisition, of innate ability, of giftedness, of self expression, of freedom, of creativity, of originality and of child art. A particular consequence of these poorly thought through ideas is the notion of the teacher, and the interventions they choose to make or choose to resist. The teacher, the choices they make and the actions they take are particularly relevant in this chapter as we move towards considering their creative and imaginative role. However, there remains the issue of the *confused rationale*. This needs to be clear if our practice is to benefit.

To guide our thoughts about teaching, about curriculum and about pupils, and to shape our rationale, we will consider a set of useful principles. In an adaptation from Steers and Swift (1999) 'A manifesto for art in schools', itself based on principles of difference, plurality and independent thought, we will identify good practice in primary art and design as outlined in Figure 10.3.

- **Teachers and pupils are encouraged to be confident in exploring personal lines of enquiry, and creative action and thought**
- **Art is seen as a relevant and meaningful activity for and by pupils**
- **The curriculum has greater range and diversity**
- **Classrooms encourage choice and self-directed activity**

Figure 10.3 Principles to guide practice

We can now consider a rationale within these principles which recognises art and design as:

> Not merely a non-verbal means through which to communicate ideas that already exist; it is a powerful way of generating and exploring new ideas and feelings, and giving them visual form and in the process making personally significant meaning. It is the way in which this meaning-making comes about through engagement in practical work and through informed personal responses to diverse works of art that is central to learning in art. (Prentice, 1999: 150)

Pause for thought

- **Have you seen different versions of art and design in the primary school, some of which reflect skill acquisition, innate ability, self-expression, or creativity and child art?**
- **Look at school policy statements for art and design. Can you identify a version of art and design education which they appear to advocate?**
- **Which version do you feel an affinity with?**
- **Can you identify principles in the policy statements which echo the principles in Figure 10.3?**
- **Write down four principles which you intend to keep in mind when teaching art and design in the primary school. Look at your principles; which areas are perhaps more complicated than you first thought? For example, how will you provide opportunities of choice and when will you prevent choice? What are the implications for you in managing this in the classroom?**

The teacher, the curriculum and pupils: flexibility, ambition and trust

The period of primary education following the 1988 Education Reform Act has been dominated by accountability and testing; it is hardly surprising that work in art and design has been limited. However, pockets of practice which have not been bound by particular constraints and which have gone out on a limb show what can be achieved (Artworks, START HEARTS – see Further information at the end of the chapter). Their achievements are in a large part due to awareness of the possibilities of art and design for children's learning, and also a willingness to challenge existing practice and to reconsider the role of those involved.

To begin to understand how primary art can be taught in a creative and imaginative way, and how learning in art can be wrapped in a creative and imaginative approach with a sense of curiosity, we need to look more closely at teachers, curriculum and pupils. We will look at these in turn and while doing so consider them in relation to three key themes: *flexibility*, *ambition* and *trust*.

Flexibility: as we will discover this is a key feature not only of artistic practice but of imaginative teaching.

Ambition: this we need to use carefully. While we may talk of 'expectations' in the primary school, and the need to establish and maintain high expectations for all pupils, there is a sense that expectations lead to work that is limited in terms of creative art work. The expectations can become negatively phrased, so thoughts are about what won't work or what won't be possible. The more ambitious projects in school, some of which are recognised nationally as examples of good practice (Artworks), are certainly ambitious in their scope, their scale and their challenge.

Trust: it is common to hear 'risk' being talked about when imaginative and creative work is undertaken. There is some truth that we might be risking things. Although the danger is probably only moderate, the stakes are often presented as being high. If we replace risk with *trust*, then the emphasis is changed to a positive way forward. We'll see in the final section how this might work out.

Underneath these key themes, and in a sense underneath other layers dedicated to values and attitudes, is the subject of primary art and design. As we have discovered this is not always clearly defined or easily understood.

The primary art and design teacher

As we move towards an identity appropriate for *you* in your role as a primary art and design teacher, we will first consider two very influential visions.

Viktor Lowenfeld, in his publication *Creative and mental growth*, first published in 1947 (revised with contributions from with W. L. Brittain in 1964) and now reprinted in its eighth edition, influenced, and continues to influence, the ways in which we think about children and their art, and consequently how we approach teaching.

It is probable that child art, and adult conceptions of art, will meet in the classroom, and Lowenfeld identifies this as a possible site of tension:

> From the discrepancy between adult taste and the way in which a child expresses himself arise most of the difficulties that prevent children from using art as a true means of self expression. (Lowenfeld, 1982: 8)

To avoid the pitfalls of such discrepancy, and to allow opportunities for self-expression and in turn to develop rounded individuals, Lowenfeld presents a clear role for the teacher:

> If it were possible for children to develop without any interference from the outside world, no special stimulation for their creative work would be necessary. Every child would use his deeply rooted creative impulses without inhibition, confident in his own means of expression. Whenever we hear children say 'I can't draw' we can be sure that some kind of interference has occurred in their lives. (Lowenfeld, 1982: 8)

This famous quotation tells us a great deal about Lowenfeld's art education and his teacher. In Lowenfeld's view, we might have had our potential for creative expression taught out of us through teacher intervention (interference). This may sound very odd in an initial teacher education setting where interventions need to be clear, making appropriate use of modelling, demonstration, instruction, questioning or directing. Lowenfeld wants a different role for the teacher. His vision of the teacher is of one who allows creativity to *unfold*. There may be truth in this vision, but it remains one of the poorly conceptualised ideas of primary school art and design teaching. As a consequence, teachers assume that to help the *unfolding* they should adopt the non-interventionist approach with little or no consideration of alternative methods.

From Herbert Read's detailed exploration of art and education, *Education through Art*, first published in 1942, his ideas about the teacher still resonate today. He too is interpreted as identifying the teacher in a supportive role. At times this interpretation is accurate, but there are other moments where his vision for a teacher is more involved and more complex, but never dominating (Ross, 1993).

Three distinct activities are present in Read's conception of art education: self-expression, observation and appreciation. For these to make sense to the pupil he sees a role for the teacher, to bring together the possibility of *spontaneous activity* with the *social activity of appreciation*. 'Generally speaking … self-expression cannot be taught …the role of the teacher is that of the attendant, the guide, inspirer, psychic midwife' (Read, 1958: 209).

He continues with an acknowledgement that there is scope for training, to improve skills of observation. As for appreciation, he says:

> This can undoubtedly be developed by teaching (but only by the age of adolescence) … Until then the real problem is to preserve the original intensity of the child's reactions to the sensuous qualities of experience – to colours, surfaces, shapes and rhythms. These are apt to be so infallibly right that the teacher can only stand over them in a kind of protective awe. (Read, 1958: 209)

This may be very difficult to imagine. Citing your teaching strategies on a lesson plan as *psychic midwifery* could well attract some close attention. However, considering Read and Lowenfeld not only helps us to see their legacy but also to consider alternatives. We are seeking a model for a teacher that fits our principles, our rationale, our version of creativity and our aims of flexibility, ambition and trust. The *artist teacher* appears to be such a model.

Pause for thought

- *Have you experienced a teacher who may fit with the examples identified by Read or Lowenfeld?*
- *If you can draw, do you put it down to not being taught, as Lowenfeld implies?*
- *If you can't draw, do you put it down to being taught, as Lowenfeld implies?*
- *Can you see a place for a teacher who takes this distanced supporting role in schools today?*
- *Can you identify the challenges they would face to their explanations of practice?*

The artist teacher

A current argument for our teacher is that of the artist-teacher or, to rephrase this slightly, one who sees teaching as an art. The *artist teacher* model (see Figure 10.4) advocates an approach to teaching which echoes that of the artist.

Eisner (1985) suggests both teaching and art as:

A source of aesthetic experience
Being independent on the perception and control of qualities
Heuristic or adventitious activity
Seeking emergent ends.

Figure 10.4 The artist teacher (Eisner, 1985: 177)

This conception is very useful as we are identifying a teacher who recognises the limitations of Read and Lowenfeld, but also sees the restrictions of orthodoxies of teaching present in current primary practice. In many examples of current practice teachers present themselves as expert, where pupils are passive, where knowledge is defined in propositional terms and privileged through numbers and words.

The artist teacher would not only work in the ways described by Eisner but they would fit our model of flexibility, ambition and trust, and also in our principled rationale for art and design education.

What does the flexible teacher do?

Adapted from Dewey (1938) Eisner (2002) recognises the importance of *flexible purposing*, and sees it in the context of 'improvisational intelligence' (Eisner, 2002: 77). In these situations pupils and teachers are encouraged to shift direction, to change their aims during the course of work, where ends are not set, and means to achieve them are constantly revised. These changing and evolving ends are encouraged through 'conversations' with work. This requires a *conversational* approach involving both the teacher and pupils and their work.

Our flexible teacher enters a conversation with work, with ideas and with pupils: this should be at the heart of all good art teaching. The conversation requires our teacher to be involved in careful *listening*. This may seem odd in the context of visual art, but where the teacher *listens* to pupil ideas, to the way materials are being used and shaped, a conversational exchange begins to emerge. This conversation needs to be set in a relationship of reciprocity: between pupils, teachers, ideas and materials. Dewey (1933) can help us further as we think about ourselves as teachers entering a conversation, and with it a sense of reflection. As with other notions of reflective practice and certainly embedded in flexible purposing is the idea of 'suspending ideas' and being 'open-minded' (Dewey, 1933; Schon, 1987). Our willingness to put things on hold, to follow personal themes, to let work develop in unpredictable ways is dependent on our established principles (Figure 10.3).

What does the ambitious teacher do?

The ambitious teacher needs to be flexible and they need to be trusting. Ambition might be better thought of as curiosity. If we are curious and ask questions, then we can begin to open up ideas with children, we can be more ambitious:

- **What will happen if ...?**
- **What might happen when ...?**
- **I wonder what this might look like?**
- **How could these things be combined?**

Equally, the ambitious teacher can see things that are not restricted by the constraints of time or space. That is not to say these constraints don't exist but to realise that positive alternatives are possible. The National Curriculum 2000 Breadth of Study (DfEE/QCA, 1999e: 121) advocates work that is collaborative and on varying scales. Unfortunately the majority of work is limited in scope by the confines of a timetable, of space and perhaps more notably by curriculum planning.

What does the trusting teacher do?

The trusting teacher is flexible, ambitious and trusting. To encourage work that is purposeful and inventive, meaningful and original, pupils must have the freedom to work in flexible and curious ways. As we have noted this may well involve an element of risk, but the suggestion is that, in the calculation of risk, trust plays an important role.

We need to trust our instincts, trust our feelings, trust pupils and trust pupils' ideas. This means some sessions may be long, others short. Rather than an hour every Wednesday, ideas could be worked on continuously in sketchbooks for 15-minute spells each day over a week or fortnight. This could encourage more personal and meaningful responses.

Seeing yourself as an artist teacher

If you've never considered yourself as an artist (teacher) you may find this concept slightly unusual.

As our identities as teachers continue to evolve, we are shaped by a range of experiences or encounters. These might include encounters with other teachers, encounters with particular subjects, encounters with theory or encounters with other learners. We continue to emerge as teachers, through a combination of theory and practice. Atkinson (2002) suggests that 'each different pathway of teaching and learning is structured by its respective values' (2002: 151).

Although the constraints of external agencies and particular regimes of control (OFSTED, TTA) may not encourage a reflection on our pathways, or the values that structure them, this chapter is very much centred on the potential we have, first, in recognising ourselves, pupils, the curriculum and the classrooms we inhabit, and second, in bringing about change. That is to say, we can establish our evolving identities not only in line with the standards set by others but by what we believe to be right. If you believe in the idea of creativity and imagination as being liberating and worthwhile, you will need to be alert to your current values, and to those which are sympathetic to creative and imaginative activity, those of the artist teacher, and create space for them in your week.

In developing an identity as a teacher, there will be times when the *pathway* is less clear, contradictory or compromised. Being aware of ourselves on a *pathway* of possibilities ranging from the didactic to the heuristic (see Figure 10.5) is the first step to bringing about change.

Activity

Look at Figure 10.5, which shows Addison and Burgess's (2000) didactic/heuristic continuum. You will see a continuum or pathway of teaching and learning approaches and possibilities.

Where would you position yourself on this scale, and where would you like to position yourself?

Use the continuum as a way of considering the roles of teachers in any art and design lessons you are able to observe.

The primary art and design curriculum

Where the interpretation of the National Curriculum is positive, interesting work has been developed. However, there is a 'gulf between the most and least successful schools' (QCA, 2005c). Prentice (1999) offers useful suggestions to extend work beyond the visual elements, by including issue-based work, including 'enquiry into personal identities, family relationships, the immediate locality or distant places' (1999: 161). He suggests materials and processes can be extended through 'combining and recombining a range of materials' (1999: 161) and tackles the difficult area of extending the range and use of artists, craftspeople and designers to include more contemporary practice.

In your emerging role as a creative and inventive teacher of art and design it is hoped you will be able to approach the National Curriculum 2000 (DfEE/QCA, 1999e) in an *extended and positive* way, seeing potential where there may otherwise have been resistance.

The flexible curriculum

To match our principles (Figure 10.3) and the NACCCE model of creativity (Figure 10.1) we need to adopt appropriate planning strategies.

Unfortunately, we have been conditioned into curriculum planning utilising a particular type of learning outcome or objective. These are specific and unambiguous; they

Centred	Learning	Teaching	Characteristics	Pupil	Teacher	Justification	Drawbacks
Teacher	Passive	Didactic	Instruction Information Demonstration Closed procedures and structures	Dependent Memoriser Imitator	Expert Provider	Outcomes are certain Introduces techniques Conditions pupils to observe, listen and record Confirms the teacher as expert	Can be authoritarian Single perspective Can alienate Pupils may become dependent Results in conformity and normative outcomes Knowledge may be lost unless reinforced using other methods
	Responsive and activity based	Directed	Rehearsing and initiating activities Response to given stimuli Working to exemplars Conditioned/determined structures Probable findings already known by teacher	Responder	Trainer Director Resourcer	Provides common experience of NC art and design Enables: Continuity and progression Identification of pupils not on task Ease of assessment Efficient transfer of skills Activity: individual/pair/group	Knowledge is given/fixed Determined by teacher's experience: often privileging making Neglects: Prior knowledge Individual needs
	Active and experiential	Negotiated	Discussion/debate Collaborative work Purposeful investigation Critical evaluation Multifaceted and flexible structures Interaction Reflexivity	Contributor Interactor	Facilitator Motivator Guide Negotiator Supporter	Provides: Intelligent making Critical thinking Learning as social activity, art as social practice Mutual trust Learner as teacher/teacher as learner Enables pupils to: Communicate ideas Evaluate their own and others' work Negotiate their own learning Cross boundaries	Time consuming Difficult to co-ordinate and resource Difficult to monitor and assess Teacher requires breadth of knowledge Teacher needs to be ready to relinquish control
	Heuristic	Empowering and liberating	Meeting needs Answering hypotheses Experimentation Unknown findings Discovery Problem-solving Investigation	Researcher Self-motivator Inventor Discoverer	Co-ordinator Reciprocator	Encourages: The application of knowledge to practical contexts Pupils as planners Divergent thinking Risk-taking	Pupils need to be ready to take on initiatives Difficult to resource Only works with self-motivation Teacher may feel insecure Teacher needs to acknowledge self as learner
Pupil	Open	Dependent Redundant	Self-determined structures, motivated by pupil interest Exploration	Agent Director	Attendant Technician	Appropriate for highly motivated, highly resourceful learners	Can be chaotic, unfocused Lacks boundaries Can invite stereotypical responses, and/or a rejection of learning

Figure 10.5: Addison and Burgess's Didactic/Heuristic continuum (2000)

refer to skills, knowledge or understanding, and in many ways indicate what can be taught. Barrett (1979) describes these as 'behavioural objectives' – behavioural in that there is an identifiable change in 'behaviour' following an experience or teaching input: a child will be able to sort, will be able to identify, will know the name of, will be able to mix, will know how many. 'In art these objectives are relevant in the processes used to develop certain skills which help pupils to reach personal solutions' (Barrett, 1979: 36).

This appears very neat. But as we all know life isn't neat and 'students learn both more and less than they are taught' (Eisner, 2002: 70). In isolation, behavioural objectives are inappropriate for our flexible curriculum. However, Eisner (1985) is helpful, and details a type of objective which encourages enquiry: an 'expressive objective':

> *An expressive objective describes an educational encounter: it identifies a situation in which children are to work, a problem with which to cope, a task in which they are to engage … With an expressive objective what is required is not homogeneity of response among students but diversity. In the expressive context the teacher hopes to provide a situation in which meanings become personalised and in which children produce products, both theoretical and qualitative, which are as diverse as themselves.* (Eisner, in Barrett, 1979: 37)

The ambitious and trusting curriculum

To gain a sense of what the ambitious and trusting curriculum might look like, an example of practice to consider is given in Figure 10.6. This example is from a project called IntoPlay, a collaborative visual art project between Mason Moor Primary School, Southampton, Winchester School of Art and University College Winchester, and funded by the Paul Hamlyn Foundation.

The project was established following an OFSTED inspection, which identified a number of art-based targets, including for children to: *express themselves or be creative in active non-verbal ways through art, music, drama and physical education.*

It was an opportunity to teach art in a way that really encouraged a unique approach to materials and processes, meeting the demands of OFSTED within our vision of what art and design might be like in the primary school.

The work is a clear testament to the pupils' commitment to learning in and about art and design. It serves as a reminder of what primary art and design might look and feel like. Not only does the work have a sense of purpose and energy, it illustrates what pupils will engage with if entrusted with a sense of ownership.

Importantly, the project highlighted how easily strategies for teaching other curriculum areas can dominate thinking in terms of pedagogy. We were able to remember that alternative teaching methodologies do exist and do work and that a more heuristic pedagogy can foster conversation that is pupil- and work-centred, rather than teacher dominated, and an outcome for children that is meaningful and purposeful.

	Initially we worked on photocopies of toys and characters, printed to card. We asked pupils to invent and imagine by playing with existing characters, cutting, pasting and transforming them into new characters. We set some rules on the transformation: either through contradiction or through similarity.
	What emerged were some inventive and playful ideas. The children explored these with interest and motivation, and then grouped their characters creating unusual scenes. We had asked the class to bring in their own toys, ones which they were prepared to cut up and change.
	A sense of ownership emerged from the simple but powerful activity of cutting up existing toys and characters. This was particularly so during the activity where the pupils cut their own toys and joined them with others to make often surreal or comic characters.
	The pupils were fully engaged with this playful repositioning and showed a willingness to try out ideas and reappraise them during the making process. This encouraged an approach that was both playful and considered. This was encouraged and emphasised throughout.
	The new characters had names and took on particular roles. Although many of the toys were from television or film, the new characters were able to cast off their original personas, defined by their cultural referent. Instead, the children were able to invent and play as we had hoped, without the constraints of predetermined and marketed characteristics. There was a sense of the children gaining confidence in the evolving 'microworlds' (Marsh and Millard, 2000), where the limitations were free from adult sanctions.

Figure 10.6 An ambitious and trusting curriculum

Activity

Although the detail is limited look at the example in Figure 10.6 and where possible identify the following as indicators of an ambitious and trusting curriculum:

- *alternative ways of starting work;*
- *the use of challenge and support;*
- *the use of rules to generate unusual responses;*
- *time for frustration and breakthrough;*
- *pupil-initiated ideas to develop and extend work;*
- *trust in pupils, their ideas and their relationships with materials.*

Flexible, ambitious and trusting pupils

For pupils to be flexible and ambitious, for them to be curious, playful and inventive, we need to present ourselves and the curriculum in a particular way, so that pupils are trusting of others. From that position pupils will be able to trust their own diverse thoughts and playful experimentation.

However, this remains a real challenge. It is perhaps the biggest of all the challenges presented: to get pupils to believe you. This requires a teacher and a curriculum that marries intention with action.

Consider the case of Clare, a final-year student, who was given an opportunity to learn and teach in a very open way as part of a college project (HEARTS) where we endeavoured to match intention with action. There was one overall aim for the project: to teach the arts in interesting and inventive ways. Clare was not bound by the constraints of the National Curriculum or the normal assessment regimes for herself as an undergraduate teacher. Her commentary reveals the move from uncertainty and limited trust, a period of being 'tricked', to trust, confidence and curiosity. Clare describes her own background as 'non-arts'.

> *There have been various points during the project when I have been very sceptical and cautious, particularly at the start. I found it very difficult to understand how Paul and Jay [tutors] could expect us to know what was expected or what the module was about when they confessed or led us to believe that they didn't know themselves. In retrospect, although this was quite scary to start with, I would say it has proved quite effective and the 'not quite telling us everything' or 'trickery' aspect seems to have been a running theme of the project, with the people running the workshops also seducing us into doing things. I found this particularly interesting as I would honestly say that if they had told us what we would have achieved at the end of each session then I wouldn't have believed I could do it. The same would probably have happened if Paul and Jay had explained what they wanted too clearly.*

The most enjoyable part for me was the school-based sessions. I found it very bene-ficial to see what we had learnt in action and to see the response we received from the children. I was still finding it hard to come up with original ideas, and at several points wanted to retreat to the safety net of the National Curriculum and behavioural objectives. However, I was managing to be a little more creative though, and if a member of the group suggested something I was often able to run with the idea and spiral from their idea. It is only since spending time in school away from the project that I have noticed a change in my thinking which has surprised me. During the pre-liminary visits to my final school placement, I have been able to watch art lessons and I was extremely surprised at how frustrated I became at the lack of investigation, play, exploration and expression and how desperately I wanted to take over the lesson, to make it more fun and thought-provoking for the children and to give own-ership back to them. I found myself sitting with a group of children talking to them about what they were doing while experiencing this whirlwind of ideas running through my head of what could be altered or developed and all the exciting things that could come out of the quite boring, mundane task that they were doing. I sud-denly stopped myself and realised how weird that was and wondered where it had come from, especially as I wasn't consciously trying to think of ideas.

I think the most surprising thing about that was that I didn't realise quite how much I had taken away from the project.

Creative and imaginative primary art and design:
a summary of key points

— **Clare's account reveals not only an aware and reflective teacher, but a developing artist teacher. We can hear her identity evolve, and with it her sense of trust. She begins to trust her teachers, her pupils and importantly herself.**

— **This account is indicative of the trusting pupil we are interested in encouraging. In addition it reveals that the pathway towards trust echoes the creative process itself. That is, there is a period of focus, withdrawal and breakthrough.**

— **If Clare's account becomes your account, and an account of pupils you work with, then you will be taking positive steps for yourself, the curriculum, and pupils to be flexible, ambitious and trusting. And the work you have conversations with is likely to be meaningful and purposeful, inventive and imaginative. You will be some way towards developing a curious classroom.**

Further information

Artworks – can be accessed at: **www.art-works.org.uk**

START – the magazine for primary and pre-school teachers of art, craft and design. Information available at **www.nsead.org/publications**

HEARTS – Higher Education, the Arts and Schools can be accessed at **www. esmeefairbairn.org.uk/HEARTS**

11 CREATIVITY IN THE MUSIC CURRICULUM

SARAH HENNESSY

Introduction

In this chapter I hope to make you aware of the potential for creative activity in music learning. Teachers are often quite anxious about their abilities to teach music – especially when it seems to be so intensely concerned with performing skills and specialist knowledge. However, as I have written elsewhere (Hennessy, 1995), I do not believe that anyone can learn to teach music by reading about it – it has to be learned through practical musical engagement with friends, colleagues and children. This chapter I hope will offer a context and rationale for that practice.

Confident teachers are much more likely to use their imagination, take risks and be responsive to their pupils. Confidence develops through sustained engagement with both musical thinking and music activity. In this way we come to understand and appreciate the nature of music-making and learning in music. David Elliott (1995) refers to this view of learning as *praxial,* that is, not only learning through doing but also music-making which is located in a social and cultural context. Music is a human activity, something we do intentionally, thoughtfully and in response to how we live.

Creativity in music learning

Creativity in music learning is not an afterthought, something we think about if there's time or as an occasional break from 'work'. Creativity is an essential component of effective learning when the purpose of learning is to enable learners to act and think independently, to grow and change and ultimately to make valuable contributions to the field. Music in schools has not always reflected this view wholeheartedly for a number of reasons:

1. Until relatively recently, music in school was viewed as a subject in which the acquisition of knowledge 'about' music (technique, theory and notation, great composers' lives and works, etc.) dominated. Music making was limited to singing and perhaps playing percussion instruments. Singing traditions in school mirrored social singing in the community (church, communal choirs) and the repertoire was largely made up of traditional songs or hymns. Singing was viewed as a healthy, socially cohesive, and disciplined activity which nurtured good behaviour and presented a positive image of the school community. Choral activity also embodied a model of teaching centred on the teacher (conductor and trainer) and therefore reinforced the kinds of desirable habits of behaviour sought in schools.

2. The National Curriculum in England was conceived in such a way as to promote a compartmentalised view of the primary curriculum with a focus on individual subjects which appeared to discourage integration across subjects around themes or topics. This meant that timetables often became increasingly rigid, making it difficult to consider innovative or flexible approaches to learning.

3. An emphasis on Literacy and Numeracy (with their attendant Strategies) has reduced teachers' energies and motivation towards the rest of the curriculum.

4. There may be a tension in teachers' minds between the notion of work (individual, product oriented, knowledge acquisition, useful, systematic) and the pleasurable, 'non-academic' image of music (and the arts in general). Music may be seen as a luxury that, when the pressure is on, becomes expendable.

5. Creativity in music is inevitably noisy. Noisiness may be viewed as a negative condition in school: a quiet environment suggests studiousness, discipline, calmness, whereas noise means lack of control. Teachers may find it difficult to reconcile this in the context of music-making – and especially when encouraging exploration and experimentation with sound – a necessary element of creative music-making.

6. Musical creativity may be construed as being found only in adult musicians.

A recent reassertion of the importance of integrated and enjoyable approaches to teaching and learning brings hope that the worst effects of recent policies may be healed by a renewed acknowledgement of the central importance of creativity in education (DfES, 2004).

Some readers might be surprised at the idea that music learning is not necessarily concerned with creativity – surely the arts are synonymous with creativity? They certainly encompass creative thinking, inventiveness, innovation, novelty, risk-taking, problem-solving, speculation and meaning-making. But of course they also involve skill training, acquisition of knowledge about the art form, and analytical and critical thinking. Perhaps music in formal education, more than other art forms, has been rather imprisoned by these latter concerns to the neglect of the creative aspects. Composing is seen as the preserve of a chosen few with exceptional talent, and the opportunities for creative music-making, more broadly defined, often struggle to be acknowledged in the other musical activities of performing and listening.

Pause for thought

Consider your own experience, as a child, of learning music in and out of school. Are your memories positive or negative?

When I ask this of my students their memories are often coloured by a mixture of strong emotions:

- *the 'buzz' of being part of a performance event, of joining in and achieving something; or*
- *the fear of failure, the misery of rejection, or the drudgery and guilt surrounding practice.*

The 'buzz' is what we should all have the opportunity to experience; negative experiences are almost always the result of a teacher's judgement or teaching habits.

Do you recall making up your own music, or working creatively in a music class?

Among generalist student teachers positive responses to this last question are rare – there is sometimes the memory of playing instruments or adding sounds to a story or drama. The impression gained is of intermittent opportunities – if they existed at all.

What is creative music-making?

> **A note to the reader**
>
> When I refer to 'musicians' I mean anyone who makes music, however simple or tentative.
>
> When I refer to the music-making behaviours of young children these are often very close to the behaviours of novice musicians of any age. Experience through listening and making, practice (i.e. ongoing practical engagement) and interactions with others will all contribute to development – whether you are a five-year-old or a 25-year-old.

Musical creativity can be viewed as both a product and a process in which the musician/music-maker expresses and communicates their ideas and feelings through:

- **interpreting the music of others in a new way;**
- **joining in with a new part;**
- **improvising;**
- **composing;**
- **making imaginative/unexpected connections with other media such as language, movement or visual images.**

We need to consider the differences between child and adult musicians – if we carry in our heads a perception of the latter then children's achievements will often seem inadequate and insubstantial. We need to learn to listen to what children's music *is* (Glover, 2000), not what is missing (not quite in tune, not in time, lacking in structure). It is easy to be critical when musical ability is based on a strict and unforgiving mastery of technical skills: if you can't sing in tune – mime; if you can't keep time – stay quiet.

Frameworks for activities should allow children even at the very earliest stages of their development to use their musical imaginations and be creative. The originality, risk-taking and novelty will be relative to their experience and ability rather than relative to all possible music. As a teacher you may well hear these musical ideas many, many times in your classroom but what you are listening for is something that is new for that child or group at that moment (consider the idea of 'small c creativity' as discussed by Craft (1999)).

All music-making has the potential to be creative. Creative activities, in which children make their own choices or decisions, add something to or adapt a given idea, all involve creative musical thinking:

- **contributing to or giving their own interpretation of a song;**
- **making an arrangement of a given piece of music (adding accompaniment and deciding how the piece is to be performed);**
- **inventing a short melodic pattern and developing it into a sequence or a complete piece;**
- **composing a backing track for a rap;**
- **improvising a rhythm in the gaps between another given rhythm;**
- **choosing sounds to represent the sound of waves on a beach, and deciding how to begin and end the 'sound picture'.**

Teaching for creativity

There needs to be a distinction between creative teaching in music and teaching for creative music-making. The former can exist without the latter but the latter is unlikely to result without the former

Creative teaching involves finding imaginative, unusual, surprising, adventurous approaches to putting across concepts and knowledge, or to making skill building enjoyable and motivating. Children may learn more effectively and engage more fully with the lesson as a result, but there may be no creative opportunities for them in the experience. Learning to read notation using colours, puppets or funny faces is still about learning to read notation. Teaching for creativity requires a kind of 'letting go' on the part of the teacher, and providing a safe space in which the children can find challenge and new insights about music and about themselves.

There is not the space here to discuss in detail the role of music in supporting and enriching creative activities in the rest of the curriculum. Suffice it to say that bringing music and music-making into humanities, other arts, core subjects and physical education not only feeds the imagination and understanding, but also puts music in its proper context of being an integral part of the cultural and social world in which children learn. This is not to suggest that music should be artificially inserted into non-music topics. But where there are obvious links the opportunities should be exploited, not least to increase children's involvement with music!

The focus of the rest of this chapter will be on creative processes and activities within music learning.

Teaching songs

The song repertoire used in primary schools should encompass a wide range of styles and traditions. Popular music (as opposed to classical/high art music) in all traditions is created to be infinitely flexible and adaptable, learned aurally through joining in and in a social setting. Each time a song is sung it will change according to the abilities and feelings of the singers and the context in which it is sung.

When teaching a song, consider the opportunities for children to create their own interpretation. The material that exists (the words, the melody and the accompaniment when there is one) is only part of the music. Making decisions about how to sing the song (expressive elements: speed, dynamics, liveliness, calmness, etc.), how to arrange the song (solos, everyone together, how to begin, how many repeats and how to vary each repeat, etc.) and what to add in the way of accompaniment are all musical choices to be made and experimented with. In this way children learn about the many ways musical material can be changed to give different meaning. Of course instrumental music can also be explored in these ways.

Activity

Suggested sequence of activities for teaching a song

- *Sing it through to give a sense of the whole. Ask children to listen out for anything they notice: repetitions, interesting words, surprises.*
- *Is the song a gentle, calming song or does it make you want to move (is it a work song or a going to sleep song, a story song or a love song, a funny/comic song or a protest song, a song for a single singer or a group)? Thinking about the meaning and context for the song will help in deciding how to sing it (i.e. how to interpret it in performance).*
- *Learn the chorus first. Children can invent their own pattern of movement (dance sequence, makaton, or just expressive gestures) to accompany it. From these the class choose movement patterns that they like (appropriate and manageable) and everyone practises – what happens if not everyone can manage it? Can the children solve the problem? Possible solutions include:*
  - *– simplify;*
  - *– break into sections for different groups to perform in sequence;*
  - *– practise;*
  - *– differentiate so that some perform a more complex version of the pattern.*
- *The possibilities for different ways of singing encourage 'possibility thinking' (what if we sing it faster, change the dynamics, vary the numbers singing together?).*
- *There are choices to be made to achieve a satisfying 'fit' of form and content. Some ideas may feel quite awkward and uncomfortable.*
- *Older children might divide into groups to perform their own version of the same song to each other.*
- *There may be a performance recorded on CD (song books often include this) – how does that performance compare?*

Skill building

Introductory skill-based activities are now a very familiar part of the music lesson. They give group focus, and introduce and establish the skills needed for listening and music-making. They are often devised as circle games: inventing and passing sounds; following the leader in making body sounds; echoing and sequencing clapped or sung patterns; keeping the pulse collectively and feeling silent beats; accompanying simple songs with actions and so on. In some ways these 'games' are disguised 'drills' – for children to practise in an enjoyable way. What will enable such games to become creative activities for the children is to invite them to make the 'game' their own – to invent variations, add new elements, play independently of the teacher as leader. Such activities should have a strong connection to the main activity of the lesson.

Improvising

Improvising and composing are considered distinct activities but in the musical behaviours of young children and the inexperienced they overlap and merge. Improvising can be seen as a form of musical play (Hennessy, 1998): spontaneous, of the moment, not fully worked out before it is sounded, a kind of musical doodling. It may not be intended to be communicated to anyone else: 'the musical stream that results may be highly structured or more exploratory' (Glover, 2000). It is, however, inevitably based on what the performer can do at that moment – and so arises out of prior learning or experience. Often the design and layout of an instrument will dictate the gestures or patterns which result. It is not something that appears out of thin air even though it may appear to do so. Improvising at a more developed stage involves knowledge, skills and practice in order to create within a given musical frame or style – this is what jazz musicians do, for example. If musicians are encouraged to play with ideas, and play by ear (without notation), to not worry about every note sounding perfect and to play and sing along with others, they are more likely to develop the confidence to improvise. Songs and musical frameworks for instrumental work which include little gaps or sections within them for improvising are a 'safe' place for children to develop their improvising abilities in this direction. The Orff approach (see Buchanan et al., 1996; Goodkin, 1997) promotes this way of working – starting from simple accessible ideas and providing supportive musical frameworks within which everyone can participate at their own level.

Composing

Composing involves a putting together of ideas – something planned and worked out. A composition is developed in stages with alterations, edits and revisions. In the hands of younger children the revision process may be barely touched upon – the inexperienced are more likely to accept the first idea which appears and stick to it. This will be compounded by lack of time in lessons and the teacher's degree of understanding of how to mediate the process of revision. Encouraging development and revisions requires careful handling – to gauge when enough is enough or when the musicians are keen (or willing) to stay with it. Knowledge of individual children, and their capacity for focus and critical thinking will inform the teacher's decision to encourage a group to work further with a piece or agree that, for now, it is ready to be performed, recorded and more or less 'fixed'.

Group compositions are more likely to have a discernible shape and structure where you can hear (and see) how the piece has been put together. You may have asked for a particular structural feature to be used (repetitions, ostinato, ABA, canon, verse/chorus) but even when you don't, children, especially when working with others, will come up with a structure which organises who plays what when. Also children, especially when working in groups, may often impose a linear 'narrative' form on their work in the absence of a given structure. Musical structures involve repetition (exact or with variations), question and answer, contrast and silence. Finding ways of encouraging children to work with these elements will lead to more developed and musical outcomes and greater musical understanding. Jo Glover provides an in depth explanation and discussion of the different ways in which children compose. She encourages us to understand children's music as a musical world quite distinct from adult music, and also argues for self-initiated composing (2000).

A note on notations

Many view musicianship as synonymous with being able to read and write conventional notation (i.e. dots on the stave), despite the fact that the vast majority of music-makers in the world do not use notations of any kind. Especially for young children in primary school, notation should always follow practical and aural engagement, not precede it. Notations of all kinds can and should, on occasion, be used to support and illuminate aspects of music learning. Paintings, sculptures and graphic art can all combine with music to offer starting points or structures for composing, responses to music or ways of analysing music. Inviting children to create their own notations will develop their understanding of the possibilities and limitations inherent in representing music in this way.

The creative process

As you can see there are different ways in which we can work creatively in music and which do not necessarily result in a completely new 'composition'. It is helpful to think of creativity in music as a process through which many different outcomes may emerge. In this process we can identify a number of phases or stages which are sequential and cumulative, but also cyclical, that is earlier stages may be revisited through the process. These stages are in many ways common to all creative processes whether in music or other disciplines. The particular aspect of the process in music which we need to acknowledge is *time*. As with dance and drama, experiencing music takes place in and through time. This temporal quality dictates much of the way we engage with music both in teaching and learning, and the process of creating in music should be framed by this understanding.

I have borrowed a model developed by Wallas (1926) and adapted it to provide a frame for how to recognise and plan for children's engagement with the creative process. Wallas identifies four phases which he names:

- preparation;
- incubation;
- illumination;
- verification.

Preparation

In the classroom this initial stage almost always commences with a 'commission' – a task instigated by the teacher as part of a unit of work. However, it could also arise from children's ideas and motives.

The preparation stage will encompass:

- **the stimulus (e.g. pattern of movement, poem, a visit to a wood, a visual image, an instrument or an existing piece of music) through which the structural or expressive framework is agreed – or given;**
- **the assembling of resources;**
- **initial focusing activity (listening game, exercise, song, conversation) exploring the elements which link the stimulus to musical ideas;**
- **establishing the mode of working (whole-class, groups, pairs) and providing some ground rules (scope of the piece and time available for working on it).**

If the composition is to be based on small-group work, the teacher may also use this phase in a quite directed way in order to take the class through a model of the suggested way of working – the kinds of decisions they will need to make, and a chance to try out and listen to how the basic ideas can be worked on.

In the teacher's planning there needs to be careful thought given to how much freedom or constraint is permitted (Burnard and Younker, 2002). Too much freedom can be as difficult as too little and the balance between them varies according to the experience and dispositions of the children.

There is a tendency to believe that creativity must be entirely free, open and unfettered – the teacher's role is to 'light the blue touch paper' and stand back. The teacher, in this view, just provides the initial stimulus, the resources, the space and the time – she has no function once the children are working other than to ensure that they stay on task and arrive at a product in the time available.

Fortunately this idea has been largely discredited and it is recognised that children learn more effectively when their experience is mediated by 'knowledgeable others' (Hennessy, 1998). This clearly supports the notion of creativity as a social phenomenon.

Pause for thought

If you were asked to compose a piece of music – anything you liked and for any purpose you chose – how would you feel? How would you approach the task?

You would have to make every decision from scratch and in effect decide on your own constraints (rules): how long, what structure, mood, melodic content, etc. If you have composed before you may feel undaunted by this and enjoy the freedom. If you have never composed or done very little, you might find this quite paralysing – even if you play an instrument or sing quite confidently.

Would this be easier alone or with others?

On the other hand composing a piece in which you can only use three notes on a recorder might feel much less threatening and more achievable. At the same time, for an experienced composer, limitations can be challenging and exciting.

It is evident that in creative activity we need both freedom and constraints – freedom to experiment, invent, find our own ideas; and constraints to support, challenge and give focus.

Incubation – exploring and experimenting

This is the phase which creates the most difficulties in the classroom context. It is likely to be noisy and therefore difficult to provide good conditions and difficult to gauge how long different groups or individuals need. Incubation might mean quite solitary thinking or a period of exploring, experimenting and the musical equivalent of doodling (noodling) with others. The teacher's role in this phase requires skills of facilitation and guidance rather than direct instruction. Children need to explore, experiment and improvise with the materials and ideas provided. Because of noise there has to be more management than perhaps seems appropriate – and more than one might need for other creative activities such as poetry, drama, or visual art, for instance. Turn-taking, listening to each other, short periods of free play, whole-class involvement with opportunities for individual suggestions to be tried and tested, all need planning (many publications offer ideas on how to achieve this).

If you are able to use time flexibly you might consider planning for small groups to explore and experiment at different times through the week – if there is an adjacent space available. If this phase is stretched over several days in this way children may want to record their ideas for recall (i.e. audio recording or finding a way to notate).

If using electronic keyboards or computer software children can use headphones – and save or record their ideas.

Illumination – choosing and organising

This is the phase in which decisions are made about what to work with and what to discard. Once choices are made the process of organising and refining takes place. As mentioned earlier young children may arrive at this stage very quickly – choosing the first idea they come up with. As they develop their understanding and skills they will become more discerning and more confident to discard or revise ideas. The teacher's role is to encourage and nurture this awareness through listening, sensitive questioning, suggestions for development, even challenging their decisions – in fact, scaffolding their learning (Hennessy, 1998).

Verification – rehearsing, performing and evaluating

Once the piece is composed (organised, assembled, fully fashioned) there comes the phase of 'fixing'. Rehearsal may still involve changes but essentially this is the stage prior to performing. In the classroom this is likely to be an event in which the composition is performed 'live' to others (the rest of the class, another class, at an assembly) or recorded and played back.

Traditionally the final product is viewed as the end of the process and the achievement should be celebrated. The accumulated experience will resonate in various ways and there should be time, after the event, for the children to evaluate their work and what they feel they learned. Articulating their reflections through writing, drawing or talking should help in developing a sense of ownership and independence.

We can see and hear what children can do in their acoustic compositions – no one is likely to compose something they cannot play themselves as most composing arises out of personal trial and error, so there is likely to be a close link between performing ability, musical understanding and the kinds of compositions children produce.

It is often suggested that there is no 'right' and 'wrong' in creative music-making – however, there is fitness and unfitness, appropriateness and inappropriateness. These are in many ways subjective terms but they are inevitably informed by common cultural experiences and ideas about balance, the relationships between certain patterns and gestures in sound and what they signify in terms of feelings, movements, natural phenomena, etc. For instance, there are very recognisable and common musical representations of different intensities of rain. Young children will tend to find simple and literal responses to events or moods in a story – often fairly predictable. As they become more experienced and exposed to more and more possibilities they will challenge themselves and be challenged to move away from clichés and experiment with more novel ideas. They develop their musical imagination and the knowledge and skills to realise it.

The contexts for musical creativity

Children are steeped in music from the moment they are born (and before) (Young, 2003) – in contemporary Britain it is impossible to avoid regular, daily contact and immersion in music. By the time children enter school they are likely to have acquired a well developed repertoire of music through TV, radio, background music in shops and, hopefully, songs and bits of music encountered in play and social settings. In this way children learn to recognise how music is structured, to respond to rhythms, to predict the shape of a tune, to separate the familiar from the unfamiliar. They learn to move and dance to music and to recognise its mood. They adopt and adapt music within their play activity: babbling, cooing, chanting, singing, using objects as instruments and dancing. They are already musically experienced. This is part of enculturation – as we learn language, ways of behaving and ways of interacting in the family and social groups, we also absorb musical behaviours.

When children enter school we need to recognise and build on this knowledge and experience. Children will already be immersed in the music of their home culture and its relationship to what is offered in school can affirm or deny their own emerging musical self. A valuable and authentic way for teachers to learn about their children's musical lives is not only to invite them to create and share their own music in the classroom, but also to listen in on how children use music in their play.

Creative music-making will:

- **reinforce and help to develop their musical ideas;**
- **increase and strengthen their abilities in controlling sound (technique);**
- **encourage social interactions through and around music;**
- **give meaning to their music learning.**

School is only one of many places where music learning for children happens and one might argue that 'school' music is a genre all of its own – made up of an exclusive repertoire never heard outside of school (unless to invoke 'school'). What primary schools can provide is a structured, safe and sociable setting for music-making. They can foster musical interactions so that children can then take their music-making into other settings: at home, with friends, at after-school clubs and community-based activities.

Creative activity carries a certain momentum which can depend on many factors:

- **the relevance and imaginative potential of the initial stimulus and purpose of the task;**
- **an appropriate balance between constraint and freedom within the task;**
- **children having some real control over musical decisions – feeling that the music is theirs;**
- **the quality of the resources and environment in which the children are working;**
- **the successful match between the demand of the task and the abilities of the children; and**
- **responsive and encouraging teachers.**

Activity

Atmospheric winds
The purpose of the lesson is to explore the contrast between long and short sounds; to develop skills in controlling long and short sounds; vocally and on wind instruments, and to create a composition which exploits the sound qualities they have explored.

Preparation
- *Play an introductory 'game' to establish group focus for listening and vocal control, and to think about and invent long sounds and short sounds*

- *Pass a vocal sound round the circle on the end of your finger – a steady horizontal movement, but wiggly or stabbing action will change the sound. First everyone reproduces the same then each invents their own. Different physical movement triggers a 'matching' vocal response and vice versa.*

- *Listen to a piece of music made up entirely of sustained sound and move to it (e.g. an excerpt from Atmosphere by Ligeti).*

- *In the circle listen to the music again and ask the group what they hear, how it makes them feel or what they imagine.*

- *Ask them to make long continuous sounds with their mouths or voices (humming, blowing, quiet singing on a single note, whistling) – contrast with very short sounds. Ask individual children to find gestures for conducting the class performing these two contrasting sounds.*

Incubation
- *Introduce lots of cardboard and plastic tubes of different lengths and diameters and ask children to find different ways of sounding them (blowing across the opening, blowing into the tube, tapping it on the ground). If there are children who play blown instruments (recorder, penny whistle, flute, trumpet, etc.) they can include these (as part of the overall texture or perhaps a specific contrasting section). This could lead to an exploration of pitched notes and how they sound in different combinations (do some tubes produce the same note? Do some notes sound comfortable together? why? can you alter the sound of your tube and control the way you play it – quietly, gradually getting louder? ... and so on).*

- *Conduct (and let the children conduct) everyone playing short sounds and long sounds – altogether, in small groups, solos, combinations of short and long, only long high sounds, only short low sounds and so on.*

Illumination
- *Create a whole-class piece based on these sounds and patterns – considering repetitions and contrast. Don't forget silence! (Children decide on the content and structure, and fix this by showing the sequence visually – how?: graphics, streamers/ribbons and unifix blocks, ... do different colours show different 'colours' of sound?)*

NB Blowing is quite tiring and might make children dizzy so you could add a contrasting section based on percussive sounds made with their soundmakers – maybe free improvisation (represented in the score by a scribble!).

Verification
- *Once the piece is constructed and the score is fixed, the piece should be rehearsed to ensure everyone knows what they are doing and get a feel for the overall sound and structure. Invite individual children to sit out and listen – to give feedback on balance, quality, etc. Record or perform to others. It could be combined with dance or become the atmospheric music for a drama.*

Creating a musical environment

- For individual explorations and musical play for young children, a sound corner works well: devise an area of the classroom where instruments are available, perhaps at certain times of the day or week, e.g. a few chime bars, a xylophone with a variety of beaters, two or three different sized drums (see Hennessy, 1998, for detailed guidelines), or headphones plugged into a keyboard and an audio recorder for children to record their stories and songs.

- Build up the best possible range and quality of instruments for the classroom. This will take time, but resist buying cheap as the sound will be disappointing.

- Use poems and stories which have sound content or which evoke movement or atmospheres which can stimulate music-making.

- Exploit the musicality of speech and enjoy the sounds and rhythms of words.

- Look for opportunities to include music in other areas of the curriculum – not only as support for learning in that area but also to further musical aims.

- Include music for listening wherever possible – to feed the imagination, and enrich sensory experience.

- Invite parents or colleagues who play instruments to play to the children.

- Involve secondary school pupils in performing and helping with music-making.

- Exploit opportunities for involving community and professional musicians in special projects or ongoing support.

Creativity in the music curriculum:
a summary of key points

- *Teaching for creativity involves taking risks and being confident in your ability to use the imagination of your pupils, allowing the power and responsibility to shift between you and the children. It requires everyone to engage in the process, however limited their contribution might be: this includes the teacher.*

- *The music teacher's role is often one of managing the activity, asking questions, capturing interesting ideas and ensuring that all the children are able to participate at an appropriate level. It may also be necessary to arbitrate among different ideas (or where little is forthcoming, offer some) and suggest some structure.*

——— *It is impossible to produce simple formulae for success as so much depends on the particular children you are working with, your knowledge of them and your own musical interests and enthusiasms. Creative activities you plan may not work, or work beautifully sometimes and not at other times.*

——— *Teachers need to see themselves as artists alongside their pupils so that they can enter the musical world of children and thus come to understand how to nurture and support their explorations and discoveries.*

Teaching materials (a selection)

Buchanan, K. and Chadwick, S. (1996) *Music Connections*. Cramer Music.
MacGregor, H. (1995/6) *Listening to Music, Elements 5+*. A & C Black.
MacGregor, H. (1995/6) *Listening to Music, Elements 7+*. A & C Black.
MacGregor, H. (1995/6) *Listening to Music, History*. A & C Black.
MacGregor, H. and Gargrave, B. (2004) *Let's Go Shoolie-shoo*. A & C Black.
MacGregor, H. and Gargrave, B. (2002) *Let's Go Zudie-o*. A & C Black.
Music Express (2003) A & C Black.
Orff-Schulwerk American Edition (1977–82) *Music for Children*, vols I and 2. Schott.
Richards, C. (1995) *Listen to This (KSI)*. Saydisc.
Richards, C. (1995) *Listen to This (KS2)*. Saydisc.

Song books

Birkenshaw-Fleming L. (1990) *Come on Everybody Let's Sing*. Holt, Rinehart & Winston.
Clark, V. (2002) *High Low Dolly Pepper*. A & C Black.
East, H. (1989) *Singing Sack*. A & C Black.
Gadsby, D. and Harrop, B. (1982) *Flying A Round*. A & C Black.
Sanderson, A. (1995) *Banana Splits*. A & C Black.
Stannard, K. (2004) *Junior Voiceworks* series. OUP.
Thompson, D. and Winfield, S. (1991) *Junkanoo*. Longman.
Thompson, D. and Winfield, S. (1991) *Whoopsy Diddledy Dandy Dee*. Longman.

Websites

www.bbc.co.uk – ideas for teachers, information and links to other sites.
www.creativepartnerships.org.uk – Arts Council initiative creating arts projects between schools and artists.
www.gridclub.com – teaching materials.
ictadvice.org.uk – BECTA site.
www.mtrs.co.uk – ideas.
www.ncaction.org.uk – advice on assessment and case studies.
www.o-music.tv

www.orff.org.uk – Orff Society holds courses for teachers in creative approaches to music teaching and learning.

www.standards.dfee.gov.uk/schemes/music – schemes of work for music devised by QCA.

www. youthmusic.org.uk – major source of funding for out-of-school music making.

12 WHAT HAS CREATIVITY GOT TO DO WITH CITIZENSHIP EDUCATION?

HILARY CLAIRE

Introduction

This chapter will raise some questions about citizenship education to help you think about:

- **the importance, for the future of our society, of creative people with vision;**
- **values in citizenship education;**
- **qualities and characteristics of people who can think creatively about citizenship issues;**
- **the creative teacher of citizenship;**
- **the creative curriculum in citizenship.**

This chapter will not concentrate on explaining citizenship education, but on exploring the conditions and possibilities in the curriculum for creative responses to citizenship education. If you are unsure about its concepts and remit, look at Part 1 of *Teaching Citizenship in Primary Schools* (Claire, 2004).

The global context of citizenship education

In the last 15 years there have been arresting examples of citizens confronting their history and creatively developing new systems of governance to promote social justice – Northern Ireland, nations which were part of the former USSR, South Africa. Historically, there are many examples of people dissatisfied with existing systems who determined to develop democracy and citizenship in new ways – Ancient Athens, England at the time of the Civil War, the Glorious Revolution and throughout the nineteenth century, America and France at the end of the eighteenth century, the Russian Revolution. Now, international conflict, global warming and other environmental hazards challenge the future of our children. Recently, Nelson Mandela appealed to the rich world to take on its responsibility to the poor in Africa and elsewhere.

In all these circumstances – historical and contemporary – people have to think with vision – not just pragmatically – about the nature of society and people's relationship to government and each other, locally and globally. The Robinson Report (NACCCE, 1999) was unequivocal, claiming that Britain's economic prosperity and social cohesion depended on unlocking the potential of every young person and enabling them to face an uncertain and demanding future (pp. 6 and 7). We have every reason to believe that as the twenty-first century rolls on, creative as well as pragmatic and principled thinking about social, economic and political problems and solutions will be essential. When children are asked about their future, they tell us clearly that they fear war, racism, crime, and environmental meltdown (Hicks and Holden, 1995; Holden, 2005).

Creativity, citizenship and children's education

The Aims, Visions and Purposes statement at the beginning of the National Curriculum document acknowledges that children's education should encourage wider visions of a future society, not just fit them for the status quo. Sometimes encapsulated in the terms 'minimalist' and 'maximalist', there is a continuum in citizenship education: at one pole, a conservative desire to maintain the status quo, at the other, a conviction that citizenship education (CE) is about moving us along the road towards social justice; (see Claire, 2001: 1 – 2). The former concentrates on knowing about public systems and obedience to the law; the latter envisions and is prepared to work for wider ideals.

But even the conservatives, who would like to keep things as they are, are forced to deal with changing, often unexpected, circumstances. The old ideas don't always work; old dogs must learn new tricks; creative solutions become essential.

So, creativity becomes fundamental to citizenship, whether at the radical or the conservative end of the continuum, or at points in between. Participative, active citizens of all political persuasions will need the ability to construe problems and consider creative solutions. Conformist/conventional thinking and attitudes will not lead to solutions in a changing world.

Creativity, democracy and values

CE is imbued with values – as has been recognised from its inception in the curriculum. Government bodies have tried with little success to establish a set of common values that everyone should live by and ended up with lists that offend nobody and still leave us with controversies. Because CE is about the ways we organise society and live alongside one another, it is imperative that principles of human rights and social justice are the yardstick for systems and proposed changes. Still, the detail will always be contentious. When we ask children to consider creative solutions to social issues we must make sure that they constantly measure them against values which we debate in terms of principles and consequences. When we ask them to judge other people's creative proposals they must also refer to values.

This is because creativity can be the handmaid of evil as well as benign change. People are capable of creative problem-setting and creative solutions, but creativity does not automatically ensure justice. No doubt, gas chambers were perceived by Nazis as 'creative'. In South Africa in the early 1950s, the Nationalist Government came up with the 'creative' solution of apartheid, to solve what they had defined as the 'problem' of diverse groups living alongside one another. For the next forty years appalling injustice was perpetrated to carry out the so-called creative solution. Contrast a very different creative solution to economic and political problems: the New Deal in 1930s America. Following Keynesian economic theory which turned classical economics on its head, Roosevelt tackled poverty by providing work through government programmes.

Democracy requires citizens who can:

- **analyse and synthesise ideas and information from a variety of sources;**
- **evaluate the ways problems are defined and the possible consequences of proposed solutions;**
- **resist brainwashing by powerful – even hegemonic – arguments.**

They will need to be independent and capable of principled, creative lateral thought and imagination. They need the education and value systems to reject arguments such as perpetrated by Nazis, white supremacists or fundamentalists, and realise that the problem itself has been wrongly defined. There are arguments that people who allow themselves to be led by the nose by their leaders have experienced an education which encouraged conformity and obedience, and punished any questioning of authority figures (Adorno, 1950). I am not advocating anarchy in the classroom: order is fundamental to successful teaching. However, I believe that being open-minded to alternative perspectives grows with the experience of creative debate and opportunities to come up with your own creative solutions to issues.

Pause for thought

I am suggesting that citizenship is linked to creativity through the following requirements for a free democratic society:

- *creative thinking about problems and solutions in society*
- *independent minds governed by principled moral thinking and capable of resisting pressure to conform*
- *the presence of an opposition which critiques the status quo and offers alternative programmes and goals.*

Any critique which can't offer alternatives will be negative, limited and backwards looking:

- *envisioning alternatives – whether radical or conservative – requires thinking outside the box, perceiving possibilities and being psychologically prepared to take risks and face challenges.*

What is citizenship education about anyway?

The brainstorm shown in Figure 12.1 and developed by a group of practising teachers and teacher educators may help you with an overview of its concepts.

Figure 12.1: A brainstorm of what CE should be about

The diagram shows that citizenship education comprises a number of concepts, skills and personal characteristics.

Activity

In Table 12.1 I have started to develop the concepts in Figure 12.1 under headings with examples. Try to complete this table, adding any other examples that you think should have been included.

Table 12.1 Development of CE concepts

Knowledge and understanding	Skills	Attitudes/personal characteristics
Human rights and children's rights	Investigation – research, critical thinking	Commitment to human rights and social justice Concern for people beyond own circle
Ideas about possible futures	Creative thought	?
Knowing about political systems/democracy	Knowing how to participate effectively; make your voice heard	?
Knowing about community organisations and issues	?	Values and concern about society
Knowing about different roles and responsibilities	Knowing how to approach people in different roles and how to exercise responsibility oneself	Willingness to take responsibility and take on different roles
Identity/multiple identities, of self and others	?	?

In what respects can citizenship education be creative?

In Figure 12.1 and your completed version of Table 12.1 there are two possible ways to consider creativity. One relates to the approaches (pedagogy) you adopt to help children understand concepts or acquire particular gobbets of knowledge. The other relates to the possibilities you provide for children to think creatively themselves about issues and possible solutions. Both require *creative teaching* but the intentions will be different. Curriculum and pedagogy which encourage children's creativity are empowering and liberatory for children; it will be part of your professional intention to develop *their* vision, hopes and dreams. It will be your investment in the future of the planet.

What sort of person is capable of thinking creatively about issues in society and their own role?

SELF-ESTEEM AND IDENTITY DEVELOPMENT – LINKS WITH CREATIVITY AND CITIZENSHIP

In the National Curriculum guidelines for primary, Personal, Social and Health Education (PSHE) and Citizenship Education are yoked together. Though PSHE may appear to be about personal qualities, they are essential to CE because pupils will grow into and hopefully influence the *social world*. High self-esteem and identity development are central to citizenship: to respect others' identity, understand their situation and grant them 'worth', even if they are very different from you, you must first respect yourself and your own worth, and feel confident about your own identity. George Mead (1934) explained how judgements and responses from 'significant others' contribute to identity development and self-esteem. Peers and teachers in school as well as parents/carers and community members are critically significant for young children.

More recently, Jeffrey (2004) explained, using his own research, that we develop our identity and our capabilities in a social world: the very experience of creative learning in a creative context, contributes to positive self-esteem and social identity – all the more when a young learners' group experience is enjoyable, active, social and emotionally engaging! Indeed, the NACCCE Report (1999) emphasised two justifications for creative approaches in education: to address the kind of future we want for the human race, but also because creative teaching and learning can promote children's self-esteem. It follows that we need to consider the environment and ethos that children will experience and how these can help them develop a strong sense of their own worth and identity, alongside an appreciation of others.

Citizenship, creativity and taking risks

Much theoretical writing about creativity emphasises the centrality of taking risks in one's thinking and planning. If your 'big new idea' goes against conventional thinking, you may not dare voice it for fear of an incredulous reception or jeering. Risk-taking is not just a physical thing like bungee jumping, though you may get an adrenalin rush as you prepare to argue a minority position! It's psychologically and emotionally charged: you are exposed and on your own. Even if you have a metaphorical map, it will be incomplete, warn of precipices or have blank bits. Think about the women who campaigned to be allowed to enter higher education – or any other campaign which went against the status quo. They had to be courageous, not just have persuasive arguments. We need to remember of course that something well tried and familiar for adults may not be so, for our young pupils. This applies to the risk-taking they may feel if we ask them to work in unfamiliar ways, or to think for themselves – without the water wings of the worksheets, the familiar textbooks. For some children, something as ordinary as working in a group where you have to take a role or expose your views to others will be highly risky. So along with high self-esteem, children who are asked to think creatively and unconventionally about the social world need courage – and they need the conditions which nurture their courage and do not undermine it.

Given how important their social world is to children, preparing the ground for taking risks in the ways they think about problems and solutions is essential. Do remember that taking risks with thinking is a greater challenge for some children than for others; this applies to pupils in Year 6 as well as four-year-olds. So you will want to consider a psychologically supportive environment which encourages children to think outside the box without fear of ridicule. Perhaps it means working with trusted friends and having the solidarity of a group to back your ideas. Perhaps it means working through role play or games, or with puppets, or some other distancing technique, which allows them to play safely with new ideas.

Rules, playing and creativity

Margaret Boden (2001) emphasises that the psychological ability to work without clear rules or to change the rules is an oft-ignored aspect of creativity. It follows that the classroom ethos we establish must encourage and not punish children for critiquing the rules and, where appropriate, changing them. Beyond that, the capacity to play with ideas – even play with rules – encourages creative thinking. So you might encourage your pupils to envisage a 'what if' world – where animals are in charge; where children are really adults' equals, where there are no adults, where the cars all vanish overnight. Some 'playing with ideas' will be seriously related to real events – suppose you were part of the unpredicted devastation wreaked by the tsunami in SE Asia, or a drought which turned you from a wealthy farmer to a refugee. The 'imaginings' that such work invites are part of encouraging the kind of empathy as well as creativity children will need later, as concerned and proactive global citizens.

Pause for thought

- *Children who have a strong sense of identity, self-worth and self-confidence can make choices for themselves, discuss and advocate what they would like to see happen – and why; listen carefully to alternative points of view, and be prepared to change their minds.*

- *We lay the foundations for concepts, skills and knowledge which will develop as the child matures towards adulthood. This means in practice that from the nursery and throughout primary school we consider confidence and identity building as children learn both to listen to and 'hear' others' positions and express their own ideas with confidence and without undue criticism.*

- *Thinking unconventionally and creatively can mean playing with ideas, imagining, letting go of rules and taking risks. Reducing the social and psychological risks will facilitate creative thinking.*

The school curriculum, creativity and citizenship

Creative CE is about looking at our social world with critical eyes, identifying what we would like to improve, and then developing realistic, appropriate ideas and plans.

'Mirrors and windows ... roots and wings'

Someone has said that we need mirrors to reflect our world, and windows opening out to wider horizons and possibilities; roots so that we know who we are and feel strongly connected, and wings so that we can fly, fantasise, hope and dream. These seem perfect metaphors for creative CE. You must start with the mirrors and roots, so that you are not misinformed, alienated, apathetic and disengaged. To change things you need to understand what you are dealing with in terms of economic, historical, social and political realities. But without the windows and the wings there can be no visions of the future. The notion of 'teaching for tomorrow' (Hicks and Holden, 1995) is best exemplified through the work of development education associations, the global citizenship movement and World Studies Trust (see Hicks, 2003). Their active pedagogy is admirably suited to work in citizenship. Much of their focus has been on global connections, particularly using geography as the vehicle. However, the principles of 'teaching for tomorrow' apply across the curriculum and connect at all points with CE.

Teachers and curriculum

So far, we have considered some of the personal qualities which may be important for creative thinking generally and CE specifically. Within the child's experience in school, starting with the youngest, there are some other necessary conditions for nurturing qualities and attitudes of creative citizenship.

1. *Creative, democratic and empowering teachers* who:
   - are committed to developing creative citizens for the future;
   - create a classroom climate in which children experience democracy first-hand;
   - see possibilities for developing children's ability to engage with the present and the future;
   - know how to develop an ethos of collaboration and trust – both essential because of the risks and dynamics of thinking creatively;
   - know how to set up opportunities for creative thinking about society – whether 'blue skies' thinking, or pragmatic.

2. *A creative curriculum* which:
   - enriches children's knowledge about society through biographies, stories and situations which challenge and stimulate their understandings of possible actions and ways of life in the world;
   - develops qualities and capabilities of empathy, creative problem-setting and problem-solving;
   - develops and encourages higher order thinking skills.

The creative teacher

Having your own vision about creative teaching

We have said that CE can be either at the minimalist or the maximalist end of a continuum. Creativity in your classroom will depend on your philosophy of education and interpretation of your own role. People with a highly instrumental and minimalist view of CE are unlikely to want to encourage creativity or open-ended situations in which children pose problems about society and try to tackle them. But we do need to consider that we are preparing young children for the rapidly changing twenty-first century.

Being able to take risks as a teacher

Many experienced teachers know that it is possible to crush children's creativity into ready-made moulds where they parrot the expected answers and do what they have

to do to get good marks or teacher approval or stay out of trouble. Moving children on from this conformist, uncreative approach to their own learning may have to start with the teacher her/himself being prepared to take some risks. In *Teaching Citizenship in Primary Schools* I wrote about a teacher called Paula who, faced with discipline problems in her Year 6 class, responded empathetically and creatively to the children — and simultaneously found solutions to their and her difficulties (see Claire, 2004: 87–9). An important message from Paula's story was that she had to take a number of risks herself. She had to break free from a repressive school system which did not give children space to bring their concerns to teachers' attention; she had to take a risk that listening to children's perspective on some difficult issues might open 'Pandora's box', as she put it herself. Basically, she had to be prepared to trust herself and the children sufficiently to set something new moving without knowing quite where it would go. This is a really important message to those of you who hope to encourage children's creative response to citizenship issues. It's not just yourself you'll have to trust, your own good sense, judgement, ability to create and manage a much more open classroom — but you'll have to trust the children.

Managing a collaborative and trusting classroom

To get 'there' from 'here' will be quite easy if the school ethos already ensures that children work collaboratively, take responsibility seriously and know how to manage themselves in situations where they have considerable autonomy. For others, the very opposite may be the case. You will need to set yourself and the children small achievable goals towards greater collaboration, responsibility and autonomy on the journey towards a more distant goal of encouraging creative responses to citizenship issues. You'll need to make your 'responsibility objectives' as clear as you would the day's plans for literacy. You'll need to use all the strategies you know for positive behaviour management, clear boundary setting, discussion about how they're doing and the progress you hope for (e.g. listening to each other, working with people who are not part of their clique, actively participating, etc.). You'll go for group reward systems, intrinsic motivation and collaboration, not individual competition and extrinsic rewards. You'll avoid damaging criticism. Your 'further goal' will be about working together towards solutions to societal problems — because they think it's worthwhile, not because they'll get a gold star.

Your goal of building greater trust between children shouldn't be confined to Circle Time. Use games and PE. Think about puppets, role play, pair and small-group work on stories, design, art and maths as possible opportunities for children to learn to talk more openly, listen and work together in trusting respectful ways.

Creative teaching – perceiving opportunities

Your vision of your role as a teacher and how you encourage learning and your intention to build greater trust and autonomy may mean some quite creative curriculum innovations. You'll need to look for opportunities and plan to implement them.

Boden (2001) explores the relationship between knowledge and creativity and points out that creative thinking develops from what we already know, not in a vacuum. We transform what we already know by changing some of the rules; we think more creatively through engaging with other people's ideas – maybe through reading or through collaborative planning or conversation. CE is privileged, because you can use any other subject you choose to further its aims – and combine them in any ways you think will work. So you might get children to consider how they would like to improve an area of wasteland near their school (which would certainly be a citizenship topic) and your work could include some design and technology, science, art, letter writing, making a PowerPoint presentation and role play. You might use a painting in a museum to reflect on emblematic, cultural representations of power, celebration or religious difference (for example, André Fougeron's *American Civilisation* which is in the Tate Modern – in the centre a man worships a car, surrounded by images of war and poverty – or the *Delhi Durbar* painting in the Bristol Museum of Empire and Commonwealth History (see Harnett *et al.*, 2005)). This will be the starting point for children to think about their own values, the people with power in their own society and how it is expressed.

Or you might start with the traditional Indian art of puppet-making to help children think about deforestation (Growney, 2005). Growney taught a primary class about puppet-makers substituting papier mâché for wood through a cross-curricular project in global citizenship, involving picture books like *The People Who Hugged Trees*, making puppets, perspective taking about the different people involved in forestry, and work on sustainable development.

It's important to give yourself permission to think outside the box and to know that after the rather repressive years when the National Curriculum was first introduced, creative cross-curricularity is encouraged in a variety of recent official documents, whose very titles hint at their agenda: for example, the Primary National Strategy: *Excellence and Enjoyment*(DfES, 2003) and *All Our Futures: Creativity, Culture and Education* (DfEE, 1999a).

Pause for thought

Reflect on some work that you have recently done with children. Could you have introduced a citizenship theme, for example about rights and responsibilities, identity, understanding other people's perspectives, what we might do when people feel excluded or bullied? Perhaps you asked children to write poems, or explore themes in a text – could this have gone in other directions? One Year 4 teacher I know got her children to develop and role-play alternative non-violent endings to Romeo and Juliet – which is about peaceful conflict resolution in CE. In Table 12.2 I have started a grid – try to add some examples from your own curriculum knowledge and work.

Table 12.2 Introdcing CE themes

Existing curriculum work	Creative extension	CE concepts, etc.
Learning about Anne Frank in history	Discussion and research about current examples of 'race hatred' and discrimination on religious grounds. Decisions about what the class can do to make its views known	Human rights; racism, courage of people who defied Nazis and hid the the Franks – challenging discrimination; considering socially just solutions to problems
Reading *Charlotte's Web* in English	Setting up a debate about how we treat farm animals; whether we should eat meat	Values; tolerance of diversity
Data handling using stats to create bar graphs and pie charts	Using statistics from web about the different languages people speak in Britain (or local area if multi cultural); finding out from council the age spread in the borough and graphing these	Discussing the composition ethnically and in age terms of our society. Considering what these mean for schools or wider community –school support, translation services, services for elderly and children
Measure	Finding out whether you could get round the school easily if you were in a wheelchair	??
??	??	??

The creative curriculum – beyond instrumentalism

Inspiring children and enriching their knowledge base

You can support children's creative thinking about their own and others' identity, human rights, possible futures, their potential power and their relationships through introducing them to a range of analytic tools and concepts that move them beyond their current experiences and understandings. This is Vygotsky's zone of proximal development in practice – building into the unknown with scaffolding. It's fundamental to a wider vision of education, beyond instrumentalism. For citizenship it may mean helping children think about their world in terms of such concepts as the following:

- *The individual's relationship to society*, e.g. how far aspects of a competitive, individualistic, materialist society create difficulties between individuals, communities and internationally, and how far such characteristics promote dynamism and progress. You could use a story like *The Selfish Giant* to help children grasp these difficult ideas, going beyond the story itself, to talk about contemporary, real issues, and where we need to share and work collaboratively in society.

- *Gender relationships*, e.g. how far conventional ideas about roles, rights and responsibilities get skewed into oppressive power plays and how far they serve stability. (Perhaps Anthony Browne's *Piggybook* could stimulate such thinking?)
- *Self-expression and instrumentalism*, e.g. what is the point of artistic endeavours whether personal or communal – should the government spend money on free art galleries and sculptures in public places?
- *Should the wealthy 'north' take responsibility for the poverty and instability in some parts of the 'south'* (less developed countries)? Are we 'our brother's keeper'? A story from the Bible could be the starting point.
- *Is war always justified?* Perhaps start with songs about soldiers like The Dixie Chicks' *Travellin' soldier* which was banned at the time of the 2004 Iraq War, Bruce Springsteen's *Youngstown* or John Lennon's *Imagine*.

You're unlikely to use the abstract words but stories, poetry, music and art are important ways to open children's minds to critiquing their own society and possibilities for progress. Remember that everyone needs ideas to bounce off – even the most creative people stand on the shoulders of the giants who came before them! It's also about progression in learning – you offer images, stories and ideas which young children may not comprehend in depth but which will form the basis for their conceptualisation of possibilities in the future.

Here are some more ideas:

- *Using a poem* – some examples

White Comedy

I waz whitemailed
By a white witch,
Wid white magic
An white lies,
Branded by a white sheep
I slaved as a whitesmith
Near a white spot
Where I suffered whitewater fever.
Whitelisted as a whiteleg
I waz in de white book
As a master of white art,
It waz like white death.

Benjamin Zephaniah, from 'Propa Propaganda'

Vegan Steven

There was a young vegan
Called Steven,
Who just would not kill for no reason,
This kid would not eat
No cheese or no meat
And he hated the foxhunting season

Benjamin Zephaniah in 'A Little Book of Vegan Poems'

Another Day in Paradise

She calls out to the man on the street
'Sir, can you help me?
It's cold and I've nowhere to sleep,
Is there somewhere you can tell me?'

He walks on, doesn't look back
He pretends he can't hear her
Starts to whistle as he crosses the street
Seems embarrassed to be there

Oh think twice, it's another day for
You and me in paradise
Oh think twice, it's just another day for you,
You and me in paradise

Phil Collins

(www.benjaminzephaniah.com/rhymin.html#british and www.poemhunter.com/)

- *a story* – **Anthony Browne:** *Willy and Hugh* **(all about bullying, friendship, the power of gangs) or** *Piggybook* **(a mum refuses to do the housework and her children and husband find out just what women's work entails); Mary Hoffman:** *Amazing Grace* **(possible futures, breaking the stereotypes);**
- *a role play* – **between a group who'd like to stop parents taking their kids to school in individual cars, and those who support it (individual rights** *vs.* **environmental pollution and traffic);**
- **diamond-ranking with an artist and musician included with the doctor, teacher, childminder (see Claire, 2004: 11–12; Clough and Holden, 2002: 55–7);**
- *art* – **such as Figure 12.2 from Southern Africa, showing people working communally and Figure 12.3: from nineteenth-century Venice, a world turned upside down – what would it be like if we lived there … ;**
- *philosophy for children* – **text (could be from a newspaper), a cartoon, a photo or painting act as stimuli for children's own questions (see Claire, 2004: ch. 3 for more on philosophy for children).**

Figure 12.2 – 'Scrumbling for water' – lithograph showing 'Crossroads' squatter camp outside Cape Town South Africa, by Patrick Holo, 1994
(original in author's possession)

Figure 12.3: 'Il mondo alla rovescia' – 'The world turned upside down'
(original print in author's possession)

Children can't be expected to think creatively about an environment with beautiful innovative buildings or inspiring landscapes if they've never seen any – even in pictures. So perhaps bring in pictures of Gaudi's architecture in Barcelona, or Corbusier's estates on the outskirts of Paris, which in their time were supposed to offer a brave new world to working people – but have not fulfilled this vision. Perhaps photographs like Figure 12.4 or 12.5 could get them thinking about the kind of world they might like to live in …

Figure 12.4 Oscar Niemayer's Cathedral in Brasilia,
the official capital of Brazil

Figure 12.5 A rural hotel near Lake Wanchi in Ethiopia
(photograph Hilary Claire, 2004)

Some more ideas for stimulating creative thinking about citizenship concepts

Historical and current examples

For opportunities to learn about values and issues starting with people and groups who wanted to change things:

- **Martin Luther King, Mahatma Gandhi, Nelson Mandela, Maya Angelou, Eglantine Jebb (who founded Save the Children Fund) – all concerned with social justice and human rights.**

- **People concerned with the environment and uses and abuses of science and technology, e.g. Rachel Carson, a progenitor of the environmental movement; Arundhati Roy who campaigns in India; Greenpeace; WWF.**

- **People concerned with the effects of war and conflict, e.g. Save the Children Fund, UNICEF, Amnesty, Anne Frank Educational Trust, Holocaust Trust, Red Cross, Médecins sans Frontières.**

Starting with fiction

Much children's fiction is about 'quest' and challenge, difficult choices, fighting the dragons and the giants or confronting evil, and personal qualities – courage, vision. From Philip Pullman, Anne Fine or Lemony Snicket to feminist and traditional fairy tales, myths and legends, there are opportunities to get children thinking about their values, concerns and their own willingness to become engaged. Frank Zipes (1987) and Bob Dixon (1977) have explored the power of traditional fairy stories and children's fiction to socialise girls and boys into conventional and conservative discourses. More recently, Bronwyn Davies has used feminist versions of familiar stories to get primary children thinking about gender and power (Davies, 2003). Familiar children's material has been used by a serious academic to get people thinking about how they make choices, and what the consequences of alternative choices might have been. For instance, was the Little Mermaid wise to accept the appalling conditions of life on earth or should she have stayed beneath the sea with her sisters? What did Humpty think he was doing sitting on a wall with such a fragile shell and so little mobility? (Dowie, 1999, 2005) The important thing for teachers is to consider how pupils can engage with dominant discourses and critiques, moving from the metaphorical and fictional to today's real world. What are 'our dragons'? What qualities do we need to slay them? What choices should we carefully think through?

Linking with art and music

Certain artists represent reality or challenge the status quo, so that we see the world differently. Some theorists believe that without exposure to critical art we are 'dumbed down' into passivity and political apathy (Adorno, 1991). To harness this material for creative CE means being prepared to include the political and social content of art and music, not just concentrate on form. Beyond the examples illustrated above, think about Picasso's *Guernica*, Dubuffet's drawings of wartime Paris or poster art from round the world. These resources are intended to do more than extend children's cultural base. After the discussion, children should themselves try and use art, photography or posters to interpret contemporary issues.

Drama techniques

Role-play, simulations and other drama techniques might well be your most powerful vehicle for creative work in CE: they can liberate creativity, allowing children to play with new ideas and new personae in safe contexts, to imagine and consider 'what if?'.

Preparing for local study in the primary history curriculum, some of my own students worked with newspaper cuttings about various historical campaigns, which included keeping a hospital open, stopping nuclear waste going through the borough, a *Rock Against Racism* concert in the late 1970s, the dustmen's strike and a march of unemployed workers in the 1920s.

They quickly appreciated the opportunity to use cross-curricular approaches to explore historical issues about rights, responsibilities and advocacy and take this into contemporary concerns. So, their plans included using the photos and articles to set up freeze-frames, with children taking different positions which were then animated, the class writing letters to the press, holding a debate, making a simulated TV programme and learning some of the songs from the old campaigns. They would follow through by identifying a contemporary concern and planning a campaign themselves, learning about the range of possible ways to make your voice heard: making banners, designing leaflets and holding meetings.

What has creativity got to do with CE? :

a summary of key points

In this short chapter it has only been possible to skim the surface of a huge subject, but I hope that creative teachers will use these ideas as a springboard, and in turn empower their pupils to think and plan creatively for their own future. Toss a pebble into a pool – watch the ripples spread. The surprises and the rewards are great when you become a creative teacher, so that CE for your pupils is creative, liberating and empowering.

- *Creativity is fundamental to citizenship. Participative, active citizens of all political persuasions will need the ability to construe problems and consider creative solutions. They will need to be independent, and capable of principled, lateral thought and imagination; they will also need to be able to realise when 'problems' have been wrongly defined. Creativity does not automatically ensure justice.*
- *Central to citizenship education are high self-esteem and development of identity. To respect others' identity, understand their situation and grant them 'worth', you must first respect yourself and your own worth, and feel confident about your own identity.*
- *Remember that taking risks with children and working with them to explore and change perceptions are greater challenges for some children than for others; this applies to pupils in Year 6 as well as four-year-olds.*
- *Try to conceptualise citizenship education as a journey towards a more distant goal of encouraging creative responses to wider societal issues. Set yourself and the children small achievable goals towards greater collaboration, responsibility and autonomy on this journey. Make your 'responsibility objectives' as clear as you would the day's plans for literacy.*
- *Citizenship education is privileged, because you can use any other subject you choose to further its aims – and combine them in any ways you think will work. Your goal of building greater trust between children shouldn't be confined to circle time.*

Introduction

Design and technology (D&T) can claim to be at the heart of any curriculum that seeks to develop children's creativity, and was originally conceived as such. In the original proposals for the subject in the National Curriculum, the Design and Technology Working Group (1988) suggested that it involves:

> The development of design and technology capability to operate effectively and *creatively* in the made world. (para 1.2, our italics)

Activity

In the current National Curriculum (NC), an 'Importance of ...' statement for each subject is included prior to the programmes of study. How many of these statements refer to creativity?

You will have discovered that all but two of the introductory 'importance of' statements for subjects in the current National Curriculum (DfEE, 1999c) claim to contribute to children's creativity, yet design and technology is the only one to mention it twice! What makes D&T such a creative subject?

Well, firstly, if we take oft-quoted definition from the highly influential report *All Our Futures* (NACCCE, 1999): 'imaginative activity fashioned so as to *produce outcomes* that are both original and of value' (our italics), we can see that the emphasis upon *production* is central to D&T activities. D&T is a hands-on activity in which children make real, tangible objects. It is, however, also 'minds-on', involving a balance between doing and thinking, action and reflection. The act of designing inevitably involves imagining something that does not yet exist. At its best, D&T offers children open-ended tasks which do not have a prescribed 'right answer' and involve an element of choice (of shape, colour, materials, function, etc.) so that their outcomes will all be original. Evaluation is also central to the 'minds-on' dimension of D&T; children need to learn to appraise others' designs as well as their own.

Secondly, Koestler's (1964) definition of creativity as 'the ability to make connections between previously unconnected ideas' seems to describe well the sorts of ways in which designers think (e.g. linking clockwork and radio, or cyclones and vacuum cleaners). D&T can provide children with opportunities to bring together ideas from different areas of the curriculum (e.g. knowledge about materials, electricity or nutrition from science, understanding of 3D shapes and measurement from maths, people's different needs and lifestyles from geography). D&T draws particularly on children's 'visual literacy' – their abilities to 'read' colour and form, patterns and symbols, and to reassemble these elements into aesthetically pleasing outcomes. It shares this with art and design, and can perhaps claim to represent a third major form of representation, alongside words and numbers.

Thirdly, accounts of creative *processes* also seem to echo those that designers or children might undertake in the course of a D&T project. For example, Dust (1999) suggests that at least four phases of creativity are commonly identified, to which we have added imaginary examples from the development of the Dyson vacuum cleaner:

1. *Preparation* – investigating the problem and gathering data (e.g. trying out many vacuum cleaners to measure their loss of suction as the bag fills up);
2. *Incubation* – usually an unconscious/subconscious phase (e.g. going away and thinking about something else, perhaps observing tornadoes or water flowing down plugholes);
3. *Illumination/revelation* – the insight, the moment of creation (e.g. if we could make two 'mini-tornadoes', one inside the other, it would suck air into a vacuum cleaner powerfully);
4. *Verification/reframing* – the 'testing', usually through communicating the outcome to peers or 'gatekeepers' in the 'field' or domain (e.g. making hundreds of models and prototypes, taking them round trade fairs, showing them to manufacturers).

If we consider these against the processes identified in the National Curriculum Programme of Study (PoS) for D&T (Table 13.1) we can see striking correspondences. You will notice that the steps in the process do not occur in the same order, but we need to remember that in both cases they 'do not generally occur in a tidy linear path: they often overlap and the process can be entered and left at any stage' (NGfL Scotland, 2003). There is also no equivalent of 'incubation' in D&T as prescribed by the National Curriculum, although there seems to be a recognition by teachers that children should be given more time to think and discuss ideas during the school day.

Table 13.1. Correspondence between models of creative and D&T processes.

Dust's (1999) synthesis of creative processes	D&T National Curricuum Programme of Study
Preparation	4. Knowledge and understanding of materials and components
	3. Evaluating processes and products
Incubation	
Illumination/revelation	1. Developing, planning and communicating ideas
Verification/reframing	2. Working with tools, equipment, materials and components to make quality products.
	3. Evaluating processes and products

The fourth reason why D&T and creativity go together is concerned with thinking skills. One of the 'creative thinking skills' identified in the National Curriculum is 'problem-solving'. Problem-solving is a thinking skill that has received much attention over the years, and the strategies to solve practical problems have long been promoted in D&T (see, for example, Roden 1999). The extent to which it is generic or transferable is debatable (if you can solve mathematical problems, it does not necessarily mean you can solve design problems), but its importance in D&T is profound. Design problems tend to be 'wicked', that is they are not clearly defined like mathematical problems and involve many factors such as materials, technology and human lifestyles. This sometimes makes them not look like problems at all: 'design and make sandwiches for a picnic' sounds more like an opportunity for trying out new combinations of fillings. Playing around with ideas, another characteristic of creative D&T, is a problem-solving activity, although within a low-stress, relatively unstructured framework. We don't necessarily need to set children artificial 'problems' (for example, 'build a tower to support a marble') but we do need to support them in developing strategies that will help them think through problems in the midst of designing and making. For a food technologist, designing a sandwich that will stick together, taste pleasant and not make the bread too soggy presents a whole range of challenging problems — it's no picnic!

Creativity and values in D&T

Before we look in detail at classroom practice we need to consider why we want children to be creative in D&T and how we will know if they have been. This involves applying value judgements — what is your response to a child who has creatively combined materials to make an innovative weapon? If we analyse further the NC 'Importance of D&T' statement it becomes clear that design and technology is a 'future-oriented' subject in that children are being asked to imagine how things might be different and better. David Orr (1993: 16) claims that:

> Students in the [twenty-first century] will need to know how to create a civilisation that runs on sunlight, conserves energy, preserves biodiversity, protects soils and forests, develops sustainable local economies and restores the damage inflicted on the earth. In order to achieve such ecological education we need to transform our schools and universities. (Orr, 1993: 16)

Orr is applying his values, which are associated with education for sustainable development, to identify problems that, in his opinion, require creative solutions. We don't often ask children to think very far into the future — what could we design to improve people's lives in ten, twenty years' time? Perhaps in order to engage children's creativity we need to be setting more 'blue-sky' design projects, inviting children to project themselves forward in time.

Pause for thought

Hicks and Holden (1995) report on a survey of children's visions of the future. They found that while half the children at age 7 thought about their own personal futures often, less than a quarter reflected on the future for their local area.

Encouragingly, 41 per cent claimed to think about the future of the world often, with a further third considering it 'sometimes'. While the majority considered that their own futures would improve, they were less optimistic about other people and the planet as a whole. Eleven-year-olds in particular were worried about increasing pollution, poverty and wars:

> *Their choice for preferred futures indicates that many would like a future based on greater environmental awareness, and their action as individuals reinforces this as an area of concern.* (Hicks and Holden, 1995, 78)

These findings will not surprise any teacher who has discussed global issues with his or her class. The problem lies (as with all of us) in the differences between what children say and what they do. At a mundane level, their apparently wasteful use of resources in a design and technology project (cutting a circle out of the middle of a piece of card for example) may frustrate us. Often it is that they have not made the connections between the big ideas of environmentalism (e.g. deforestation) and their individual choices (how much paper to use).

So a further dimension of decision-making for children can be to introduce *eco-choice* points in a project in which they are given the relevant environmental information to make sustainable decisions. For example, a problem regarding too much litter in a school playground could be solved by designing and making litter bins or producing posters to persuade others not to drop litter. In one Bristol primary school the Year 3 class, with support from the Recycling Consortium, conducted a litter audit over three days for the whole school (except the kitchens) and analysed the results. Unsurprisingly, paper was the most common type of waste collected. The discussion of the categories of litter helped increase the pupils' awareness of what is thrown away and how this could be reduced. At a small-scale, but very practical level, they were taught how to fold crisp packets to make them less likely to be blown out of bins and around the playground. Their teacher Jayne then taught about the long-term effects on global warming of their attitudes towards energy and rubbish, and introduced children to the benefits of recycling. This led to them e-mailing the Recycling Consortium to ask for appropriate recycling boxes for the school. There was discussion about where the boxes should be placed to maximise the benefits. Although the children had not actually made the boxes themselves, they had made important decisions about the layout of their environment. Older children can be invited to deal with more sophisticated questions that involve value judgements concerned with economic, aesthetic, environmental, technical or social issues (Benson, 1992).

Activity

How could common classroom design and make assignments such as fairground rides, coats or fruit salads be adapted to engage children with values consistent with sustainable development?

Starting points for creativity in D&T

Through looking at what experienced teachers do in the classroom (Howe *et al.*, 2001), we have identified three ways that teachers provide motivational and inspirational starting points for D&T activities that support the development of children's creativity. These are:

- **building on children's interests;**
- **identifying real opportunities;**
- **using relevant contexts.**

For example, in a reception class making wheeled vehicles, we observed how the class teacher used the *children's interests* to identify a context for learning:

> [The children] had lots of experience of working with a variety of construction kits on a small scale. There was a class 'craze' for making ever-more elaborate wheeled vehicles. Katherine, the class teacher, wanted to capitalise and build on this enthusiasm. This led to her making formative assessments about what the children were able to do, their language development, their knowledge and understanding of the world and their interests. She had also identified a need to give the children opportunities to work on a larger scale and to develop the skills of cutting and joining wood... To begin the project, Katherine discussed with the class their recently made wheeled models, and introduced a new word – 'axle'. She showed them how an axle could be used to link pairs of wheels and allow them to turn. Some children were able to make freehand labelled drawings of vehicles whilst others used the models as designs for the next stage ... The children discovered how PVA glue and elastic bands might be used to join pieces of wood through this activity. At times they became engrossed in this to such an extent [Figure 13.1] that they lost a sense of time and place – they were 'in the flow ... ' (Howe et al., 2001: 22–3).

Figure 13.1: Developing wheeled vehicles from children's initial interest

Csikszentmilhalyi (1997, 2002) coined the phrase 'in the flow' to describe the most productive and fulfilling phases of the creative process, a state he characterises by intense concentration, absorption, pleasure and lack of awareness of time passing. By providing children with *real opportunities* their sense of engagement with the task can carry them into this state. For example, at Bromley Heath Infants' School in South Gloucestershire, D&T co-ordinator Sarah Stillie chose to take advantage of the new housing development being built locally to provide children with the opportunity of observing structures at various stages of completion, and consider ways in which the development would impact upon the local community. She was also anxious to provide children with a sense of the social setting within which homes are bought and sold, so set up an estate agency in the classroom role-play area, complete with ICT-generated advertisements, index files, property descriptions and key tags. When children came to undertake the design-and-make assignment (DMA) she wanted them to be able to consider the particular needs of individuals, so set up a 'fantasy' scenario in which children would design for story characters. They were to group the resulting models in a housing development ('Fairytale land') which considered issues of access, space and traffic.

A classroom role-play area is also an example of a *relevant context*. In other examples we have seen, contexts were provided through the use of story or by referring to needs within the school – to help someone, to put on an assembly or to redesign a library. Relevant contexts are particularly important in helping young children to design for others, because without significant scaffolding many find it very difficult to think beyond their own needs and wants. For example, the children in the autumn of Year 1 at St Philip's Primary School, Bath, carried out a DMA to make a sandwich that they would like to eat. The starting point was, therefore, a discussion about their own preferences. Their teacher had judged that it would be too demanding for them to think of the needs of others while, at the same time, meeting the requirements to plan before making and remembering safe and hygienic practices. Later in the year, when the children were more secure with the notion of designing and making, she 'scaffolded' their transition from egocentricity to awareness of the perspectives of *others* during work on playgrounds. The class went to look at a playground as the starting point for thinking about the equipment different age groups would like and where a playground should be sited so as not to offend residents.

Pause for thought

Are the teachers above teaching for creativity, teaching creatively or both?

Helping children to generate creative ideas

Having 'good ideas' is fundamental to creativity; it is an obvious point to make, yet do we actually teach children in a way that develops their ability to think creatively? By 'good' ideas we refer here not only to inventing new products but also to considering new ways of looking at things and doing things. It is important to note that we are using the 'ideas' in the plural here. We want children to be able to come up with a *number* of possibilities, *then* evaluate their potential before proceeding. We want to avoid situations where children say 'I can't think of anything!' or on the other hand proceed with the first idea that occurred to them. This is not to say that every time children do D&T they should come up with three ideas and chose the 'best' one. That would be too formulaic. We do believe children should have the opportunity to think before proceeding.

The D&T curriculum provides a framework for allowing children time to think by suggesting they should investigate and evaluate 'a range of familiar products' (DfEE, 1999c:93). Although the processes of D&T can occur in any order and begin at any point (see Table 13.1) we believe there is a strong case for beginning with *evaluation*. D&T and evaluation have a 'special relationship', and it is difficult to think of a great innovation in design that has come about without a keen awareness of what has been done before. We need not worry that by exposing children to existing products they will simply 'copy' them – some degree of transformation is inevitable in the process of making an idea their own. The key to making an investigation and evaluation activity (IEA) a spur to generative thought is the teachers' choice of a range of different design solutions around a common theme, and the 'scaffolding' of children's ability to 'interrogate' these objects (Figure 13.2).

Figure 13.2 'Interrogating' a collection of musical instruments to provide design ideas

For example, we can use questioning which focuses children's attention on key aspects of the objects being evaluated. This needs to begin with questions that encourage closer observation and initial investigation, such as:

- **What shapes can you see?**
- **What materials have been used?**
- **How many pieces have been used in construction?**
- **What does it feel/taste/smell like?**

Next, we can ask children to consider the human factors behind the design of the product being evaluated, and to think about future developments as this may provide a springboard for their own ideas:

- **Who do you think this product was designed for? How can you tell?**
- **Describe how they would use it – can you imagine any difficulties they might have?**

- **Could you improve upon the product, and if so, how?**
- **How would you redesign it for a different user (perhaps for a child, an elderly person, an astronaut, a fictional character)?**

So, through evaluation of the made world, children's ideas can be sparked and their creativity enhanced. Handled in the wrong way, however, looking at what already exists can be an inhibitor to creative thought. Such a situation could arise of the children see only one or two alternatives, if they think the teacher values one solution above others, or if one product seems perfectly suited to the specifications set for the children's design-and-make assignment.

Another common way of supporting idea generation is *brainstorming* or *blue-sky thinking*. Essentially this is an uninterrupted process during which a teacher might invite immediate responses to a given scenario, e.g. a 'wolf-proof house' for the three little pigs. Children throw any words or ideas that occur to them into the 'pot' for recording on a large sheet of paper or interactive whiteboard. The ground rules are to avoid evaluating the ideas immediately, and certainly not to laugh at them! Such a flow of ideas in response to a problem or scenario can be enhanced if the thinkers work in small groups initially to allow a chance for discussion. The discussion may start from a very open-ended question – 'what winds you up?' – or completing the statement – 'we really must do something about … ' Another technique is for ideas to be written or drawn on paper aeroplanes – this literally allows ideas to be 'tossed around' for others to pick up and add to. The playfulness of the situation can encourage playfulness in thinking. Once the initial 'storm' has passed, we can then sort through the contributions and evaluate them against criteria decided by the group, e.g. practicality, aesthetics, expense.

Another strategy for idea generation is called *linking-thinking*. Linking ideas, as we have seen, is a fundamental part of creativity. There are a number of techniques that can help this 'linking-thinking' in the classroom. Relating a product in an analogous way can throw up new possibilities, e.g.:

> *'Packages are like … '*
> *… nuts (strong, keep the contents safe, hard to open)*
> *… homes (keep contents dry, secure, insulated, reflect the owner's character)*

Develop the analogy for the item to be packaged:

'If my new sweet was growing on a tree, it would look like this … be displayed like this … dispersed like this … be consumed by … ' and so on.

Some children might find the visual a more powerful stimulation than words. Visual triggers might come from:

- **random shapes/scribbles/doodles;**
- **images from photos or clippings;**
- **digital photos that have been manipulated;**
- **shapes in nature – fruits, river deltas, frost patterns.**

In generating ideas, children might be asked to act out an aspect of the life of the intended user or even the intended product. Some adult designers have actually done this – dressing like a pregnant woman or visually impaired person. Examples for role-play could include:

- **looking after a baby;**
- **coping in a classroom without bending;**
- **if I were a package I would be …;**
- **a day in the life of a shoe.**

Social creativity in D&T

As teachers, should we concentrate on enabling individuals to be creative or should we concentrate on developing a creative classroom ethos? Siraj-Blatchford (1996) discusses how, in the classroom, children can move from being involved in 'collective design' – working as a group with support from the teacher – to, in later years, a 'design collective' in which children draw on earlier experiences and learned skills to design and make with autonomy alongside their peers. He suggests that if children are part of successful design collectives during the primary years then they are more likely to progress to challenging tasks with confidence.

Pause for thought

Harrington (1990) explores the notion of social or distributed creativity by using the biological analogy of an ecosystem. Just as a biological ecosystem consists of a complex interrelationship of organisms, habitats and environmental conditions, he argues that:

> *… social creativity does not 'reside' in any single cognitive or personality process, does not 'occur' at any single point in time, does not 'happen' at any particular place, and is not the product of a single individual. (p. 149)*

Through analysing descriptions of creative episodes, Harrington identifies common process features and argues that, in a similar way that life processes make biochemical demands upon organisms and their ecosystems, these creative processes make psychosocial demands upon individuals and their support networks, which must provide sufficient resources to enable creativity ('life') to be sustained. The resources of Harrington's 'ecosystem' in which creativity may flourish are:

- *an atmosphere or 'ambience' of creativity;*
- *stimulation;*
- *opportunities for 'play';*
- *easy access to resources;*
- *mentors and role models;*
- *permission/support;*
- *motivation/encouragement;*
- *information;*
- *open-ended assignments.*

One of the key findings from research into children's creativity is the central importance of peers, supportive adults and role models in inspiring and stimulating children. Our own research in this field – the Young Designers on Location project (Davies *et al.,* 2004) – suggests that the most important kinds of encounters for stimulating children's creativity are those involving practising designers, technologists, artists, architects and engineers – we will call them 'design-related professionals'. Children respond instinctively to the apprenticeship model of education offered by the designer in the classroom, rather than to the more rigid, curriculum-led attempts to 'teach children to design'. By sharing their own work practices with examples, it seemed that the designers working on the project helped to create a climate of confidence and trust, while maintaining 'high ambient levels of creative activity' through acting as 'co-workers', modelling behaviours and demonstrating practice. The professionals also demonstrated 'explicit expressions of confidence in the creative abilities of those within the environment' (Harrington, 1990) through a discussion of children's own creativity – demonstrating both a democratic view of creativity and a metacognitive dimension to their teaching. By the end of the project, when relationships had had time to establish, the interactions between children and designers were very productive. They were genuinely able to 'bounce ideas' off each other and challenge formulaic thinking.

The project described above describes a situation where the distinction between the roles of adult and child had begun to dissolve. This poses the class teacher a real challenge – can this radical shift of roles be allowed to happen in a 'normal' classroom? The role of the 'more knowledgeable other' is like that suggested by Bruner (1996) in 'scaffolding' children's learning, as evidenced in the way Steve Heal works with his Year 5/6 class in helping them to prioritise design criteria (Figure 13.3). Another way forward is to consider different uses of curriculum time. Many schools have made a step in this direction through 'D&T weeks', where different ways of working can be developed and where different relationships can take hold. This different use of time, when combined with some input from those who work in the design world – perhaps in the form of an afternoon visit or short residency – can provide an ideal context for a 'creative ecosystem' to be developed.

Figure 13.3 'Scaffolding' children's prioritising of design criteria for a shelter

Creative making in D&T

We have discussed creative and generative thinking as a part of designing, yet there is more thinking to be done when making. At any point, the introduction of one of the strategies we have described above might refresh or refocus minds. D&T is an iterative process moving backwards and forwards between activities 'inside' and 'outside the head' (Kimbell *et al.*, 1991) so it is appropriate for children to employ procedures in different orders – for example by starting with making. In order to develop their creative ideas, children may find it helpful and motivating to get their hands on materials as soon as possible. This can involve play, by which we mean handling objects and exploring them in a relatively unstructured way. In a primary classroom children might be encouraged to handle objects such as the materials they will later be using (as in the wheeled vehicles example above). This will allow children to develop their knowledge of the properties of materials and will allow them to imagine how the materials might be put to use. Ideal materials that allow shapes and forms to be developed in a temporary way include:

- clay – to explore a form for a storage container, candle holder or vehicle body;
- pipe-cleaners or art straws – to allow exploration of stable shapes for a photo frame, furniture or playground equipment;
- paper – to allow exploration of card mechanisms, patterns for garments, patterns for bags or shoes;
- construction kits – to allow exploration of mechanisms for vehicles or toys, hinges for storage boxes, stable shapes, strong shapes.

The power of ICT in developing children's ideas before and during making is considerable. For example, using a site such as **www.dtonline.org** to explore packaging design, simple computer-aided design software such as TABS+ which allows children to make 3D models and prints out 2D nets, or 'My World' which allows young children to make a number of decisions, for example in relation to designing a house, can all help to develop creative solutions.

Pause for thought

Should teachers give children freedom to design and make, or should they teach them skills beforehand? This question of balance between intervention and non-intervention has been at the heart of debates about teaching for creativity. In D&T there are certain skills that children can learn – to do with thinking and making. The tension between a skills-based approach to developing creativity (what Gardner (1999) identifies as deriving from an Eastern, Confucian tradition with an emphasis on 'mastery') and one that is more 'constructive' with an emphasis on process was highlighted in our own work with 11-year-olds and 'design-related professionals' (Davies et al., 2004). Those with more skills input produced outcomes of higher quality, though children who had been encouraged to reflect on their own creativity and 'follow their own path' were less conventional. This reflects research by DATA/Nuffield (2003) who advocate an approach combining skills input with 'surprise' activities to stimulate unusual solutions. The National Grid for Learning

(NGfL Scotland, 2003) urges teachers to go beyond the 'creative ecosystem' to a more directive role in children's capability:

Although a creative climate and an encouraging adult are essential they are not enough to develop creativity. The teacher's role, beyond encouragement, involves intervening, actively teaching creative techniques and strategies.

Although young children may exhibit 'preconventional' creativity (Rosenblatt and Winner, 1988) before exposure to specific D&T knowledge and skills, our own view is that 'postconventional' creativity (i.e. that which transcends convention) is associated with explicit teaching of knowledge and skills, through, for example, focused practical tasks (FPTs). Through making with a range of materials, children will develop knowledge of their properties, together with skills of cutting, fixing, joining and manipulating that will enable them to realise their creativity with fewer frustrations. There is no substitute for this first-hand experience.

Sometimes children can get 'stuck' and give up, or return again and again to making the same limited range of things. To move children on and help them transcend their existing set of ideas for solving the problem we can intervene in a number of ways:

- **by introducing a new set of materials;**
- **by asking the child to share their project and ideas with the rest of the class;**
- **by showing a new technique for cutting, joining or combining.**

One way in which we can support children in their development of problem-solving is to make the strategies they are using more explicit through questioning. This will promote 'self-knowledge', or 'metacognition', widely regarded as essential if you want to get better at something. For example, during an activity to design and make homes for story characters (see above) class teacher Sarah Stillie gathered the children on the carpet for a joint problem-solving session (Figure 13.4). Each pair had to present their progress and discuss their problems – plus the ways in which they had tried to overcome them – with the wider group, who made suggestions about the way forward.

Figure 13.4. A problem-solving seminar during making

Activity

Another way of looking at creative teaching of D&T is to consider what a D&T teacher should not do (Fasciato and Rogers, 2005). Can you imagine what the most uncreative D&T teaching would be like?

Creativity in primary design and technology:

a summary of key points

In this chapter, we have suggested that in order to develop children's creativity through D&T teachers should;

- *develop a supportive 'ecosystem';*
- *be playful with ideas, spaces, time and resources;*
- *make connections, when planning, between learning and children's lives;*
- *teach skills and knowledge, but in a way that helps children to solve their own problems;*
- *develop cross-curricular links with other learning areas.*

Part 4 Looking to the future: trainee teachers' potential for creativity

14 'GOING AGAINST THE FLOW': AN INTERVIEW WITH TED WRAGG

Anthony Wilson:

'Creativity' seems to be a buzzword at the moment. There's been a lot of recent emphasis on it, with *Excellence and Enjoyment* and the campaign in the *Times Ed*, for example. So I'd like just to begin to ask you about what your idea of creativity is.

Ted Wragg:

There's not much enjoyment in *Excellence and Enjoyment* at the moment. Actually, I think it was probably called Excellence, and then someone probably said – I suspect a Civil Servant: 'Teachers are complaining that it's too technical, and they won't enjoy it, so let's put enjoyment in.' If you do a word search on it, there's not an awful lot of enjoyment there. And of course the reality doesn't always match the rhetoric, so someone will say 'Well, we want you to be creative' – but then of course we still have a fairly punitive OFSTED framework.

Anthony Wilson:

What is the impact of this?

Ted Wragg:

Teachers get very apprehensive. The most common question I get when I'm talking about creative teaching to heads and teachers when I've finished is: 'Oh yes, that sounds really interesting and I'd love to do that, but what about OFSTED?'

So I think in order to create a creative climate, its not just a question of dealing with symptoms and deciding to let teachers go out and do something interesting on their own, you need a whole creative climate throughout a school. I reviewed a book called *The Creative School* and it was about a very interesting school outside Reading where they do some very interesting things but when I read it through I wondered why I wasn't getting over-excited. It was interesting, it was nice. They capitalised on the environment. Fine. They bring in people from the outside to talk to children. Fine. And then it said: 'And on Fridays we don't even do the literacy and the numeracy hour, we do projects.' And I thought, well, is that it? Does that mean that being creative means one day a week you don't do the prescription?

Anthony Wilson:

Is that creating a climate?

Ted Wragg:
It's not, no. That's kind of one device, really. And to have a truly creative climate what you need is first of all freedom from fear, because fear is not a good motivator for creativity. So that's the first thing I think, there needs to be an encouragement. Secondly, you need a structure for it, because my experience of being creative is that of course you can be creative in your attic - but actually being creative sometimes, particularly if it's to spread elsewhere, needs to have a structure.

For example, you need maybe a forum where you can talk to other teachers about what you're doing. Or you need a way of recording what you're doing, so that you can write about it and other people can read what you've done. So it needs certain structures to go with it, otherwise it's a series of one-offs, or it's entirely confined to one classroom, it's not part of the whole school's climate. On the other hand, if you over-ritualise it, then you kill it. It's like Goethe's poem about the dragonfly. He chases after a dragonfly and wants to see why it's so beautiful. He takes it to bits and he's got a crumpled heap of dead bits in his hand. So if you over-structure it, that's what you'd have with creative teaching in a school — a series of dead bits.

Anthony Wilson:
Are head teachers responsible for this, creating the climate, or would it be more like clusters or LEAs that would get together and say 'Look, this is what we're going to try out'?

Ted Wragg:
The evidence from research shows that what sometimes gets called the distal factors, the ones at a distance, are less influential on what happens in a classroom than what are called the proximal factors. The factors within the school, within the classroom, the teacher's own skills, inclinations, interests and so on, are more powerful than some dictate from outside. And so there is a limit to what LEAs can do.

They can exert influence, for example at conferences, where the people attending are encouraged to work in groups of five to ten people to talk about ideas they've had in their own classroom that seem to be successful. And then to share these with other people, who then to go back to their school and promise to try out an idea they've picked up from someone else. Now that's something valuable an LEA can do, but an LEA can't dictate a climate or an atmosphere that's conducive to creativity.

Anthony Wilson:
And at the head teacher level?

Ted Wragg:
Heads can neither be creative in every classroom, nor can they kill creativity in every classroom, but the latter is probably easier than the former. A negative Head who constantly tells staff that they've got to be worried about OFSTED and stepping out of line and doing anything other than QCA Schemes of Work is actually killing creativity stone dead before it even starts. So Heads do have a role.

But in the end, I believe that climate has to be created at the classroom level, because that's where the teaching and learning is – Heads don't teach every class in the school, teachers do that.

Anthony Wilson:
You talked about a climate of fear. Can you say how that erodes teachers' willingness to be creative?

Ted Wragg:
We've been told OFSTED is supposed to be changing. I'll believe it all when it happens. The problem is not whether you tinker around again with symptoms like the period of notice, and say you'll give less notice, well, people will just be anxious all the time – if it's a bad experience.

If it's a good experience it doesn't matter whether you give people three days' or three months' notice because they look forward to it and say 'Well, this will help us improve the school'. If it's a bad experience, then all that happens is either you give them a long notice and they're fretting all the time, or they fret permanently on the grounds that there might be a knock at the door.

That's what people are afraid of, the knock at the door. So, that climate has to change. Now, one OFSTED inspector said to me when I was talking at a conference: 'You are being very unfair, because we've just failed a school for not being innovative.' And I said 'That illustrates precisely the point I'm making: "Ve have vays off making you innovative."'

Schools respond by saying: 'Oh, look at this, it's innovative: get the tick in the box.' But it still won't be.

Anthony Wilson:
So, do you think that's the main challenge, or are there other challenges for individual teachers and schools to be creative?

Ted Wragg:
My view is that every teacher should have an obligation to invent.

Now, that doesn't mean to say that every lesson should be a fresh invention – you can't do it, you'd kill yourself. Teaching is a busy job; you've got lots of things to do. Much of the time what you do will be derivative. It will be based on ideas you got from elsewhere: textbooks, schemes of work and things you've tried and tested over many years.

But then, if that's all you do then that, for me, is a killer, because no profession can move forward in that conservative manner. If all you do is what people have always done, then actually you lose, because you lose a few bits along the way and the whole profession will diminish. Whereas, if you're encouraging everybody to invent and imagine from time to time when they can, then you add to the profession, because somebody somewhere has an idea that seems to work rather well, and then it can spread. And I would say in just the same way doctors and people who work in health are obliged to try and improve practice, save more lives, get people better quickly, use safer procedures, more hygienic procedures and so on, better therapies, better surgical techniques, better drugs. All these things are incumbent on a medical practitioner to improve. And then, once they've tested out rigorously what they've done and found it really is better than what they did before, the next step is that they then try and generalise that to other people. I think that the same duty should be felt by teachers. That your job is to try and do something that's a bit different and better. If it works, you test it out again, make sure it really is better, and then you tell other people and they tell you and you share good ideas because they're precious.

Anthony Wilson:
That's a form of research, in a way.

Ted Wragg:
It is, it's people doing research in their own classrooms – because you see the inescapable logic, whether you are talking about school improvement or teachers improving their own professional skills, you cannot improve what you're doing by staying the same. It would be nice if you could but if you carry on doing the same things you don't improve. You repeat and rehearse but you don't improve. To improve you've actually got to change. There's no alternative. You have to change for the better, and therefore if people never try out a fresh idea, never have an inspiration or whatever, they can't actually improve by just doing the same things.

Anthony Wilson:
Is there any sort of direct advice that you might have for teachers to try to do that? If you're a relatively new teacher, for example, you might be nervous about passing on new practice.

Ted Wragg:
Creativity embodies risk, in the sense that if you've done something a hundred times you've got a pretty good idea of how it'll go. If you've not done it before, then you don't have any idea of how it will go, and it might go badly. And a lot of good ideas actually, the first manifestation of them is terrible. And anybody who's tried a different idea, say in drama, would say the first time they tried it, it was a shambles. But order can come through chaos.

So I think people have to have courage to innovate and create, because you have to go through something that you may know doesn't go down as well as what you normally do, and then the big temptation is to go back to what you've always done, whereas, in fact, that's the challenge. The challenge is not so much having an idea because most people can either have an idea of their own or get one from someone else. The challenge is when you're trying out the idea to make it work. That's where people's professionalism has to come out because experienced teachers who are committed could make almost anything work. They'd find a way of making it work, if they believed it was worth doing, even if it didn't work the first three times, they could find a way of making it work. The second time they did it, it would be better, and by the third time it would probably be rather good. If it was a worthwhile idea.

Anthony Wilson:

What do you think of the way that the National Literacy and Numeracy Strategies recommend teachers to teach in certain structures? Do you have any advice to pass on about how to teach within them?

Ted Wragg:

The National Literacy and Numeracy Strategies were a hugely misplaced initiative. There is nothing wrong with having a big bash on literacy and numeracy. There is nothing wrong either with having available schemes of work or ideas about things that might be worth trying. What was wrong was to impose a uniform pattern on everybody.

The message there was compliance. And the first message people got from OFSTED – this is where it all started – was: 'If you're not doing the literacy and the numeracy hour as laid down in the book then you're probably going to be in deep trouble unless you can demonstrate that what you're doing as an alternative is far better'. And people didn't want to take that risk.

There was no reason, no research evidence – and I've worked in this field for thirty odd years – there's no research evidence either here or anywhere else, that having three parts to a numeracy hour is the best thing to have, or having four parts to a literacy hour. Why not four parts to a numeracy hour and three to a literacy hour? Who's to say?

So, that was misplaced, to pretend that there was a structure that was somehow superior and you could override the professional judgement of 200,000 primary teachers by telling them what they should do every day of the week with every age group from Reception right up to Year 6. It's crazy.

And the message was: 'Don't try and be creative, because you are going to be told what to do, and if you're not doing it, OFSTED is a compliance model, a ticking box, to see if you comply.' It may be changing, but that's the history of it.

Anthony Wilson:

Student teachers, as well as experienced teachers, find it hard, when they're being watched, to try out new things, even if they believe they are good practice. They feel, perhaps, that their ideas won't divide up neatly into the three- or four-part lesson.

Ted Wragg:

But this is across the board, you see. Here's a good example. I get head teachers saying to me now: 'Is the next generation of trainees going to be able to invent and inno-vate?' and I say they would like to, but then very often they have an idea and their classroom teacher says 'Well, I wouldn't do that if I were you, it's not in the QCA Schemes of Work.'

It's not that they don't want to; often the impression they get is: 'Play it safe, don't step out of line.'

And that's a very bad start in the profession, because among many people's motivation, not everybody, but among many people's motivation, is the belief that they can be creative, that they can use their imagination. Again, the research evidence shows over many years that if you look at why mature entrants leave a job that they've maybe done for ten or fifteen years, for teaching, very often they'll use a word like 'creative': 'I want to be able to use my imagination', 'I want to be more creative', 'I don't feel that my talents are being used in the job I'm in'. They see working with children as a creative enterprise. They then get very disappointed when they find that they are inhibited in it.

Anthony Wilson:
I know you have a story which exemplifies what you're saying a bit further.

Ted Wragg:
Bill Larr was talking to head teachers in Bristol just after there had been a sudden snow fall that had paralysed the city. And Bill said to these two hundred primary head teachers: 'Put your hand up if you did snow yesterday.' And very few hands went up. They were saying things like: 'Well, SATs are coming up' and 'We had SATs practice'. One even said: 'I was doing science'. And Bill said: 'Snow is science'. That just seems to me that that's an example of how people have lost courage.

Let me take this further. I'm not in favour of all the things that have gone on in primary education over the years, but one of the things that has been a real gain is that teachers have been willing to capitalise on something that they thought would grab children's attention: snow would be a good example. It doesn't snow every day, in fact nowadays with global warming you sometimes get five or six years with no snow at all, and when you suddenly get snow it's very exciting to kids and it's no use saying 'We do snow in May, or November'; or 'We don't do snow at all'. You know, it's there, use it while it's there. And that relates to another point, which is the literacy strategy was very weak on writing.

Everybody knew it was weak on writing from the beginning but people were scared to use their initiative and say: 'There's not enough on writing so I am going to do it.' People said: 'Well, you know, that's the Strategy, we better follow it.' But in fact, snow is a very good example of capitalising on something that will get children writing because they are interested in it.

The saddest letter I had for many years was from a primary head, who wrote to me saying that she had some boys who were not keen on writing: they couldn't see the purpose, why the hell should they write, there was no point. And she thought that if she took them to a farm to watch lambs being born, because it was the lambing season, this would move them to write: the miracle of birth.

But, unfortunately, it was OFSTED inspection week, so she said to the Registered Inspector: 'Would it be all right if we start off the literacy hour with a visit to a farm? It's not too far away. Then the kids can come back and write about it.' And he said: 'No, you have to start the literacy hour with fifteen minutes of shared text.' Well, that kind of knuckle-headed view of the curriculum just seems to me inane.

I was also talking to the geography advisor in a county where there are fantastic geographical features. He said that they look out of the window and they can see great coastal scenery and moors. But he told me the children in primary school had to study: 'Your High Street is dug up: what are the implications for traffic?' Why? Because that is what's in the QCA Schemes of Work. Well, all right, it's a perfectly interesting topic. But what about the stuff you can see out of the window? Which apparently they are not doing.

Anthony Wilson:
Projecting into the future a little, do you think that the pendulum will swing more towards a creative climate?

Ted Wragg:
It's swinging a bit.

Anthony Wilson:
But not terribly much?

Ted Wragg:
You see there's a massive, massive political terror. When the political parties lock horns, not just before an election, but between elections, they are all terrified that their image as being in control of education, which is what they see the right-wing tabloids want, will slip. They have to be seen to be telling schools what to do. It doesn't square with a policy of saying we want to trust teachers to use their imaginations more, or we want to give schools more freedom. On the one hand they say schools are going to have more freedom, then they say schools are going to have to introduce uniforms and have a house system. Well, are they free or not?

The same applies to the curriculum. Schools are told they are going to have more freedom, but then told exactly what they're going to have to teach and how. And that has been the big change in education: massive amounts have been prescribed. Back in 1980 I wrote an article called: 'State approved knowledge, ten steps down the slippery slope'. Of those ten steps, only one of them was in force at the time, which was the government having broad, generalised aspirations, like 'to give every child the opportunity to develop themselves fully'. (Only psychopaths would dissent!) But now we've got all ten, including the government saying what should be taught, the government saying how it should be taught, the government even firing teachers who don't follow their instructions. Which they have, people have been fired for not teaching the National Curriculum for example. And now, actually, you need to go further. I had to think of another ten steps because we've got all the first ten. For example, schools actually have to apply to the Minister, under the 2002 Education Act, to innovate.

Most schools don't know it, and I'm glad they don't know it, so they don't bother. But that is what you are supposed to do, and you are supposed to fill in a form describing how many people you've consulted about this innovation and what they've said. The biggest joke of all is the last section, called 'Exit Strategy'. It asks what schools will do when their licence to innovate has expired. It's beyond satire now.

Thank God they don't do that in medicine. You can imagine Christiaan Barnard going round saying: 'Me old heart's back so I'm going to have to stick it in because my licence has expired.' The whole point about innovation is that it should lead to better practice!

Anthony Wilson:
What's your response to politicians and the media complaining about 'trendy teaching methods'?

Ted Wragg:
The *Daily Mail* has a particular line on education which is that schools are full of trendy teachers doing wild unimaginable things, which bears no resemblance at all to the schools I go into. None at all. It is as remote from reality as Pluto.

For one thing, most teachers now are over forty. In fact, half the profession is over fifty. So the idea that these are wild hippies, throwing out crazy-horse ideas is nonsense.

Anthony Wilson:
If you had a handful of tips or words of advice for new trainees to remain creative, to remain 'courageous' as you put it earlier, how would you sum that up?

Ted Wragg:
Well, the first thing is that the climate will not be the same as it would have been two or three decades earlier. Now that's both a good and a bad thing. It's a bad thing, because there would have been – certainly when I started teaching in the 1960s – there was a feeling that you could have a go at something and people would say: 'Oh, well done, you had a go.' Even if it didn't work, at least you had had a go.

So the assumption was that teachers could try out ideas to see if they would work. And there was quite a feeling of excitement and a lot of new teachers in their twenties being recruited.

But then, the bad thing about it was there was no structure within which these ideas could fit.

So the good thing now is that we do have an outline National Curriculum where you can see where content fits, into the sort of work you do in Year 5, or whatever.

This puts us in a strong position, because it means that we could now have invention within a framework which is perfectly possible, unless the framework is so strong that it's a straitjacket. Then you can't have invention, because your arms are literally tied. You can't do anything imaginative. So, if people use the structure to give security and continuity and progression, but then branch out, then it's actually quite a good climate.

Second thing is that it is a matter of courage. And if new teachers are not courageous, who the hell else is going to be? People will always turn to newly qualified teachers. I think new teachers often don't realise how high the expectations are about them. They come in and see themselves as being the smallest piece of plankton in the food chain, but in practice, if they could have only eavesdropped on the conversations before they arrived, the other staff would have been saying 'Oh, we've got a new teacher coming in September, and we're hoping that they will do...' and then they'd have a long shopping list, some of which would be innovation: 'We're hoping that they'd have fresh ides on this that and the other.' Schools also look for new skills: for example, they hope their recruits will be IT literate, and more secure with new technology.

There are often high hopes that the new person will actually be miles better than the people that have been doing the job for years. Which of course you can't live up to, but at least you can capitalise on the climate of goodwill.

Anthony Wilson:
Finally, are you optimistic about the potential for the general discussion or debate about creativity to remain ongoing?

Ted Wragg:
Yes. I am positive. By nature I'm an optimist. I remember a very good biologist I know saying that to be a biologist you need to believe in regeneration. There's an analogy with forests burning down and growing again and so on: even if the teaching profession gets beleaguered and things are too prescriptive, humanity has a habit of bouncing back in the same way. We do like to look past the obstacles and see them off.

So, yes, I am optimistic. I also think the other good thing about teaching is that you've got 24,000 schools and over 400,000 teachers and therefore when you're working on that scale, there should always be some places and some individuals, some groups, who as Peter Abbs put it, go against the flow. They row upstream.

Which is not easy, but it is nice to know that there is a constituency out there that would have a go. So yes, I feel an optimist because I think the system is big enough for a number of people to buck the trend and the main thing is that they actually tell people about what they are doing, and feel proud about it, not shamed or apprehensive.

Adams, E. (2003a) *Power Drawing*. London: Drawing Power, The Campaign for Drawing.

Adams, E. (2003b) *Start Drawing*. London: Drawing Power, The Campaign for Drawing.

Addison, N. and Burgess, L. (2000) Learning in art, in *Learning to Teach Art and Design in the Secondary School*. London: Routledge Falmer.

Adorno, T. W. (1950) *The Authoritarian Personality*. New York: Harper & Bros.

Adorno, T. W. (1991) *The Culture Industry: Selected Essays on Mass Culture*. London: Routledge.

Ahtee, M. and Rikkinen, H. (1995) Luokanopettajaksi opiskelevien mielikuvia fysiikasta, kemiasta, biologiasta ja maantieteestä (Primary student teachers' images about physics, chemistry, biology and geography), *Dimensio*, 59, 54–8.

Ahtee, M. and Telia, S. (1995) Future class teachers' images of their school-time teachers of physics, mathematics and foreign languages, in S. Telia (ed.), *Juuret ja arvot: Etnisyys ja eettisyys – aineen opettaminen monikultturisessa oppimisympäristössä (Roots and Values: Ethnicity and Ethics – Teaching a Subject in a Multicultural Learning Environment)*. Proceedings of a subject-didactic symposium in Helsinki. Department of Teacher Education, University of Helsinki, Research Report 150, pp. 180–200.

Aires, J., Wright, J., Williams, L. and Adkins, R. (2004) The performing arts, in R. Jones and D. Wyse (eds), *Creativity in the Primary Curriculum*. London: David Fulton.

Amabile, T. M. (1983) *The Social Psychology of Creativity*. New York: Springer Verlag.

Amabile, T. M. (1988) A model of creativity and innovation in organizations, in B. M. Staw and L. L. Cunnings (eds), *Research in Organizational Behavior*. Greenwich, CT: JAI Press.

Amabile, T. M. (1996) *Creativity in Context (Update to The Social Psychology of Creativity)*. Boulder, CO: Westview Press.

Amabile, T. M. (1997) Motivating creativity in organisations: on doing what you love and loving what you do. *California Management Review*, 40 (1).

Andreasan, N. C. and Powers, P. S. (1974) Over-inclusive thinking in mania and schizophrenia, *British Journal of Psychiatry*, 125, 425–56.

Anning, A. and Ring, K. (2004) *Making Sense of Children's Drawings*. Maidenhead: Open University Press.

Armitage, S. (ed.) (2002) *Short and Sweet: 101 Very Short Poems*. London: Faber & Faber.

ASE (1999) *ASE Survey on the Effect of the National Literacy Strategy on the Teaching of Science*. Hatfield: ASE.

Askew, M., Brown, M., Rhodes, V., Wiliam, D. and Johnson, D. (1997) *Effective Teachers of Numeracy: A Report of a Study Carried Out for the Teacher Training Agency*. London: King's College, University of London.

Atkinson, D. (2002) *Art in Education: Identity and Practice*. London: Kluwer.

Atkinson, J. (1985) How children read poems at different ages, *English in Education*, 19 (1), 24–34.

Auden, W. H. (1979) *Selected poems*, ed. E. Mendelson. London: Faber & Faber.

Auden, W. H. and Garrett, J. (1935) Introduction to *The Poet's Tongue*, in E. Mendelson (ed.) (1996), *W. H. Auden, Prose 1926–1938: Essays and Reviews and Travel Books in Prose and Verse*. London: Faber & Faber.

Bailey, R. and Macfadyen, T. (eds) (2000) *Teaching Physical Education 5–11*. London: Continuum.

Balaam, J. and Merrick, B. (1987) *Teaching Poetry 5–8*. Sheffield: NATE.

Balke, E. (1997) Play and the arts: the importance of the 'unimportant'. *Childhood Education*, 73 (6), 353–60.

Barnes, D. (1992) The role of talk in learning, in K. Norman (ed.), *Thinking Voices*. London: Hodder & Stoughton, .p 125.

Barrett, M. (1979) *Art Education: A Strategy for Course Design*. London: Heinemann.

Barrs, M. (2000) The reader in the writer, *Reading Literacy and Language*, 34 (2), 54–60.

Barrs, M. and Cork, V. (2001) *The Reader in the Writer: The Influence of Literature upon Writing at KS2*. London: Centre for Literacy in Primary Education.

Beetlestone, F. (1998) *Creative Children, Imaginative Teaching*. Buckingham: Open University Press.

Benn, T. and Benn, B. (1992) *Primary Gymnastics – A Multi-activities Approach.* Cambridge: Cambridge University Press.

Benson, C. (1992) *Design and Technology at Key Stages 1 and 2.* York: Longman.

Benton, M. (1978) Poetry for children: a neglected art, *Children's Literature in Education,* 9 (3), 111–26.

Benton, M. and Fox, G. (1985) *Teaching Literature: Nine to Fourteen.* Oxford: Oxford University Press.

Benton, P. (1986) *Pupil, Teacher, Poem.* London: Hodder & Stoughton Educational.

Bereiter, C. and Scardamalia, M. (1987) *The Psychology of Written Composition.* Hillsdale, NJ: Lawrence Erlbaum Associates.

Berninger, V. W., Fuller, F. and Whittaker, D. (1996) A process model of writing development across the life span, *Educational Psychology Review,* 8(3), 193–218.

Board of Education (1933) *Syllabus of Physical Training for Schools.* London: HMSO.

Boden, M. (1992) *The Creative Mind.* London: Abacus.

Boden, M. A. (2001) Creativity and knowledge, in A. Craft, B. Jeffrey and M. Leibling (eds), *Creativity in Education.* London: Continuum.

Bohm, D. and Peat, P.D. (1989) *Science, Order and Creativity.* London: Routledge.

Booth, D. (1996) *Story Drama: Reading, Writing and Role Playing across the Curriculum.* Markham: Pembroke Publishers.

Bowler, T. (2002) Write off your plans and go with the flow, *Times Educational Supplement,* 16 August.

Bray, S. (1992) *Fitness Fun.* Crediton: Southgate Publishers.

Brice Heath, S. (1983) *Ways with Words: Language, Life and Work in Communities and Classrooms.* Cambridge: Cambridge University Press.

Bricheno, P., Johnston, J. and Sears, J. (2001) Children's attitudes to science, in J. Sears and P. Sorensen (eds), *Issues in the Teaching of Science.* London: Routledge.

Briggs, M. (1998) The right baggage? in A. Olivier and K. Newstead (eds), *Proceedings of the 22nd Conference of the International Group for the Psychology of Mathematics Education, Stellenbosch, South Africa,* Vol. 2, pp. 152–9.

Briggs, M. (2000) Feel free to be flexible, *Special Children.* Hertfordshire: Questions, pp. 1–8.

Briggs, M., Daniell, J., Farncombe, J., Lenton, N. and Stonehouse, A. (2002) Wizarding maths, *Mathematics Teaching,* 180, 23–7.

British Association of Advisors and Lecturers in Physical Education (BAALPE) (2004) *Safe Practice in Physical Education.* Dudley: Dudley LEA.

Britton, J. (1982) *Prospect and Retrospect,* ed. G. M. Pradl. Montclair, NJ: Boynton/Cook.

Browne, A. (1990) *Piggybook.* London: Julia MacRae Books.

Browne, A. (1999) *Willy and Hugh.* London: Julia MacRae Books.

Brownjohn, S. (1994) *To Rhyme or Not to Rhyme?* London: Hodder & Stoughton.

Bruner, J. S. (1962) *On Knowing: Essays for the Left Hand.* Cambridge, MA: Harvard University Press.

Bruner, J. S. (1979) *On Knowing: Essays for the Left Hand.* Cambridge, MA: Belknap Press of Harvard University Press.

Bruner, J. S. (1986) *Actual Minds, Possible Worlds.* Cambridge, MA: Harvard University Press.

Bruner, J. S. (1996) *The Culture of Education.* Cambridge, MA: Harvard University Press.

Buchanan, K., Chadwick, S. and Dacey, L. (1996) *Music Connections: Practical Music for All Primary Class Teachers, Key Stages 1 and 2.* London: Cramer Music.

Burnard, P. and Younker, B. A. (2002) Mapping pathways: fostering creativity in composition, *Music Education Research,* 4 (2), 245–62.

Buxton, L. (1981) *Do You Panic about Mathematics?* London: Heinemann.

CAGE (Central Advisory Council for Education in England) (1967) *Children and Their Primary Schools, Report of the Central Advisory Council for Education in England (The Plowden Report).* London: HMSO.

CARA (2005) See website: **www.creative-partnerships.com/events/27150?view= Standard**.

Carter, D. (1998) *Teaching Poetry in the Primary School: Perspectives for a New Generation.* London: David Fulton.

Carter, R. (2004) *Language and Creativity: The Art of Common Talk.* London: Routledge.

Carter, S., Mason, C. and Tagg, S. (2004) *Lifting the Barriers to Growth in UK Small Businesses: The FSB Biennial Membership Survey, Report to the Federation of Small Businesses*. London: Federation of Small Businesses.

Chalmers, F.G. (1996) *Celebrating Pluralism: Art Education and Cultural Diversity*. Los Angeles, CA: Getty Education Institute for the Arts.

Chambers, A. (1993) *Tell Me: Children, Reading and Talk*. Stroud: Thimble Press.

Chedzoy, S. (1996) *Physical Education for Teachers and Coordinators at Key Stages 1 and 2*. London: David Fulton.

Chedzoy, S. (2000) *Physical Education in the School Grounds*. Crediton: Southgate Publishers.

Childs, D. (1986) *Psychology and the Teacher* (4th edn). Chatham: Holt, Rinehart & Winston.

Claire, H. (2001) *Not Aliens: Primary School Children and the PSHE/Citizenship Curriculum*. Stoke-on-Trent: Trentham.

Claire, H. (ed.) (2004) *Teaching Citizenship in Primary Schools*. Exeter: Learning Matters.

Claxton, G. (1997) *Hare Brain, Tortoise Mind: Why Intelligence Increases When You Think Less*. London: Fourth Estate.

Claxton, G. (1999) *Wise Up*. London: Bloomsbury.

Claxton, G. (2000) The anatomy of intuition, in T. Atkinson and G. Claxton (eds), *The Intuitive Practitioner*. Buckingham and Philadelphia: Open University Press.

Clough, N. and Holden, C. (2002) *Education for Citizenship: Ideas into Action. A Practical Guide for Teachers of Pupils Aged 7–14*. London: Routledge Falmer.

Collins, A. and Gentner, D. (1980) A framework for a cognitive theory of writing, in L. W. Gregg and E. R. Steinberg (eds), *Cognitive Processes in Writing*. Hillsdale, NJ: Lawrence Erlbaum Associates.

Corden, R. (2000) *Literacy and Learning Through Talk Strategies for the Primary Classroom*. Birmingham: Open University Press.

Cosgrove, M. and Osborne, R. (1985) Lesson frameworks for changing children's ideas, in R. Osborne and P. Freyberg (eds), *Learning in Science: The Implications of Children's Learning*. Auckland: Heinemann.

Costello, P. J. M. (2000) *Thinking Skills and Early Childhood Education*. London: David Fulton.

Coulson, J. (1999) An hour a day helps them spell, read (and play!), *Teachers*, 1, 8–9.

Craft, A. (1997) Identity and creativity: education for post-modernism? *Teacher Development: International Journal of Teachers' Professional Development*, 1 (1), 83–96.

Craft, A. (2000) *Creativity Across the Primary Curriculum: Framing and Developing Practice*. London: Routledge Falmer.

Craft, A. (2001) Little c creativity, in A. Craft, B. Jeffrey and M. Leibling (eds), *Creativity in Education*. London: Continuum.

Craft, A. (2002) *Creativity and Early Years Education*. London: Continuum.

Craft, A. (2003a) Early Years education in England and little c creativity: the third wave? *Korean Journal of Thinking and Problem Solving*, 13 (1), 49–57.

Craft, A. (2003b) Limits to creativity in education: dilemmas for the educator, *British Journal of Educational Studies*, 51 (2), 113–27.

Craft, A. (2004) Creative thinking in the Early Years of education, in M. Fryer (ed.), *Creativity and Cultural Diversity*. Leeds: Creativity Centre Educational Trust.

Craft, A. (in press) *Creativity in Schools: Tensions and Dilemmas*. London: Routledge Falmer.

Craft, A., Miell, D., Joubert, M., Littleton, K., Murphy, P., Vass, E. and Whitelock, D. (2004) *Final Report for the NESTA's Fellowship Young People Project, Ignite*. September.

Crawford, R., Hart, H., Kinloch, D. and Price, R. (eds) (1995) *Talking Verse: Interviews with Poets*. St Andrews and Williamsburg, VA: University of St Andrews and College of William and Mary.

Creative Partnerships (2004) See website: **www.creative-partnerships.com/news/ pressreleases/28584** (last accessed 28/1/05).

Creative Partnerships (2005) website: **www.creatve-partnerships.com/** (last accessed 26/1/05).

Crick, B. (1998) *Education for Citizenship and the Teaching of Democracy in Schools: Final Report of the Advisory Group on Citizenship* (The Crick Report). London: QCA.

Cropley, A. J. (2001) *Creativity in Education and Learning: A Guide for Teachers and Educators*. London: Kogan Page.

Cross, K. (2004) Engagement and excitement in mathematics, *Mathematics Teaching*, 189, 4–6.

Csikszentmihalyi, M. (1997) *Creativity, Flow and the Psychology of Discovery and Invention*. London: Rider.

Csikszentmihalyi, M. (2002) *Flow*. London: Rider.

Csikszentmihalyi, M. and Epstein, R. (1999) A creative dialog, *Psychology Today*, July.

Cullingford, C. (1996) Changes in primary education, in C. Cullingford, *The Politics of Primary Education*. Buckingham: Open University Press.

Daniels, H. (2002) *Literature Circles: Choice and Voice in Book Clubs and Reading Groups*. Portland, OR: Stenhouse Publishers.

Davies, B. (2003) Working with primary school children to deconstruct gender, in C. Skelton and B. Francis (eds), *Boys and Girls in the Primary Classroom*. Buckingham: Open University Press.

Davies, D., Howe, A. and Haywood, S. (2004) Building a creative ecosystem – the Young Designers on Location Project, *International Journal of Art and Design Education*, 23 (3), 278–89.

de Bono, E. (1992) *Serious Creativity*. London: HarperCollins.

de Bóo, M. (1999) *Enquiring Children: Challenging Teaching*. Buckingham: Open University Press.

de Bóo, M. (ed.) (2004) *Early Years Handbook. Support for Practitioners in the Foundation Stage*. Sheffield: Curriculum Partnership/Geography Association.

De Mello, A. (1984) *The Song of the Bird*. New York: Doubleday.

Department for Education (DfE) (1995) *English in the National Curriculum*. London: HMSO.

Department for Education and Employment (DfEE) (1998) *The National Literacy Strategy: Framework for Teaching*. London: HMSO.

Department for Education and Employment (DfEE) (1999a) *All Our Futures: Creativity, Culture and Education. The National Advisory Committee's Report on Creative and Cultural Education*. London: HMSO.

Department for Education and Employment (DfEE) (1999b) *The National Curriculum for England: Information and Communication Technology*. London: DfEE.

Department for Education and Employment (DfEE) (1999c) *The National Curriculum: Handbook for Primary Teachers in England*. London: DfEE.

Department for Education and Employment (DfEE) (1999d) *The National Numeracy Strategy*. London: DfEE.

Department for Education and Employment (DfEE) (2000) *Curriculum Guidance for the Foundation Stage*. London: QCA.

Department for Education and Employment/Qualifications and Curriculum Authority (DfEE/QCA) (1999a) *English: The National Curriculum for England (Key Stages 1–4)*. London: Stationery Office.

Department for Education and Employment/Qualifications and Curriculum Authority (DfEE/QCA) (1999b) *The National Curriculum: Handbook for Primary Teachers in England, Key Stages 1 and 2*. London: QCA.

Department for Education and Employment/Qualifications and Curriculum Authority (DFEE/QCA) (1999c) *The National Curriculum: Handbook for Teachers in Key Stages 3 and 4*. London: QCA.

Department for Education and Employment/Qualifications and Curriculum Authority (DfEE/QCA) (1999d) *Physical Education: The National Curriculum for England*. London. HMSO.

Department for Education and Employment/Qualifications and Curriculum Authority (DfEE/QCA) (1999e) *The National Curriculum*. London: HMSO.

Department for Education and Skills (DfES) (2000) *The National Curriculum for England and Wales*. London: HMSO.

Department for Education and Skills (DfES) (2003) *Excellence and Enjoyment*. London: HMSO.

Department for Education and Skills (DfES) (2004a) *A National Conversation about Personalised Learning*. Nottingham: DfES Publications.

Department for Education and Skills (DfES) (2004b) *Excellence and Enjoyment: A Strategy for Primary Schools*. London: DfES.

Department for Education and Skills (DfES) (2004c) *High Quality PE and Sport for Young People: A Guide to Recognising and Achieving High Quality PE and Sport in Schools*. London: DfES.

Department for Education and Skills (DfES) (2004d) *Personalised Learning for Every Child, Personalised Contact for Every Teacher*, Press Notice 2004/0050.

Department for Education and Skills (DfES) (2004e) Personalised learning around each child. See website: **www.standards.dfes.gov.uk/personalisedlearning/about/** (last accessed December 2004).

Department for Education and Skills (DfES) (2005a) See website: **www.standards.dfee. gov.uk/excellence** (last accessed 24/1/05).

Department for Education and Skills (DfES) (2005b) See website: **www.teachernet. gov.uk/ professionaldevelopment/resourcesandresearch/bprs/search/** (last accessed 24/1/05)

Department for Education and Skills/Department for Culture, Media and Sport (DfES/DCMS) (2004) *Learning Through Physical Education and Sport: A Guide to the School Sport and Club Links Strategy.* London: DfES.

Department for Education and Skills/Department for Culture, Media and Sport (DfES/DCMS) (2005) *Do You Have High Quality PE and School Sport in Your School?* London: DfES.

Department for Education and Skills/Qualifications and Curriculum Authority (DfES/QCA) (1999) *Mathematics: The National Curriculum in England and Wales.* London: DfES.

Department for Education and Skills/Qualifications and Curriculum Authority (DfES/QCA) (2003a) *Speaking, Listening, Learning: Working with Children in Key Stages 1 and 2.* London: DfES.

Department for Education and Skills/Qualifications and Curriculum Authority (DfES/QCA) (2003b) *Creativity: Find It! Promote It!* London: DfES.

Department of Education and Science (DES) (1967) *Children and Their Primary School. A Report of the Central Advisory Council for Education (England) Vol. 1: Report.* London: HMSO.

Department of Education and Science (DES) (1972) *Movement – Physical Education in the Primary Years.* London: HMSO.

Department of Education and Science (DES) (1975) *A Language for Life: A Report of the Committee of Inquiry into Reading and the Use of English* (The Bullock Report). London: HMSO.

Department of Education and Science (DES) (1987) *Teaching Poetry in the Secondary School: An HMI View.* London: HMSO.

Department of Education and Science (DES) (1989) *English in the National Curriculum.* London: HMSO.

Department of Education and Science/Welsh Office (DES/WO) (1991) *Physical Education for Ages 5 to 16: Proposals of the Secretary of State for Education and Science and the Secretary of State for Wales.* London: HMSO.

Department of Education and Science/Welsh Office (DES/WO) (1990) *English in the National Curriculum.* London: HMSO.

Department of Trade and Industry (DTI) (2005) See website: **www.dti.gov.uk/ bestpractice/innovation/innovation-creativity.htm** (last accessed 26/1/05).

Design and Technology Association (DATA)/Nuffield Foundation (2003) *Creativity in Crisis?* Wellesbourne, Warwickshire: DATA.

Devon Local Education Authority (LEA) (2002) *A Devon Approach to Physical Education: Curriculum Gymnastics.* Devon: Devon Curriculum Advice.

Dewey, J. (1933) *How We Think.* Boston, MA: Heath & Co.

Dewey, J. (1938) *Experience and Education.* New York: Macmillan.

Dixon, B. (1977) *Catching Them Young with Political Ideas.* London: Pluto Press.

Dixon, B. (1977) *Catching Them Young: Sex, Race and Class in Children's Fiction.* London: Pluto Press.

Donaldson, Margaret (1978) *Children's Minds.* London: Fontana.

Dowie, J. (1999) Against risk, *Risk Decision and Policy,* 4 (1), 57–73.

Dowie, J. (2005) The Mermaid and the Bayesian (in circulation). Available by sending an e-mail with subject 'Send Mermaid' to **jack.dowie@lshtm.ac.uk**.

Duffy, B. (1998) *Supporting Creativity and Imagination in the Early Years.* Buckingham: Open University Press.

Dunn, J., Styles, M. and Warburton, N. (1987) *In Tune with Yourself: Children Writing Poetry: A Handbook for Teachers.* Cambridge: Cambridge University Press.

Dunn, S. (2001) *Walking Light: Memoirs and Essays on Poetry* (new and expanded edition). New York: BOA Editions.

Durant, A. (2003) *Dear Tooth Fairy.* London: Walker Books.

Dust, K. (1999) *Motive, Means and Opportunity: Creativity Research Review.* London: NESTA.

Johnston, J., Ahtee, M. and Hayes, M. (1998) Elementary teachers' perceptions of science and science teaching: comparisons between Finland and England, in S. Kartinen (ed.), *Matemaattisten aineiden opetus ja opiminem*. Oulu: Oulun yliopistopaino, pp. 13–30.

Jones, A. and Mulford, J. (1971) *Children Using Language: An Approach to English in the Primary School*. Oxford: Oxford University Press.

Jones, C. (2000) The role of language in the learning and teaching of science, in M. Monk and J. Osborne (eds), *Good Practice in Science Teaching. What Research Has to Say*. Buckingham: Open University Press.

Kahn, P. H. Jr (1999) *The Human Relationship with Nature*. Cambridge, MA: MIT Press.

Karplus, R. (1977) *Science Teaching and the Development of Reasoning*. Berkeley, CA: University of California Press.

Kellogg, R. T. (1994) *The Psychology of Writing*. Oxford: Oxford University Press.

Keogh, B. and Naylor, S. (2000) Assessment in the Early Years, in M. de Bóo (ed.), *Laying the Foundations in the Early Years*. Hatfield: ASE.

Kerr, A. (2002) An ode to the literacy hour, *Times Educational Supplement*, 22 November, p. 25.

Kessler, R. (2000) *The Soul of Education: Helping Students Find Connection, Compassion and Character at School*. Alexandria, VA: Association for Supervision and Curriculum Development.

Kimbell, R. (2000) Creativity in crisis. *Journal of Design and Technology Education*, 5 (3), 206–11.

Kimbell, R., Stables, K., Wheeler, T., Wozniak, A. and Kelly, A. V. (1991) *The Assessment of Performance in Design and Technology*. London: Evaluation and Monitoring Unit (EMU), School Examinations and Assessment Council (SEAC).

King, J. (1992) *The Art of Mathematics*. New York and London: Plenum Press.

King, J. (1998) *Take a Lesson in Poetry*. Slough: Foulsham Educational.

Klassen, S. and Struthers, B. (eds) (1995) *Poets in the Classroom*. Markham, Ont.: Pembroke Publishers.

Koch, K. (1991) *Selected Poems*. Manchester: Carcanet Press.

Koch, K. (1996) *The Art of Poetry: Poems, Parodies, Interviews, Essays, and Other Work*. Ann Arbor, MI: University of Michigan Press.

Koch, K. (1999) *Making Your Own Days: The Pleasures of Reading and Writing Poetry*. New York: Simon & Schuster.

Koestler, A. (1964) *The Act of Creation*. London: Macmillan.

Koulaidis, V. and Ogborn, J. (1989) Philosophy of science: an empirical study of teachers' views, *International Journal of Science Education*, 11 (2), 173–84.

Lave, J. and Wenger, E. (1991) *Situated Learning. Legitimate Peripheral Participation*. Cambridge: Cambridge University Press.

Leach, J. (2001) A hundred possibilities: creativity, community and ICT, in A. Craft, B. Jeffrey and M. Leibling (eds), *Creativity in Education*. London: Continuum.

Lederman, N. G. and Zeidler, D. L. (1987) Science teachers' conceptions of the nature of science: do they really influence teaching behaviour? *Science Education*, 71, 721–34.

Longbottom, J. (1999) *Science Education for Democracy: Dilemmas, Decisions, Autonomy and Anarchy*. Paper presented to the European Science Education Research Association Second International Conference, Kiel, Germany.

Loveless, A. (1999a) *Art on the Net Evaluation – Report to South East Arts, Lighthouse and DCMS*. Brighton: University of Brighton.

Loveless, A. (1999b) A digital big breakfast: the Glebe School Project, in J. Sefton-Green (ed.), *Young People, Creativity and New Technology: The Challenge of Digital Arts*. London: Routledge.

Loveless, A. and Taylor, T. (2000) Creativity, visual literacy and ICT, in M. Leask and J. Meadows (eds), *Teaching and Learning with ICT in the Primary School*. London: Routledge, pp. 65–80.

Loveless, A., Burton, J. and Turvey, K. (2006) Developing conceptual frameworks for creativity, ICT and teacher education. *International Journal of Teaching for Thinking and Creativity*, 1(1).

Lowenfeld, V. and Brittain, W. L. (1982) *Creative and Mental Growth*. New York: Macmillan.

Macdonald, A. M. (1972) *Chambers Twentieth Century Dictionary*. London: W & R Chambers.

Macdonald, S. (2004) *The History and Philosophy of Art Education*. Cambridge: Lutterworth Press.

Mahy, M. (1981) *The Great Piratical Rumbustification and The Librarian and the Robbers*. London: Puffin.

Edwards, C. P. and Springate, K. W. (1995) *Encouraging Creativity in Early Childhood Classrooms*, ERIC Digest. Washington, DC: ERIC Clearing House on Elementary and Early Childhood Education.

Efland, A. (1990) *A History of Art Education: Intellectual and Social Currents in Teaching the Visual Arts*. New York: Teachers College Press.

Eisner, E. W. (1985) *The Educational Imagination: On the Design and Evaluation of School Programmes*. London: Macmillan.

Eisner, E. W. (2002) *The Arts and the Creation of Mind*. New Haven, CT: Yale University Press.

Elliott, D. J. (1995) *Music Matters*. New York: Oxford University Press.

Emig, J. (1988) Writing, composition and rhetoric, in N. Mercer (ed.), *Language and Literacy from an Educational Perspective*, Vol. 1. Buckingham: Open University Press.

Erikson, E. H. (1950) *Childhood and Society*. New York: Norton.

Ernest, P. (2000) Teaching and learning mathematics, in V. Koshy, P. Ernest and R. Casey, *Mathematics for Primary Teachers*. London: Routledge.

Fasciato, M. and Rogers, M. (2005) *Creativity in Practice*, Design Technology Association Annual Conference, Sheffield Hallam University, 7–9 July.

Feldman, D. H. (1999) The development of creativity, in R. J. Sternberg (ed.), *Handbook of Creativity*. Cambridge: Cambridge University Press, pp. 169–88.

Feldman, D. H., Csikszentmihalyi, M. and Gardner, H. (1994) *Changing the World: A Framework for the Study of Creativity*. Westport, CT and London: Praeger.

Fensham, P. J. (2001) Science content as problematic – issues for research, in H. Behrendt, H. Dahncke, R. Duit, W. Graber, M. Komorek, A. Kross and P. Reiska (eds), *Research in Science Education – Past, Present and Future*. Dordrecht: Kluwer Academic.

Fischmann, W., Solomon, B., Greenspan, D. and Gardner, H. (2004) *Making Good: How YA Cope with Moral Dilemmas at Work*. Cambridge, MA: Harvard University Press.

Fisher, R. (2002) Shared thinking: metacognitive modelling in the literacy hour, *Reading: Literacy and Language*, 36 (2), 63–7.

Fisher, R. (2003) *Teaching Thinking*. London: Continuum.

Flutter, J. (2000) *Words Matter: Thinking and Talking about Writing in the Classroom*. NFERTopicOnline, 1, 23.

Fox, C. (1993) *At the Very Edge of the Forest: The Influence of Literature on Storytelling by Children*. London: Cassell.

Fox, R. (ed.) (1996) *Perspectives on Constructivism*. Exeter: University of Exeter Media and Resources Centre.

Fraser, B. and Tobin, K. (1993) Exemplary science and mathematics teachers, in B. Fraser (ed.), *Research Implications for Science and Mathematics Teachers*, Vol. 1. Perth, WA: National Key Centre for School Science and Mathematics, Curtin University of Technology.

Frater, G. (2001) *Effective Practice in Writing at Key Stage 2: Essential Extras*. London: Basic Skills Agency.

Fryer, M. (1996) *Creative Teaching and Learning*. London: Paul Chapman Publishing.

Gardner, H. (1983) *Frames of Mind: The Theory of Multiple Intelligences*. London: Heinemann.

Gardner, H. (1991) *The Unschooled Mind*. London: Fontana.

Gardner, H. (1999) *The Disciplined Mind*. New York: Simon & Schuster.

Gardner, H. (2004) *Can There Be Societal Trustees in America Today?* Working paper, Harvard Graduate School of Education, November.

Glover, J. (2000) *Children Composing 4–14*. London: Routledge Falmer.

Goodkin, D. (1997) *A Rhyme in Time: Rhythm, Speech Activities and Improvisation for the Classroom*. Miami, FL: Warner Bros Publications.

Goodwin, P. (2005) *The Literate Classroom* (2nd edn). London: David Fulton.

Gower, K. (2005) Planning in PE, in S. Capel (ed.), *Learning to Teach Physical Education in the Secondary School*. Abingdon: Routledge Falmer.

Graham, G. (1997) *Philosophy of the Arts: An Introduction to Aesthetics*. London: Routledge.

Graham, L. and Johnson, A. (2003) *Writing Journals*. Cambridge: United Kingdom Reading Association.

Graham, L (2001) 'From *Tyrannosaurus Rex* to Pokemon: autonomy in the teaching of writing'. *Reading, Literacy and Language*, 35(1): 18–26

Grainger, T. (1997) *Traditional Storytelling in the Primary Classroom*. Milton Keynes: Scholastic.

Grainger, T. (2003a) Creative teachers and the language arts: possibilities and potential, *Education 3–13*, 31 (1), 43–8.

Grainger, T. (2003b) Exploring the unknown: drama, ambiguity and meaning making, in E. Bearne, H. Dombey and T. Grainger (eds), *Classroom Interactions in Literacy*. Buckingham: Open University Press.

Grainger, T. and Cremin, M. (2001) *Resourcing Classroom Drama 5–8*. Sheffield: National Association for the Teaching of English.

Grainger, T., Goouch, K. and Lambirth, A. (2003) Playing the game called writing: children's views and voices, *English in Education*, 37(2), 4–15.

Grainger, T., Goouch, K. and Lambirth, A. (2004) *Creative Activities for Plot, character and setting, 5–7, 7–9, 9–11*. Milton Keynes: Scholastic.

Grainger, T., Goouch, K. and Lambirth, A. (2005) *Creativity and Writing: Developing Voice and Verve in the Classroom*. London: Routledge.

Griffiths, M. and Woolf, F. (2004) *Report on Creative Partnerships Nottingham Action Research*. Nottingham: Nottingham Trent University.

Growney, C. (2005) *Primary Design and Technology and Citizenship*. See website: **www.citized. info/pdf/commarticles/Cathy_Growney.pdf**.

Grugeon, E. and Gardner, P. (2000) *The Art of Storytelling for Teachers and Pupils*. London: David Fulton.

Guilford, J. P. (1950) Creativity, *American Psychologist*, 5, 444–54.

Guilford, J. P. (1967) *The Nature of Human Intelligence*. New York: McGraw-Hill.

Halliwell, S. (1993) Teacher creativity and teacher education, in D. Bridges and T. Kerry (eds), *Developing Teachers Professionally*. London: Routledge.

Hardy, B. (1977) Towards a poetics of fiction: an approach through narrative, in M. Meek, A. Warlow and G. Barton (eds), *The Cool Web*. London: The Bodley Head.

Hardy, G. H. (1941) *A Mathematician's Apology*. London: Cambridge University Press.

Harnett, P. *et al.* (2005) *My 'Self' and the Wider World: Interpreting the British Empire and Commonwealth Museum*. See website: **www.citized.info/pdfycommarticles/Penelope_ Harnett.pdf**.

Harrington, D. M. (1990) The ecology of human creativity: a psychological perspective, in M. A. Runco and R. S. Albert (eds), *Theories of Creativity*. London: Sage.

Hartley. D. (2003) The instrumentalisation of the expressive in education. *British Journal of Educational Studies*, 51 (1), 6–19.

Hawkey, R. (2001) Science beyond school: representation or re-presentation? in A. Loveless and V. Ellis (eds), *ICT, Pedagogy and the Curriculum: Subject to Change*. London: Routledge.

Hayes, J. R. and Flower, L. S. (1980) Identifying the organisation of writing processes, in L. W. Gregg and E. R. Steinberg (eds), *Cognitive Processes in Writing*. Hillsdale, NJ: Lawrence Erlbaum Associates.

Heaney, S. (1988) *The Government of the Tongue: the 1986 T. S. Eliot Memorial Lectures and Other Critical Writings*. London: Faber & Faber.

Hennessy, S. (1995) *Music 7–11: Developing Primary Teaching Skills*. London: Routledge.

Hennessy, S. (1998a) *Coordinating Music Across the Primary School*. London: Falmer Press.

Hennessy, S. (1998b) Teaching composing in the primary curriculum, in M. Littledyke and L. Huxford (eds), *Teaching the Primary Curriculum for Constructive Learning*. London: David Fulton.

Henry, J. (2001) Warning to cool the test frenzy, *Times Educational Supplement*, 2 November, p. 8

Herbert, W. N. and Hollis, M. (eds) (2000) *Strong Words: Modern Poets on Modern Poetry*. Newcastle upon Tyne: Bloodaxe Books.

Hicks, D. (2003) Thirty years of global education: a reminder of key principles and precedents, *Educational Review*, 55 (3), 265–75.

Hicks, D. and Holden, C. (1995) *Visions of the Future: Why We Need to Teach for Tomorrow*. Stoke-on-Trent: Trentham.

HMI (2003) *Expect the unexpected: creativity in successful primary schools*. E-publication.

Hobsbaum, A., Gamble, N. and Reedy, D. (2002) *Guiding Reading*. London: Institute of Education.

Hoffman, M. (1991) *Amazing Grace*. London: Frances Lincoln.

Holden, C. (2005) The citizenship challenge: educating children about the real world and real issues, in A. Ross (ed.), *Teaching Citizenship*. London: CiCe, University of North London.

Holden, J. (2004) *Creative Reading: Young People, Reading and Public Libraries*. London: DEMOS.

Hopper, B., Grey, J. and Maude, T. (2000) *Teaching Physical Education in the Primary School*. London: Routledge Falmer.

Hornsby, A. (1991) Sports day: a cross-curricular approach to planning, *Primary P.E. Focus*, Summer, 11–12.

Howe, A., Davies, D. and Ritchie, R. (2001) *Primary Design and Technology for the Future: Creativity, Culture and Citizenship in the Curriculum*. London: David Fulton.

Hubbard, R. S. (1996) *A Workshop of the Possible: Nurturing Children's Creative Development*. York, ME: Stenhouse Publishers.

Hughes, M. (1999) The National Numeracy Strategy: are we getting it right? *Psychology of Education Review*, 23 (2), 3–7.

Hughes, T. (1967) *Poetry in the Making*. London: Faber & Faber.

Hughes, T. (1988) Myth and education, in K. Egan and D. Nadaner (eds), *Imagination and Education*. Milton Keynes: Open University Press, pp. 30–44.

Imison, T. (2001) Creative leadership: innovative practices in a secondary school, in A. Craft, B. Jeffrey and M. Leibling (eds), *Creativity in Education*. London: Continuum.

Inkpen, M. (1992) *Kipper's Toybox*. London: Hodder & Stoughton.

Jeffrey, B. (2001a) Challenging prescription in ideology and practice: the case of Sunny first school, in J. Collins, K. Insley and J. Soler (eds), *Developing Pedagogy: Researching Practice*. London: Paul Chapman Publishing.

Jeffrey, B. (2001b) Primary pupils' perspectives and creative learning, *Encyclopaideia*, 9, Spring (Italian journal).

Jeffrey, B. (2003a) Countering student instrumentalism: a creative response. *British Educational Research Journal*, 29 (4), 489–503.

Jeffrey, B. (2003b) Creative learning and student perspectives. See website: **opencreativity.open.ac.uk**.

Jeffrey, B. (2004a) *End of Award Report: Creative Learning and Student Perspectives (CLASP) Project*, submitted to ESRC, November.

Jeffrey, B. (2004b) *Meaningful Creative Learning: Learners' Perspectives*. Paper given at the ECER conference, Crete. See website: **opencreativity.open.ac.uk/pdf/ECER04-CL+ Meaningfulness.pdf**.

Jeffrey, B. and Craft, A. (2001) The universalization of creativity in education, in A. Craft, B. Jeffrey and M. Leibling (eds), *Creativity in Education*. London: Continuum.

Jeffrey, B. and Craft, A. (2004) Teaching creatively and teaching for creativity: distinctions and relationships. *Educational Studies*, 30 (1), 77–87.

Jeffrey, B. and Woods, P. (1997) The relevance of creative teaching: pupils' views, in A. Pollard, D. Thiessen and A. Filer (eds), *Children and Their Curriculum: The Perspectives of Primary and Elementary School Children*. London: Falmer Press.

Jeffrey, B. and Woods, P. (2003) *The Creative School: A Framework for Success, Quality and Effectiveness*. London and New York: Routledge Falmer.

Jennings, P. (1997) Ex Poser, in W. Cooling (ed.), *Thirteen Unpredictable Tales*. London: Puffin.

John-Steiner, V. (2000) *Creative Collaboration*. New York: Oxford University Press.

Johnston, J. (1996) *Early Explorations in Science*. Buckingham: Open University Press.

Johnston, J. (2002) The changing face of teaching and learning, in J. Johnston, M. Chater and D. Bell (eds), *Teaching the Primary Curriculum*. Buckingham: Open University Press.

Johnston, J. (2003) *Teachers' Philosophies on Science Teaching*. Paper presented to the European Science Educational Research Conference 2003, University of Utrecht, The Netherlands.

Johnston, J. (2004) The value of exploration and discovery, *Primary Science Review*, 85, 21–3.

Johnston, J. (2005) *Early Explorations in Science* (2nd edn). Buckingham: Open University Press.

Johnston, J. and Ahtee, M. (2005) What are primary student teachers' attitudes, subject knowledge and pedagogical content knowledge needs in a physics topic? *Teaching and Teacher Education*. Forthcoming.

Johnston, J. and Gray, A. (1999) *Enriching Early Scientific Learning*. Buckingham: Open University Press.

Marsh, J. and Millard, E. (2000) *Literacy and Popular Culture: Using Children's Culture in the Classroom*. London: Paul Chapman Publishing.

Martin, B. (2000) Teaching outdoor and adventurous activities, in R. Bailey and T. Macfadyen (eds), *Teaching Physical Education 5–11*. London: Continuum.

Martin, T. (2005) in P. Goodwin (ed.), *The Literate Classroom* (2nd edn). London: David Fulton.

McNaughton, C. and Kitamura, S. (2004) *Once Upon an Ordinary School Day*. London: Andersen Press.

McNeill, C., Marland, J. and Palmer, P. (1992) *Orienteering in the National Curriculum: A Practical Guide*. London: Harveys.

McNeill, C., Ramsden, J. and Renfrew, T. (1987) *Teaching Orienteering*. London: Harveys.

Mead, G. (1934) *Mind, Self, and Society*, ed. C. W. Morris. Chicago, IL: University of Chicago.

Medawar, P. B. (1969) *Induction and Intuition in Scientific Thought. Memoirs of the American Philosophical Society. Jayne Lectures 1968*. London: Methuen.

Meek, M. (1985) Play and paradoxes: some considerations of imagination and language, in G. Wells and J. Nicholls (eds), *Language and Learning: An International Perspective*. London: Falmer Press.

Meissner, H. (2000) Creativity in mathematics education, in *Proceedings of the Mathematics Education Study Group (MESG)*, 7–8 August, Tokyo, Japan.

Mendelson, E. (ed.) (1996) *W. H. Auden, Prose 1926–1938: Essays and Reviews and Travel Books in Prose and Verse*. London: Faber & Faber.

Mercer, N. (2000) *Words and Minds: How We Use Language to Think Together*. London: Routledge.

Midi, S. and Harackiewicz, J. M. (2000) Motivating the academically unmotivated: a critical issue for the 21st century, *Review of Educational Research*, 70 (2), 151–79.

Miell, D. and Littleton, K. (2004) *Collaborative Creativity*. London: Free Association Books.

Ministry of Education (1953a) *Planning the Programme: Physical Education in the Primary School*. London: HMSO.

Ministry of Education (1953b) *Moving and Growing: Physical Education in the Primary School*. London: HMSO

Monk, M. and Dillon, J. (2000) The nature of science knowledge, in M. Monk and J. Osborne (eds), *Good Practice in Science Teaching: What Research Has to Say*. Buckingham: Open University Press.

Munn, N. (1966) *Psychology* (5th edn). London: Harrap.

Murdock, E. (2005) NCPE 2000 – where are we so far? in S. Capel (ed.), *Learning to Teach Physical Education in the Secondary School*. Abingdon: Routledge Falmer.

Murphy, P., McCormick, B., Lunn, S., Davidson, M. and Jones, H. (2004) Electronics in schools, *Final Evaluation Report, Executive Summary*. London and Buckingham: Department of Trade and Industry and Open University.

Myhill, D.A. (2001) Writing: creating and grafting, *English in Education*, 35 (3), 13–20.

Nachmanovitch, S. (1990) *Free Play: Improvisation in Life and Art*. New York: Jeremy P. Tarcher/Putnam.

National Advisory Committee on Creative and Cultural Education (NACCCE) (1999) *All Our Futures: Creativity, Culture and Education* (The Robinson Report). London: DfEE.

National College for School Leadership (NCSL) (2005) See website: **www.ncsl.org.uk/index.cfm?pageid=randd-activities-creativity** (last accessed 26/1/05).

National Curriculum Council (1989) *Mathematics: Non-Statutory Guidance*. York: NCC/HMSO.

National Curriculum Council (1990) *The Arts 5–16: Practice and Innovation*. Harlow: Oliver & Boyd.

National Curriculum Design and Technology Working Group (1988) *Interim Report*. London: DES/WO.

Neelands, J. (2001) Drama: it sets you free, or does it? in J. Moss and J. Davison (eds), *Issues in English Teaching*. London: Routledge.

Neelands, J. and Goode, T. (1990) *Structuring Drama Work*. Cambridge: Cambridge University Press.

Ng, A. K. (2003) A cultural model of creative and conforming behaviour, *Creativity Research Journal*, 15(2 & 3), 223–233.

NGfL Scotland (2003) *Creativity in Education Online*. See website: **www.ltscotland.org.uk/creativity**.

Nicholson, H. (2000) Dramatic literacies and difference, in E. Bearne and V. Watson (eds), *Where Texts and Children Meet*. London: Routledge.

Nisbettt, R. E. (2003) *The Geography of Thought*. New York: Free Press.

Nixon, J. and Topping, K. (2001) Emergent writing: the impact of structured peer interaction, *Educational Psychology*, 21 (1) 41–58.

O'Hara, F. (2003) '*Why I Am Not a Painter' and Other Poems*. Manchester: Carcanet Press.

O'Hara, M. (1988) No parent ever complains about poetry, *Education 3–13*, 16 (3), 55–8.

O'Neill, C. (1995) *Drama Worlds: A Framework for Process Drama*. Portsmouth, NH: Heinemann.

Office for Standards in Education (OFSTED) (2003a) *Expecting the Unexpected: Developing Creativity in Primary and Secondary Schools*, HMI Report 1612. E-publication, August. See website: **www.ofsted.gov.uk**.

Office for Standards in Education (OFSTED) (2003b) *Improving City Schools: How the Arts Can Help*, HMI Report 1709. E-publication, August.

Office for Standards in Education (OFSTED) (2003c) *The Education of Six Year Olds in England, Denmark and Finland*. London: HMI.

Office for Standards in Education (OFSTED) (2004) *Excellence in Cities Primary Extension: Real Stories*, Document reference HMI2394. See website: **www.ofsted. gov.uk** (last accessed 24/1/05).

Orr, D. (1993) Schools for the 21st century, *Resurgence*, 160 (September/October).

Osgood, C. E., Suci, G. J. and Tannenbaum, P. H. (1967) *The Measurement of Meaning*. Chicago, IL: University of Illinois Press.

Papert, S. (1993) *The Children's Machine: Rethinking School in the Age of the Computer*. New York and London: Harvester Wheatsheaf.

Paterson, D. (2004) Rhyme and reason, *Guardian Review*, 6 November, pp. 34–5.

Pirrie, J. (1994) *On Common Ground: A Programme for Teaching Poetry* (2nd edn). Godalming: World Wide Fund for Nature.

Pollard, A. (2002) *Reflective Teaching*. London: Continuum.

Porter, L. (2005) *Gifted Young Children: A Guide for Teachers and Parents* (2nd edn). Buckingham: Open University Press.

Prentice, R. (1999) Art: visual thinking, in J. Riley and R. Prentice (eds), *The Curriculum for 7–11 Year Olds*. London: Paul Chapman Publishing.

Prentice, R. (2000) Creativity: a reaffirmation of its place in early childhood education, *Curriculum Journal*, 11 (2), 145–58.

PSR (2004) Primary science review, *Creativity and Science Education*, No. 81.

Qualifications and Curriculum Authority (QCA) (2000) *A Scheme of Work for Key Stages 1 and 2 – Science*. London: QCA.

Qualifications and Curriculum Authority (QCA) (2003) *Creativity: Find It! Promote It!* London: QCA/DFEE.

Qualifications and Curriculum Authority (QCA) (2005a) *Creativity: Find It! Promote It! – Promoting Pupils' Creative Thinking and Behaviour across the Curriculum at Key Stages 1, 2 and 3 – Practical Materials for Schools*. London: Qualifications and Curriculum Authority.

Qualifications and Curriculum Authority (QCA) (2005b) See website: **www.ncaction.org.uk/creativity/about.htm**.

Qualifications and Curriculum Authority (QCA) (2005c) Art and design subject report. See website: **www.qca.org.uk/11457.html**.

Read, H. (1958) *Education through Art*. London: Faber.

Renner, J. (1982) The power of purpose, *Science Education*, 66, 709–16.

Resnick, L. B. (1987) *Education and Learning to Think*. Washington, DC: National Academy Press.

Reynolds, T. (2000) Teaching gymnastics, in R. Bailey and T. Macfadyen (eds), *Teaching Physical Education 5–11*. London: Continuum.

Rhyammar, L. and Brolin, C. (1999) Creativity research: historical considerations and main lines of development. *Scandinavian Journal of Educational Research*, 43 (3), 259–73.

Ritchart, R. (2002) *Intellectual Character: What It Is, Why It Matters and How to Get It*. San Francisco, CA: Jossey-Bass.

Robinson, D. and Koshy, V. (2004) Creative mathematics: allowing caged birds to fly, in R. Fisher and M. Williams (eds), *Unlocking Creativity: Teaching Across the Curriculum*. London: David Fulton.

Robinson, K. (2001) *Out of Our Minds: Learning to be Creative*. Chichester: Capstone.

Robinson, M. and Ellis, V. (2000) Writing in English and responding to writing, in J. Sefton Green and R. Sinker (eds), *Evaluating Creativity: Making and Learning by Young People*. London: Routledge.

Roden, C. (1999) How children's problem solving strategies develop at Key Stage I, *Journal of Design and Technology Education*, 4 (I), 21–7.

Rosen, H. (1988) The irrepressible genre, in M. Maclure, T. Phillips and A. Wilkinson (eds), *Oracy Matters*. Buckingham: Open University Press.

Rosen, M. (1989) *Did I Hear You Write?* London: André Deutsch.

Rosen, M. (1997) Making poetry matter, in M. Barrs and M. Rosen (eds) *A Year with Poetry: Teachers Write about Teaching Poetry*. London: Centre for Language in Primary Education.

Rosenblatt, E. and Winner, E. (1988) The art of children's drawing, *Journal of Aesthetic Education*, 22: 3–15.

Ross, M. (1993) Living there: Herbert Read's education through art fifty years on, *Journal of Art and Design Education*, 12 (2), 135–41.

Rowling, J. K. (1997) *Harry Potter and the Philosopher's Stone*. London: Bloomsbury.

Runco, M. (2004) Everyone has creative potential, in E. L. Grigorenko and R. J. Sternberg (eds), *Creativity: From Potential to Realization*. Washington, DC: American Psychological Association.

Ryhammar, L. and Brolin, C. (1999) Creativity research: historical considerations and main lines of development. *Scandinavian Journal of Educational Research*, 43 (3): 259–73.

Ryle, G. (1949) *The Concept of Mind*. London: Hutchinson.

Sansom, P. (1994) *Writing Poems*. Newcastle upon Tyne: Bloodaxe Books.

Schon, D. (1987) *Educating the Reflective Practitioner*. San Fransisco, CA: Jossey-Bass.

Schools Council and Assessment Authority (SCAA) (1997) *Expectations in Physical Education at Key Stages I and 2*. London: SCAA.

Scott, P. (1987) *A Constructivist View of Teaching and Learning Science*. Leeds: Leeds University.

Sedgwick, F. (1997) *Read My Mind: Young Children, Poetry and Learning* London: Routledge.

Seltzer, K. and Bentley, T. (1999) *The Creative Age: Knowledge and Skills for the New Economy*. London: Demos.

Shallcross, D. J. (1981) *Teaching Creative Behavior: How to Teach Creativity to Children of All Ages*. Englewood Cliffs, NJ: Prentice-Hall.

Sharp, J., Potter, J., Alien, J. and Loveless, A. (2002) *Primary ICT: Knowledge, Understanding and Practice* (2nd edn). Exeter: Learning Matters.

Sharples, M. (1999) *How We Write: Writing as Creative Design*. London: Routledge.

Siraj-Blatchford, J. (1996) *Learning Technology, Science and Social Justice*. Nottingham: Education Now Publishing.

Sonnenburg, S. (2004) Creativity in communication: a theoretical framework for collaborative product creation. *Creativity and Innovation Management*, 13 (4), 254–62.

Steers, J. (2003) Art and design in the UK: the theory gap, in N. Addison and L. Burgess (eds), *Issues in Art and Design*. London: Routledge Falmer.

Steers, J. and Swift, J. (1999) A manifesto for art in schools, *Journal of Art and Design Education*, 18 (I), 7–14.

Steinberg, H., Sykes, E., Moss, T., Lowery, S., Leboutillier, N. and Dewey, A. (1997) Exercise enhances creativity independently of mood, *British Journal of Sports Medicine*, 31, 240–5.

Sternberg, R. J. (1988) *The Nature of Creativity*. Cambridge: Cambridge University Press.

Sternberg, R. J. and Lubart, T. I. (1999) The concept of creativity: prospects and paradigms, in R. J. Sternberg (ed.), *Handbook of Creativity*. Cambridge: Cambridge University Press.

Strauss, P. (1993) *Talking Poetry: A Guide for Students, Teachers and Poets*. Cape Town and Pietermaritzburg: David Philip Publishers and University of Natal Press.

Styles, M. (1992) Just a kind of music: children as poets, in M. Styles, E. Bearne and V. Watson (eds), *After Alice: Exploring Children's Literature*. London: Cassell.

Synectics Education Initiative, Esmee Fairbairn Foundation, Department for Education and Skills and the Open University (2004) *Excite! Excellence, Creativity and Innovation in Teacher Education*. London: SEI.

Taber, K. S. (2002) *The Constructivist View of Learning: How Can It Inform Assessment?* Invited presentation to the University of Cambridge Local Examinations Syndicate (UCLES) Research and Evaluation Division (RED), 27 May.

Tall, D., Gray, E., Bin Ali, M., Crowley, L., De Marios, P., McGovern, M., Pitta, D., Pinto, M., Thomas, M. and Yusof, Y. (2001) Symbols and bifurification between procedural and conceptual thinking, *Canadian Journal of Mathematics and Technology Education*, 1 (1), 81–104.

Tarleton, R. (1983) Children's thinking and poetry, *English in Education*, 17 (3), 36–46.

Thistlewood, D. (1992) *Histories of Art and Design Education – Cole to Coldstream*. Corsham: Longman/NSEAD.

Torrance, E. P. (1962) *Guiding Creative Talent*. Englewood Cliffs, NJ: Prentice-Hall.

Torrance, E. P. (1963) *Education and the Creative Potential*. Minneapolis, MN: University of Minnesota Press.

Torrance, E. P. (1979) *The Search for Satori and Creativity*. Buffalo, NY: Bearly Ltd.

Torrance, E. P. (1984) *Mentor Relationships: How They Aid Creative Achievement, Endure, Change and Die*. Buffalo, NY: Bearly.

Torrance, E. P. and Myers, R. E. (1971) *Creative Learning and Teaching*. New York: Dodd, Mead.

Underwood, M. (1991) *Agile*. Nelson.

van den Bergh, H. and Rijlaarsdam, G. (2001) Changes in cognitive activities during the writing process and relationships with text quality, *Educational Psychology*, 21 (4), 373–82.

Viguers, S. T. (1983) Nonsense and the language of poetry, *Signal*, 42, 137–49.

Vygotsky, L. (1978) *Mind in Society*. Cambridge, MA: MIT Press.

Wade, B. and Sidaway, S. (1990) Poetry in the curriculum: a crisis of confidence, *Educational Studies*, 16 (1), 75–83.

Wallas, B. (1926) *The Art of Thought*. New York: Harcourt Brace & World.

Walter, C. (1990) Sound in content: some under-regarded possibilities for the teaching of poetry in school, *Education Today*, 40 (2), 54–60.

Wegerif, R. (2004) Reason and creativity in classroom dialogues. Unpublished paper based on seminar given at The Open Creativity Centre Seminar Series, Milton Keynes, UK, March 2003.

Wenger, E. (1998) *Communities of Practice: Learning, Meaning and Identity*. Cambridge: Cambridge University Press.

Whitehead, M. R. (2004) *Language and Literacy in the Early Years* (3rd edn). London: Sage.

Wilkins, V. A. (1993) *Dave and the Tooth Fairy*. London: Tamarind.

Wilkins, V. A. (1996) *Toyin Fay*. London: Tamarind.

Williams, A. (1997) *National Curriculum Gymnastics*. London: Hodder & Stoughton.

Wilson, A. (1996) *How Far From Here Is Home?* Exeter: Stride Publications.

Wilson, A. (2002) *Nowhere Better Than This*. Tonbridge: Worple Press.

Wilson, A. with Hughes, S. (eds) (1998) *The Poetry Book for Primary Schools*. London: Poetry Society.

Wilson, K. and Briggs, M. (2002) Able and gifted: judging by appearances? *Mathematics Teaching*, 180, 34–6.

Wilson, S. and Ball, D. L. (1997) Helping teachers meet the standards: new challenges for teacher educators, *Elementary School Journal*, 97 (2), 121–38.

Wood, D. (1988) *How Children Think and Learn*. Oxford: Blackwell.

Woods, P. (1990) *Teacher Skills and Strategies*. London: Falmer Press.

Woods, P. (1993) *Critical Events in Teaching and Learning*. Lewes: Falmer Press

Woods, P. (1995) *Creative Teachers in Primary Schools*. Buckingham: Open University Press.

Woods, P. (2002) Teaching and learning in the new millennium, in C. Sugrue and D. Day (eds), *Developing Teachers and Teaching Practice: International Research Perspectives*. London and New York: Routledge Falmer.

Woods, P. and Jeffrey, B. (1996) *Teachable Moments: The Art of Teaching in Primary Schools*. Buckingham: Open University Press.

Young, S. (2003) *Music with the Under Fours*. London: Routledge Falmer.

Zipes, F. (1996) *Creative Storytelling: Building Communities, Changing Lives*. London: Routledge.

Zipes, J. (ed.) (1987) *Don't Bet on the Prince: Contemporary Feminist Fairy Tales in North America and England*. New York: Routledge.

5146